Four Greek Plays

Four Greek Plays

Edited by Dudley Fitts

The Agamemnon of Aeschylus
Translated by Louis MacNeice

The Oedipus Rex of Sophocles
Translated by Dudley Fitts and Robert Fitzgerald

The Alcestis of Euripides
Translated by Dudley Fitts and Robert Fitzgerald

The Birds of Aristophanes
Translated by Dudley Fitts

A HARVEST BOOK • HARCOURT, INC
San Diego   New York   London

Requests for permission to make copies of any part of the work should be
mailed to the following address: Permissions Department, Harcourt, Inc.,
6277 Sea Harbor Drive, Orlando, Florida 32887-6777.

Library of Congress Cataloging-in-Publication Data
Four Greek Plays
"A Harvest book."
Contents: The Agamemnon of Aeschylus/translated
by Louis MacNeice—The Oedipus Rex of Sophocles/translated
by Dudley Fitts and Robert Fitzgerald—The Alcestis of Euripides/translated
by Dudley Fitts and Robert Fitzgerald — [etc.]
1. Greek drama — Translations into English.
2. English Drama — Translations from Greek.
I. Fitts, Dudley, 1903-1968
PA3626.A2F48   1985   882'.01'08   84-22535
ISBN 0-15-602795-X

Printed in the United States of America

A C E G I J H F D B

CONTENTS

THE AGAMEMNON
OF AESCHYLUS

TRANSLATED BY

LOUIS MacNEICE

INTRODUCTORY NOTE

Aeschylus was born in 525 B.C. At the time of his death in 456 he had written some ninety plays, of which only seven have come down to us. The *Oresteia*, produced in 458, comprises three of them: *Agamemnon, Choephoroe*, and *Eumenidês*. These dramas, which deal with the murder of King Agamemnon and the subsequent vengeance taken by his son Orestês, are the only complete trilogy that has survived from classical times, and they would be of the greatest importance, critically and historically, for that reason alone. But this particular trilogy, whatever its accidental values may be, stands on its own merits as one of the noblest expressions of man's spirit; and the *Agamemnon* is, by common consent, the most urgent and moving utterance of Aeschylus in this vein. It is, of course, the first of three closely linked plays, and it loses a certain amount of philosophical depth when we read it apart from its companion pieces; but it is an artistic whole nevertheless, and as such it has been admired and pondered for centuries. No dramatist has set forth more profoundly, or more excitingly, an allegory of human crime and divine retribution.

The mythological material that Aeschylus uses is terrible enough even when it has been transfigured by his art. The primitive saga is a nightmare of cannibalism, incest, adultery, murder, and madness. We must assume that the gods will curse an entire family, meaninglessly and mercilessly, and that the succeeding generations will each enact, helplessly, bloody variations of the ancestral curse. It is Aeschylus's purpose in the trilogy to show that this primeval horror may be tamed, to suggest the possibility of a more civilized idea of justice. Accordingly, in the *Eumenidês* he is audacious enough to represent Apollo, a young god embodying a new order in Heaven, as unseating the Furies of blind chaotic vengeance and subduing the irrational by

3

the persuasive power of intellect. In the *Agamemnon*, however, we are still lost in darkness, watching evil punish
evil to no apparent end. The cause of all this trouble is
the original curse. That is to say, bluntly, that the gods
force man to sin and then punish him for sinning. It is not
an exalted concept of divinity.

The name of Helen rings like a death-cry through this
play. An extraordinary series of bitter puns calls her

> Helen, bride of spears and conflict's
> Focus, who as was befitting
> Proved a hell to ships and men,
> Hell to her country—

and the Chorus returns again and again to the idea that
Helen, as the prime reason for the Trojan War, is the
adulterous origin of the calamities that follow it. Another
fatal name is that of Iphigeneia, Agamemnon's eldest daughter, whom the king offered up as a sacrifice to Artemis in
order that the army might be allowed to sail from Aulis
to the plains of Troy. It is her death that Clytemnestra
makes the pretext for murdering Agamemnon: a mother's
just vengeance for a child slaughtered. Neither imputation
is wholly true or wholly false. It is true that Helen ran away
from her husband Menelaus to live with Prince Paris in
Troy; but the ensuing war was a thing out of all proportion
to the offence—an indulgence, really, of mass vanity and
old-school-tie cliquishness. As for Iphigeneia, it was undeniably true that the gods would not permit the fleet to
sail until she had been sacrificed on the altar of Artemis;
but that is not the same thing as saying that it was *right*
to sacrifice her, or that the fleet *had* to sail. Should a war
for so nearly worthless a woman have been undertaken in
the first place? Does military success in any war, let alone
a war of vanity, justify a father's killing his child? Is this
the story of Abraham and Isaac, an act of unquestioning
submissiveness to God's will, or is it the less edifying story
of a proud man who horribly distorts God's will to serve his
own vain purpose? He could not have conquered Troy if
he had not killed his daughter. Was it necessary that he
conquer Troy? And who says that it was necessary?

These questions are not intended to take away any of the blame from Clytemnestra. She is an adulteress and a murderess. Whatever she may say about Iphigeneia, her real motive for killing her husband is Aegisthus, the despicable paramour whom she wants to make an honest man. We can not pardon her for that; nor does her son Orestês, who comes back from exile, in the second of the plays, and kills her and her paramour. It is with the guilt of Agamemnon that we are concerned at the moment. It may be that in the primitive myth he was fated to kill Iphigeneia, just as he was undeniably held by an oath to go to the aid of Menelaus in recovering Helen. Aeschylus does not deny these probabilities. Nevertheless, he has added the decidedly unmyth-like idea that Agamemnon really had a choice in these matters, that he chose wrong, and that the reason for his error was pride.

We can hardly discuss the *Agamemnon* or any other of the Greek tragedies without coming up sooner or later against the sin of human pride: so, at any rate, we may compress the various connotations of the term *hybris*, which in its basic sense means arrogance or insolence. *Hybris* exists when a man forgets his due place in the order of things and aspires to be more than the gods will permit. These deathless gods—Olympian, but all too obviously made after man's image—are touchy creatures, cruelly jealous of their own prerogatives. Like insecure masters (yet why should the eternal feel insecure?) they are quick to crush any human attempt to rise above the human lot. The attempt may not be an act of revolt, or even of presumptuous ambition—like the building of the Tower of Babel, for instance. It may seem, to our eyes, no more than a self-respecting assertion of human worth, or a step taken without the customary groveling before divinity, or a simple and forgivable indulgence of more than the usual measure of happiness. Any kind of success, any kind of happiness, is therefore suspect because it may lead a man, however innocently, to regard himself with too much confidence. The theory seems to be instinctive; at all events, we ought not to laugh at it until we ourselves are able to boast without feeling that we should touch wood. When we read these plays, we must take literally the statement that 'I, the Lord thy God, am a jealous God,' understanding 'jealous' exactly as we should understand it man to man or man to woman: a superior's insistence, which seems basically ignoble, upon privileges that take precedence of those of anyone else and that are not, without blasphemy, to be impinged upon. This, again, may be an unworthy way of thinking about God; but it is the primitive way that underlies the Aeschylean tragedy.

Agamemnon, where the concepts are most basic and savage, is full of *hybris* and symbols of *hybris*. The sacrifice of Iphigeneia is the real thing—success in war is preferable to the sanctities of kinship—and it brings retribution. The arrogant posturing of Clytemnestra as an instrument of retributive justice is the real thing, and eventually it brings about her destruction. Cassandra pathetically boasts of how she once set her wits against those of the god Apollo. Aegisthus struts comically as a king in the palace that a woman has usurped for him. And Agamemnon walks on a purple carpet to meet his death. This last is the most notorious example of all, but it is not the real thing: it is a symbol merely, very carefully and cleverly brought about by Clytemnestra. Purple is a royal color, and Agamemnon is a king; but to assert one's royalty of nature in so overt a manner is rash, even unhealthy, since the gods are what they are. Agamemnon is aware of the danger; that is why he takes off his shoes, so that at least the dust of ruined Troy will not soil the trodden splendor; but Clytemnestra has taunted him so for his reluctance, even comparing him unfavorably with that silly oriental despot Priam, that his vanity overcomes his better judgment and he enacts a charade of Pride:

> Well, if such is your wish, let someone quickly loose
> My vassal sandals, underlings of my feet,
> And stepping on these sea-purples may no god
> Shoot me from afar with the envy of his eye.
> Great shame it is to ruin my house and spoil
> The wealth of costly weavings with my feet.

. . . .

> But since I have been prevailed on by your words
> I will go to my palace home, treading on purples.

For ten years, every step that the man has taken has been ruinous to his house, and now he worries about spoiling the draperies. His whole history, from his departure for Troy till his return home this very day, has been one of self-inflation and intemperate action. 'I will go to my palace home.' All his life he has been preparing himself for the entangling net and the stroke of the two-edged cleaver.

DF

PREFACE

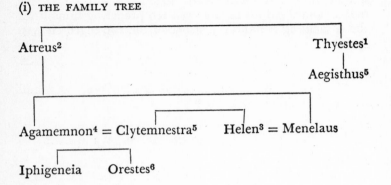

(ii) THE CHAIN OF CRIMES

Two brothers, Agamemnon and Menelaus, were kings of Argos. They married two sisters, Clytemnestra and Helen; each married to his cost. On the Greek view Helen and Clytemnestra were not just bad women; they were agents rather than creators of evil. Nobody on this view is either simply a protagonist of evil or simply a victim of circumstance. The family is physically, and therefore morally, a unit: the same blood runs in all, and through it descends an inherited responsibility which limits, without wholly destroying, the power of choice in each. The sins of the fathers are visited on the children, so the children are victims of circumstance. But the children, because they are of the same blood, are tempted to sin in their turn. If a man holds such a view he will tend simultaneously to vindicate the ways of God and kick against the pricks of chance. It is this paradox that gives tension to a play like the Agamemnon. Here we have a chain of crimes, one leading to another from generation to generation by a logic

8

immanent in the blood and working through it. But the cause of the crimes, not only of the first link, the first crime, but present in every one of them, is the principle of Evil which logic cannot comprehend.

The chain of crimes in this play is as follows (see Family Tree above):

Past.

(1) Thyestes seduced Atreus' wife.

(2) Atreus killed Thyestes' young children and gave him them as meat.

(3) Helen forsook her husband and went to Troy with Paris.

(4) Agamemnon, to promote the Trojan War, sacrificed his daughter Iphigeneia.

Present.

(5) Aegisthus and Clytemnestra murder Agamemnon.

Future.

(6) Orestes will kill Aegisthus and his mother Clytemnestra.

(iii)

I have written this translation primarily for the stage. I have consciously sacrificed certain things in the original—notably the liturgical flavour of the diction and the metrical complexity of the choruses. It is my hope that the play emerges as a play and not as a museum piece.

My thanks are very much due to my friend, Professor E. R. Dodds, who, with a tolerance rare among scholars and a sympathy rare in anyone, read through the whole of my unacademic version and pointed out to me its more culpable inadequacies. The translation of certain passages is our joint product; but for the faults which remain I alone am responsible.

It is intended that this version of the Agamemnon shall be produced on the stage in the autumn of this year by Mr. Rupert Doone and the Group Theatre.

1 August 1936   **L.M.**

PERSONS REPRESENTED

WATCHMAN
CHORUS OF OLD MEN OF THE CITY
CLYTEMNESTRA
HERALD
AGAMEMNON
CASSANDRA
AEGISTHUS

SCENE. *A space in front of the palace of Agamemnon in Argos. Night. A* WATCHMAN *on the roof of the palace.*

WATCHMAN:
   The gods it is I ask to release me from this watch
   A year's length now, spending my nights like a dog,
   Watching on my elbow on the roof of the sons of Atreus
   So that I have come to know the assembly of the nightly
      stars
   Those which bring storm and those which bring summer
      to men,
   The shining Masters riveted in the sky—
   I know the decline and rising of those stars.
   And now I am waiting for the sign of the beacon,
   The flame of fire that will carry the report from Troy,
   News of her taking. Which task has been assigned me
   By a woman of sanguine heart but a man's mind.
   Yet when I take my restless rest in the soaking dew,
   My night not visited with dreams—
   For fear stands by me in the place of sleep
   That I cannot firmly close my eyes in sleep—

Whenever I think to sing or hum to myself
As an antidote to sleep, then every time I groan
And fall to weeping for the fortunes of this house
Where not as before are things well ordered now.
But now may a good chance fall, escape from pain,
The good news visible in the midnight fire.

> [*Pause. A light appears, gradually increasing,
> the light of the beacon.*

Ha! I salute you, torch of the night whose light
Is like the day, an earnest of many dances
In the city of Argos, celebration of Peace.
I call to Agamemnon's wife; quickly to rise
Out of her bed and in the house to raise
Clamour of joy in answer to this torch
For the city of Troy is taken—
Such is the evident message of the beckoning flame.
And I myself will dance my solo first
For I shall count my master's fortune mine
Now that this beacon has thrown me a lucky throw.
And may it be when he comes, the master of this house,
That I grasp his hand in my hand.
As to the rest, I am silent. A great ox, as they say,
Stands on my tongue. The house itself, if it took voice,
Could tell the case most clearly. But I will only speak
To those who know. For the others I remember nothing.

> [*Enter* CHORUS OF OLD MEN. *During the following
> chorus the day begins to dawn.*

CHORUS:

The tenth year it is since Priam's high
Adversary, Menelaus the king
And Agamemnon, the double-throned and sceptred
Yoke of the sons of Atreus
Ruling in fee from God,
From this land gathered an Argive army
On a mission of war a thousand ships,
Their hearts howling in boundless bloodlust
In eagles' fashion who in lonely
Grief for nestlings above their homes hang

Turning in cycles
Beating the air with the oars of their wings,
   Now to no purpose
   Their love and task of attention.

But above there is One,
Maybe Pan, maybe Zeus or Apollo,
Who hears the harsh cries of the birds
Guests in his kingdom,
Wherefore, though late, in requital
He sends the Avenger.
Thus Zeus our master
Guardian of guest and of host
Sent against Paris the sons of Atreus
For a woman of many men
Many the dog-tired wrestlings
Limbs and knees in the dust pressed—
   For both the Greeks and Trojans
   An overture of breaking spears.

Things are where they are, will finish
In the manner fated and neither
Fire beneath nor oil above can soothe
The stubborn anger of the unburnt offering.
As for us, our bodies are bankrupt,
The expedition left us behind
And we wait supporting on sticks
Our strength—the strength of a child;
For the marrow that leaps in a boy's body
Is no better than that of the old
For the War God is not in his body;
While the man who is very old
And his leaf withering away
Goes on the three-foot way
No better than a boy, and wanders
A dream in the middle of the day.

But you, daughter of Tyndareus,
Queen Clytemnestra,

What is the news, what is the truth, what have you learnt,
On the strength of whose word have you thus
Sent orders for sacrifice round?
All the gods, the gods of the town,
Of the worlds of Below and Above,
By the door, in the square,
Have their altars ablaze with your gifts,
From here, from there, all sides, all corners,
Sky-high leap the flame-jets fed
By gentle and undeceiving
Persuasion of sacred unguent,
Oil from the royal stores.
Of these things tell
That which you can, that which you may,
Be healer of this our trouble
Which at times torments with evil
Though at times by propitiations
A shining hope repels
The insatiable thought upon grief
Which is eating away our hearts.

Of the omen which powerfully speeded
That voyage of strong men, by God's grace even I
Can tell, my age can still
Be galvanized to breathe the strength of song,
To tell how the kings of all the youth of Greece
Two-throned but one in mind
Were launched with pike and punitive hand
Against the Trojan shore by angry birds.
Kings of the birds to our kings came,
One with a white rump, the other black,
Appearing near the palace on the spear-arm side
Where all could see them,
Tearing a pregnant hare with the unborn young
Foiled of their courses.
    Cry, cry upon Death; but may the good prevail.

But the diligent prophet of the army seeing the sons
Of Atreus twin in temper knew

That the hare-killing birds were the two
Generals, explained it thus—
'In time this expedition sacks the town
Of Troy before whose towers
By Fate's force the public
Wealth will be wasted.
Only let not some spite from the gods benight the bulky
    battalions,
The bridle of Troy, nor strike them untimely;
For the goddess feels pity, is angry
With the winged dogs of her father
Who killed the cowering hare with her unborn young;
Artemis hates the eagles' feast.'
    Cry, cry upon Death; but may the good prevail.

'But though you are so kind, goddess,
To the little cubs of lions
And to all the sucking young of roving beasts
In whom your heart delights,
Fulfil us the signs of these things,
The signs which are good but open to blame,
And I call on Apollo the Healer
That his sister raise not against the Greeks
Unremitting gales to baulk their ships,
Hurrying on another kind of sacrifice, with no feasting,
Barbarous building of hates and disloyalties
Grown on the family. For anger grimly returns
Cunningly haunting the house, avenging the death of a
    child, never forgetting its due.'
So cried the prophet—evil and good together,
Fate that the birds foretold to the king's house.
In tune with this
    Cry, cry upon Death; but may the good prevail.

Zeus, whoever He is, if this
Be a name acceptable,
By this name I will call him.
There is no one comparable

When I reckon all of the case
Excepting Zeus, if ever I am to jettison
The barren care which clogs my heart.

Not He who formerly was great
With brawling pride and mad for broils
Will even be said to have been.
And He who was next has met
His match and is seen no more,
But Zeus is the name to cry in your triumph-song
And win the prize for wisdom.

Who setting us on the road
Made this a valid law—
   'That men must learn by suffering.'
Drop by drop in sleep upon the heart
Falls the laborious memory of pain,
Against one's will comes wisdom;
The grace of the gods is forced on us
   Throned inviolably.

So at that time the elder
Chief of the Greek ships
Would not blame any prophet
Nor face the flail of fortune;
For unable to sail, the people
Of Greece were heavy with famine,
Waiting in Aulis where the tides
   Flow back, opposite Chalcis.

But the winds that blew from the Strymon,
Bringing delay, hunger, evil harbourage,
Crazing men, rotting ships and cables,
By drawing out the time
Were shredding into nothing the flower of Argos,
When the prophet screamed a new
Cure for that bitter tempest
And heavier still for the chiefs,

Pleading the anger of Artemis so that the sons of Atreus
Beat the ground with their sceptres and shed tears.

Then the elder king found voice and answered:
'Heavy is my fate, not obeying,
And heavy it is if I kill my child, the delight of my house,
And with a virgin's blood upon the altar
Make foul her father's hands.
Either alternative is evil.
How can I betray the fleet
And fail the allied army?
It is right they should passionately cry for the winds to
      be lulled
By the blood of a girl. So be it. May it be well.'

But when he had put on the halter of Necessity
Breathing in his heart a veering wind of evil
Unsanctioned, unholy, from that moment forward
He changed his counsel, would stop at nothing.
For the heart of man is hardened by infatuation,
A faulty adviser, the first link of sorrow.
Whatever the cause, he brought himself to slay
His daughter, an offering to promote the voyage
To a war for a runaway wife.

Her prayers and her cries of father,
Her life of a maiden,
Counted for nothing with those militarists;
But her father, having duly prayed, told the attendants
To lift her, like a goat, above the altar
With her robes falling about her,
To lift her boldly, her spirit fainting,
And hold back with a gag upon her lovely mouth
By the dumb force of a bridle
The cry which would curse the house.

Then dropping on the ground her saffron dress,
Glancing at each of her appointed

Sacrificers a shaft of pity,
Plain as in a picture she wished
To speak to them by name, for often
At her father's table where men feasted
She had sung in celebration for her father
With a pure voice, affectionately, virginally,
The hymn for happiness at the third libation.

The sequel to this I saw not and tell not
But the crafts of Calchas gained their object.
To learn by suffering is the equation of Justice; the Future
Is known when it comes, let it go till then.
To know in advance is sorrow in advance.
The facts will appear with the shining of the dawn.

> [*Enter* CLYTEMNESTRA.

But may good, at the least, follow after
As the queen here wishes, who stands
Nearest the throne, the only
   Defence of the land of Argos.

LEADER OF THE CHORUS:
   I have come, Clytemnestra, reverencing your authority.
   For it is right to honour our master's wife
   When the man's own throne is empty.
   But you, if you have heard good news for certain, or if
   You sacrifice on the strength of flattering hopes,
   I would gladly hear. Though I cannot cavil at silence.
CLYTEMNESTRA:
   Bearing good news, as the proverb says, may Dawn
   Spring from her mother Night.
   You will hear something now that was beyond your hopes.
   The men of Argos have taken Priam's city.
LEADER OF THE CHORUS:
   What! I cannot believe it. It escapes me.
CLYTEMNESTRA:
   Troy in the hands of the Greeks. Do I speak plain?
LEADER OF THE CHORUS:
   Joy creeps over me, calling out my tears.

CLYTEMNESTRA:
  Yes. Your eyes proclaim your loyalty.
LEADER OF THE CHORUS:
  But what are your grounds? Have you a proof of it?
CLYTEMNESTRA:
  There is proof indeed—unless God has cheated us.
LEADER OF THE CHORUS:
  Perhaps you believe the inveigling shapes of dreams?
CLYTEMNESTRA:
  I would not be credited with a dozing brain!
LEADER OF THE CHORUS:
  Or are you puffed up by Rumour, the wingless flyer?
CLYTEMNESTRA:
  You mock my common sense as if I were a child.
LEADER OF THE CHORUS:
  But at what time was the city given to sack?
CLYTEMNESTRA:
  In this very night that gave birth to this day.
LEADER OF THE CHORUS:
  What messenger could come so fast?
CLYTEMNESTRA:
  Hephaestus, launching a fine flame from Ida,
  Beacon forwarding beacon, despatch-riders of fire,
  Ida relayed to Hermes' cliff in Lemnos
  And the great glow from the island was taken over third
  By the height of Athos that belongs to Zeus,
  And towering then to straddle over the sea
  The might of the running torch joyfully tossed
  The gold gleam forward like another sun,
  Herald of light to the heights of Mount Macistus,
  And he without delay, nor carelessly by sleep
  Encumbered, did not shirk his intermediary role,
  His farflung ray reached the Euripus' tides
  And told Messapion's watchers, who in turn
  Sent on the message further
  Setting a stack of dried-up heather on fire.
  And the strapping flame, not yet enfeebled, leapt
  Over the plain of Asopus like a blazing moon

And woke on the crags of Cithaeron
Another relay in the chain of fire.
The light that was sent from far was not declined
By the look-out men, who raised a fiercer yet,
A light which jumped the water of Gorgopis
And to Mount Aegiplanctus duly come
Urged the reveille of the punctual fire.
So then they kindle it squanderingly and launch
A beard of flame big enough to pass
The headland that looks down upon the Saronic gulf,
Blazing and bounding till it reached at length
The Arachnaean steep, our neighbouring heights;
And leaps in the latter end on the roof of the sons of
    Atreus
Issue and image of the fire on Ida.
Such was the assignment of my torch-racers,
The task of each fulfilled by his successor,
And victor is he who ran both first and last.
Such is the proof I offer you, the sign
My husband sent me out of Troy.

LEADER OF THE CHORUS:

To the gods, queen, I shall give thanks presently.
But I would like to hear this story further,
To wonder at it in detail from your lips.

CLYTEMNESTRA:

The Greeks hold Troy upon this day.
The cries in the town I fancy do not mingle.
Pour oil and vinegar into the same jar,
You would say they stand apart unlovingly;
Of those who are captured and those who have conquered
Distinct are the sounds of their diverse fortunes,
For *these* having flung themselves about the bodies
Of husbands and brothers, or sons upon the bodies
Of aged fathers from a throat no longer
Free, lament the fate of their most loved.
But *those* a night's marauding after battle
Sets hungry to what breakfast the town offers
Not billeted duly in any barracks order
But as each man has drawn his lot of luck.
So in the captive homes of Troy already

They take their lodging, free of the frosts
And dews of the open. Like happy men
They will sleep all night without sentry.
But if they respect duly the city's gods,
Those of the captured land and the sanctuaries of the
    gods,
They need not, having conquered, fear reconquest.
But let no lust fall first upon the troops
To plunder what is not right, subdued by gain,
For they must still, in order to come home safe,
Get round the second lap of the doubled course.
So if they return without offence to the gods
The grievance of the slain may learn at last
A friendly talk—unless some fresh wrong falls.
Such are the thoughts you hear from me, a woman.
But may the good prevail for all to see.
We have much good. I only ask to enjoy it.

LEADER OF THE CHORUS:
Woman, you speak with sense like a prudent man.
I, who have heard your valid proofs, prepare
To give the glory to God.
Fair recompense is brought us for our troubles.

        [CLYTEMNESTRA *goes back into the palace.*

CHORUS:
O Zeus our king and Night our friend
Donor of glories,
Night who cast on the towers of Troy
A close-clinging net so that neither the grown
Nor any of the children can pass
The enslaving and huge
Trap of all-taking destruction.
Great Zeus, guardian of host and guest,
I honour who has done his work and taken
A leisured aim at Paris so that neither
Too short nor yet over the stars
    He might shoot to no purpose.

From Zeus is the blow they can tell of,
This at least can be established,

They have fared according to his ruling. For some
Deny that the gods deign to consider those among **men**
Who trample on the grace of inviolate things;
It is the impious man says this,
For Ruin is revealed the child
Of not to be attempted actions
When men are puffed up unduly
And their houses are stuffed with riches.
Measure is the best. Let danger be distant,
This should suffice a man
With a proper part of wisdom.
    For a man has no protection
    Against the drunkenness of riches
    Once he has spurned from his sight
    The high altar of Justice.

Sombre Persuasion compels him,
Intolerable child of calculating Doom;
All cure is vain, there is no glozing it over
But the mischief shines forth with a deadly light
And like bad coinage
By rubbings and frictions
He stands discoloured and black
Under the test—like a boy
Who chases a winged bird.
He has branded his city for ever.
His prayers are heard by no god.
Who makes such things his practice
The gods destroy him.
    This way came Paris
    To the house of the sons of Atreus
    And outraged the table of friendship
    Stealing the wife of his host.

Leaving to her countrymen clanging of
Shields and of spears and
Launching of warships
And bringing instead of a dowry destruction to Troy
Lightly she was gone through the gates daring

Things undared. Many the groans
Of the palace spokesmen on this theme—
'O the house, the house, and its princes,
O the bed and the imprint of her limbs;
One can see him crouching in silence
Dishonoured and unreviling.'
Through desire for her who is overseas, a ghost
Will seem to rule the household.
    And now her husband hates
    The grace of shapely statues;
    In the emptiness of their eyes
    All their appeal is departed.

But appearing in dreams persuasive
Images come bringing a joy that is vain,
Vain for when in fancy he looks to touch her—
Slipping through his hands the vision
Rapidly is gone
Following on wings the walks of sleep.
Such are his griefs in his house on his hearth,
Such as these and worse than these,
But everywhere through the land of Greece which men
    have left
Are mourning women with enduring hearts
To be seen in all houses; many
Are the thoughts which stab their hearts;
    For those they sent to war
    They know, but in place of men
    That which comes home to them
    Is merely an urn and ashes.

But the money-changer War, changer of bodies,
Holding his balance in the battle
Home from Troy refined by fire
Sends back to friends the dust
That is heavy with tears, stowing
A man's worth of ashes
In an easily handled jar.
And they wail speaking well of the men how that one

Was expert in battle, and one fell well in the carnage—
But for another man's wife.
Muffled and muttered words;
And resentful grief creeps up against the sons
Of Atreus and their cause.
    But others there by the wall
    Entombed in Trojan ground
    Lie, handsome of limb,
    Holding and hidden in enemy soil.

Heavy is the murmur of an angry people
Performing the purpose of a public curse;
There is something cowled in the night
That I anxiously wait to hear.
For the gods are not blind to the
Murderers of many and the black
Furies in time
When a man prospers in sin
By erosion of life reduce him to darkness,
Who, once among the lost, can no more
Be helped. Over-great glory
Is a sore burden. The high peak
Is blasted by the eyes of Zeus.
    I prefer an unenvied fortune,
    Not to be a sacker of cities
    Nor to find myself living at another's
    Ruling, myself a captive.

AN OLD MAN:
    From the good news' beacon a swift
    Rumour is gone through the town.
    Who knows if it be true
    Or some deceit of the gods?
ANOTHER OLD MAN
    Who is so childish or broken in wit
    To kindle his heart at a new-fangled message of flame
    And then be downcast
    At a change of report?

ANOTHER OLD MAN
 It fits the temper of a woman
 To give her assent to a story before it is proved.
ANOTHER OLD MAN
 The over-credulous passion of women expands
 In swift conflagration but swiftly declining is gone
 The news that a woman announced.
LEADER OF THE CHORUS:
 Soon we shall know about the illuminant torches,
 The beacons and the fiery relays,
 Whether they were true or whether like dreams
 That pleasant light came here and hoaxed our wits.
 Look: I see, coming from the beach, a herald
 Shadowed with olive shoots; the dust upon him,
 Mud's thirsty sister and colleague, is my witness
 That he will not give dumb news nor news by lighting
 A flame of fire with the smoke of mountain timber;
 In words he will either corroborate our joy—
 But the opposite version I reject with horror.
 To the good appeared so far may good be added.
ANOTHER SPEAKER:
 Whoever makes other prayers for this our city,
 May he reap himself the fruits of his wicked heart.

  [*Enter the* HERALD, *who kisses the ground before
                                          speaking.*

HERALD:
 Earth of my fathers, O the earth of Argos,
 In the light of the tenth year I reach you thus
 After many shattered hopes achieving one,
 For never did I dare to think that here in Argive land
 I should win a grave in the dearest soil of home;
 But now hail, land, and hail, light of the sun,
 And Zeus high above the country and the Pythian king—
 May he no longer shoot his arrows at us
 (Implacable long enough beside Scamander)
 But now be saviour to us and be healer,
 King Apollo. And all the Assembly's gods

I call upon, and him my patron, Hermes,
The dear herald whom all heralds adore,
And the Heroes who sped our voyage, again with favour
Take back the army that has escaped the spear.
O cherished dwelling, palace of royalty,
O august thrones and gods facing the sun,
If ever before, now with your bright eyes
Gladly receive your king after much time,
Who comes bringing light to you in the night time,
And to all these as well—King Agamemnon.
Give him a good welcome as he deserves,
Who with the axe of judgment-awarding God
Has smashed Troy and levelled the Trojan land;
The altars are destroyed, the seats of the gods,
And the seed of all the land is perished from it.
Having cast this halter round the neck of Troy
The King, the elder son of Atreus, a blessed man,
Comes, the most worthy to have honour of all
Men that are now. Paris nor his guilty city
Can boast that the crime was greater than the atonement.
Convicted in a suit for rape and robbery
He has lost his stolen goods and with consummate ruin
Mowed down the whole country and his father's house.
The sons of Priam have paid their account with interest.

LEADER OF THE CHORUS:
Hail and be glad, herald of the Greek army.

HERALD:
Yes. Glad indeed! So glad that at the god's demand
I should no longer hesitate to die.

LEADER OF THE CHORUS:
Were you so harrowed by desire for home?

HERALD:
Yes. The tears come to my eyes for joy.

LEADER OF THE CHORUS:
Sweet then is the fever which afflicts you.

HERALD:
What do you mean? Let me learn your drift.

LEADER OF THE CHORUS:
Longing for those whose love came back in echo.

HERALD:
Meaning the land was homesick for the army?

LEADER OF THE CHORUS:
Yes. I would often groan from a darkened heart.

HERALD:
This sullen hatred—how did it fasten on you?

LEADER OF THE CHORUS:
I cannot say. Silence is my stock prescription.

HERALD:
What? In your masters' absence were there some you
  feared?

LEADER OF THE CHORUS:
Yes. In your phrase, death would now be a gratification.

HERALD:
Yes, for success is ours. These things have taken time.
Some of them we could say have fallen well,
While some we blame. Yet who except the gods
Is free from pain the whole duration of life?
If I were to tell of our labours, our hard lodging,
The sleeping on crowded decks, the scanty blankets,
Tossing and groaning, rations that never reached us—
And the land too gave matter for more disgust,
For our beds lay under the enemy's walls.
Continuous drizzle from the sky, dews from the marshes,
Rotting our clothes, filling our hair with lice.
And if one were to tell of the bird-destroying winter
Intolerable from the snows of Ida
Or of the heat when the sea slackens at noon
Waveless and dozing in a depressed calm—
But why make these complaints? The weariness is over;
Over indeed for some who never again
Need even trouble to rise.
Why make a computation of the lost?
Why need the living sorrow for the spites of fortune?
I wish to say a long goodbye to disasters.
For us, the remnant of the troops of Argos,
The advantage remains, the pain can not outweigh it;
So we can make our boast to this sun's light,
Flying on words above the land and sea:

'Having taken Troy the Argive expedition
Has nailed up throughout Greece in every temple
These spoils, these ancient trophies.'
Those who hear such things must praise the city
And the generals. And the grace of God be honoured
Which brought these things about. You have the whole
    story.

LEADER OF THE CHORUS:

I confess myself convinced by your report.
Old men are always young enough to learn.

                    [*Enter* CLYTEMNESTRA *from the palace.*

This news belongs by right first to the house
And Clytemnestra—though I am enriched also.

CLYTEMNESTRA:

Long before this I shouted at joy's command
At the coming of the first night-messenger of fire
Announcing the taking and capsizing of Troy.
And people reproached me saying, 'Do mere beacons
Persuade you to think that Troy is already down?
Indeed a woman's heart is easily exalted.'
Such comments made me seem to be wandering but yet
I began my sacrifices and in the women's fashion
Throughout the town they raised triumphant cries
And in the gods' enclosures
Lulling the fragrant, incense-eating flame.
And now what need is there for you to tell me more?
From the King himself I shall learn the whole story.
But how the best to welcome my honoured lord
I shall take pains when he comes back—For what
Is a kinder light for a woman to see than this,
To open the gates to her man come back from war
When God has saved him? Tell this to my husband,

To come with all speed, the city's darling;
May he returning find a wife as loyal
As when he left her, watchdog of the house,
Good to *him* but fierce to the ill-intentioned,
And in all other things as ever, having destroyed
No seal or pledge at all in the length of time.

I know no pleasure with another man, no scandal,
More than I know how to dye metal red.
Such is my boast, bearing a load of truth,
A boast that need not disgrace a noble wife.

[*Exit.*

LEADER OF THE CHORUS:

Thus has she spoken; if you take her meaning,
Only a specious tale to shrewd interpreters.
But do you, herald, tell me; I ask after Menelaus
Whether he will, returning safe preserved,
Come back with you, our land's loved master.

HERALD:

I am not able to speak the lovely falsehood
To profit you, my friends, for any stretch of time.

LEADER OF THE CHORUS:

But if only the true tidings could be also good!
It is hard to hide a division of good and true.

HERALD:

The prince is vanished out of the Greek fleet,
Himself and ship. I speak no lie.

LEADER OF THE CHORUS:

Did he put forth first in the sight of all from Troy,
Or a storm that troubled all sweep him apart?

HERALD:

You have hit the target like a master archer,
Told succinctly a long tale of sorrow.

LEADER OF THE CHORUS:

Did the rumours current among the remaining ships
Represent him as alive or dead?

HERALD:

No one knows so as to tell for sure
Except the sun who nurses the breeds of earth.

LEADER OF THE CHORUS:

Tell me how the storm came on the host of ships
Through the divine anger, and how it ended.

HERALD:

Day of good news should not be fouled by tongue
That tells ill news. To each god his season.
When, despair in his face, a messenger brings to a town

The hated news of a fallen army—
One general wound to the city and many men
Outcast, outcursed, from many homes
By the double whip which War is fond of,
Doom with a bloody spear in either hand,
One carrying such a pack of grief could well
Recite this hymn of the Furies at your asking.
But when our cause is saved and a messenger of good
Comes to a city glad with festivity,
How am I to mix good news with bad, recounting
The storm that meant God's anger on the Greeks?
For they swore together, those inveterate enemies,
Fire and sea, and proved their alliance, destroying
The unhappy troops of Argos.
In night arose ill-waved evil,
Ships on each other the blasts from Thrace
Crashed colliding, which butting with horns in the
        violence
Of big wind and rattle of rain were gone
To nothing, whirled all ways by a wicked shepherd.
But when there came up the shining light of the sun
We saw the Aegean sea flowering with corpses
Of Greek men and their ships' wreckage.
But for us, our ship was not damaged,
Whether someone snatched it away or begged it off,
Some god, not a man, handling the tiller;
And Saving Fortune was willing to sit upon our ship
So that neither at anchor we took the tilt of waves
Nor ran to splinters on the crag-bound coast.
But then having thus escaped death on the sea,
In the white day, not trusting our fortune,
We pastured this new trouble upon our thoughts,
The fleet being battered, the sailors weary,
And now if any of *them* still draw breath,
They are thinking no doubt of us as being lost
And we are thinking of them as being lost.
May the best happen. As for Menelaus
The first guess and most likely is a disaster.

But still—if any ray of sun detects him
Alive, with living eyes, by the plan of Zeus
Not yet resolved to annul the race completely,
There is some hope then that he will return home.
So much you have heard. Know that it is the truth.

[*Exit.*

CHORUS:
Who was it named her thus
In all ways appositely
Unless it was Someone whom we do not see,
Fore-knowing fate
And plying an accurate tongue?
Helen, bride of spears and conflict's
Focus, who as was befitting
Proved a hell to ships and men,
Hell to her country, sailing
Away from delicately-sumptuous curtains,
Away on the wind of a giant Zephyr,
And shielded hunters mustered many
On the vanished track of the oars,
Oars beached on the leafy
Banks of a Trojan river
For the sake of bloody war.

But on Troy was thrust a marring marriage
By the Wrath that working to an end exacts
In time a price from guests
Who dishonoured their host
And dishonoured Zeus of the Hearth,
From those noisy celebrants
Of the wedding hymn which fell
To the brothers of Paris
To sing upon that day.
But learning this, unlearning that,
Priam's ancestral city now
Continually mourns, reviling
Paris the fatal bridegroom.
The city has had much sorrow,

Much desolation in life,
From the pitiful loss of her people.

So in his house a man might rear
A lion's cub caught from the dam
In need of suckling,
In the prelude of its life
Mild, gentle with children,
For old men a playmate,
Often held in the arms
Like a new-born child,
Wheedling the hand,
Fawning at belly's bidding.

But matured by time he showed
The temper of his stock and payed
Thanks for his fostering
With disaster of slaughter of sheep
Making an unbidden banquet
And now the house is a shambles,
Irremediable grief to its people,
Calamitous carnage;
For the pet they had fostered was sent
By God as a priest of Ruin.

So I would say there came
To the city of Troy
A notion of windless calm,
Delicate adornment of riches,
Soft shooting of the eyes and flower
Of desire that stings the fancy.
But swerving aside she achieved
A bitter end to her marriage,
Ill guest and ill companion,
Hurled upon Priam's sons, convoyed
By Zeus, patron of guest and host,
Dark angel dowered with tears.

Long current among men an old saying
Runs that a man's prosperity

When grown to greatness
Comes to the birth, does not die childless—
His good luck breeds for his house
Distress that shall not be appeased.
I only, apart from the others,
Hold that the unrighteous action
Breeds true to its kind,
Leaves its own children behind it.
But the lot of a righteous house
Is a fair offspring always.

Ancient self-glory is accustomed
To bear to light in the evil sort of men
A new self-glory and madness,
Which sometime or sometime finds
The appointed hour for its birth,
And born therewith is the Spirit, intractable, unholy,
    irresistible,
The reckless lust that brings black Doom upon the house,
A child that is like its parents.

But Honest Dealing is clear
Shining in smoky homes,
Honours the god-fearing life.
Mansions gilded by filth of hands she leaves,
Turns her eyes elsewhere, visits the innocent house,
Not respecting the power
Of wealth mis-stamped with approval,
But guides all to the goal.

> [*Enter* AGAMEMNON *and* CASSANDRA *on chariots.*

CHORUS:
Come then my King, stormer of Troy,
Offspring of Atreus,
How shall I hail you, how give you honour
Neither overshooting nor falling short
    Of the measure of homage?
There are many who honour appearance too much
Passing the bounds that are right.
To condole with the unfortunate man

Each one is ready but the bite of the grief
   Never goes through to the heart.
And they join in rejoicing, affecting to share it,
Forcing their face to a smile.
But he who is shrewd to shepherd his sheep
Will fail not to notice the eyes of a man
Which seem to be loyal but lie,
   Fawning with watery friendship.
Even you, in my thought, when you marshalled the troops
For Helen's sake, I will not hide it,
Made a harsh and ugly picture,
Holding badly the tiller of reason,
Paying with the death of men
   Ransom for a willing whore.
But now, not unfriendly, not superficially,
I offer my service, well-doers' welcome.
In time you will learn by inquiry
Who has done rightly, who transgressed
   In the work of watching the city.

AGAMEMNON:

First to Argos and the country's gods
My fitting salutations, who have aided me
To return and in the justice which I exacted
From Priam's city. Hearing the unspoken case
The gods unanimously had cast their vote
Into the bloody urn for the massacre of Troy;
But to the opposite urn
Hope came, dangled her hand, but did no more.
Smoke marks even now the city's capture.
Whirlwinds of doom are alive, the dying ashes
Spread on the air the fat savour of wealth.
For these things we must pay some memorable return
To Heaven, having exacted enormous vengeance
For wife-rape; for a woman
The Argive monster ground a city to powder,
Sprung from a wooden horse, shield-wielding folk,
Launching a leap at the setting of the Pleiads,
Jumping the ramparts, a ravening lion,
Lapped its fill of the kingly blood.

To the gods I have drawn out this overture
But as for your concerns, I bear them in my mind
And say the same, you have me in agreement.
To few of men does it belong by nature
To congratulate their friends unenviously,
For a sullen poison fastens on the heart,
Doubling the pain of a man with this disease;
He feels the weight of his own griefs and when
He sees another's prosperity he groans.
I speak with knowledge, being well acquainted
With the mirror of comradeship—ghost of a shadow
Were those who seemed to be so loyal to me.
Only Odysseus, who sailed against his will,
Proved, when yoked with me, a ready tracehorse;
I speak of him not knowing if he is alive.
But for what concerns the city and the gods
Appointing public debates in full assembly
We shall consult. That which is well already
We shall take steps to ensure it remain well.
But where there is need of medical remedies,
By applying benevolent cautery or surgery
We shall try to deflect the dangers of disease.
But now, entering the halls where stands my hearth,
First I shall make salutation to the gods
Who sent me a far journey and have brought me back.
And may my victory not leave my side.

> [*Enter* CLYTEMNESTRA, *followed by women slaves*
> *carrying purple tapestries.*

CLYTEMNESTRA:
Men of the city, you the aged of Argos,
I shall feel no shame to describe to you my love
Towards my husband. Shyness in all of us
Wears thin with time. Here are the facts first hand.
I will tell you of my own unbearable life
I led so long as this man was at Troy.
For first that the woman separate from her man
Should sit alone at home is extreme cruelty,
Hearing so many malignant rumours—First
Comes one, and another comes after, bad news to worse,

Clamour of grief to the house. If Agamemnon
Had had so many wounds as those reported
Which poured home through the pipes of hearsay, then—
Then he would be gashed fuller than a net has holes!
And if only he had died . . . as often as rumour told us,
He would be like the giant in the legend,
Three-bodied. Dying once for every body,
He should have by now three blankets of earth above
    him—
All that above him; I care not how deep the mattress
    under!
Such are the malignant rumours thanks to which
They have often seized me against my will and undone
The loop of a rope from my neck.
And this is why our son is not standing here,
The guarantee of your pledges and mine,
As he should be, Orestes. Do not wonder;
He is being brought up by a friendly ally and host,
Strophius the Phocian, who warned me in advance
Of dubious troubles, both your risks at Troy
And the anarchy of shouting mobs that might
Overturn policy, for it is born in men
To kick the man who is down.
This is not a disingenuous excuse.
For me the outrushing wells of weeping are dried up,
There is no drop left in them.
My eyes are sore from sitting late at nights
Weeping for you and for the baffled beacons,
Never lit up. And, when I slept, in dreams
I have been waked by the thin whizz of a buzzing
Gnat, seeing more horrors fasten on you
Than could take place in the mere time of my dream.
Having endured all this, now, with unsorrowed heart
I would hail this man as the watchdog of the farm,
Forestay that saves the ship, pillar that props
The lofty roof, appearance of an only son
To a father or of land to sailors past their hope,
The loveliest day to see after the storm,
Gush of well-water for the thirsty traveller.

Such are the metaphors I think befit him,
But envy be absent. Many misfortunes already
We have endured. But now, dear head, come down
Out of that car, not placing upon the ground
Your foot, O King, the foot that trampled Troy.
Why are you waiting, slaves, to whom the task is assigned
To spread the pavement of his path with tapestries?
At once, at once let his way be strewn with purple
That Justice lead him toward his unexpected home.
The rest a mind, not overcome by sleep
Will arrange rightly, with God's help, as destined.

AGAMEMNON:

Daughter of Leda, guardian of my house,
You have spoken in proportion to my absence.
You have drawn your speech out long. Duly to praise me,
That is a duty to be performed by others.
And further—do not by women's methods make me
Effeminate nor in barbarian fashion
Gape ground-grovelling acclamations at me
Nor strewing my path with cloths make it invidious.
It is the gods should be honoured in this way.
But being mortal to tread embroidered beauty
For me is no way without fear.
I tell you to honour me as a man, not god.
Footcloths are very well—Embroidered stuffs
Are stuff for gossip. And not to think unwisely
Is the greatest gift of God. Call happy only him
Who has ended his life in sweet prosperity.
I have spoken. This thing I could not do with confidence.

CLYTEMNESTRA:

Tell me now, according to your judgment.

AGAMEMNON:

I tell you you shall not override my judgment.

CLYTEMNESTRA:

Supposing you had feared something . . .
Could you have vowed to God to do this thing?

AGAMEMNON:

Yes. If an expert had prescribed that vow.

CLYTEMNESTRA:
And how would Priam have acted in your place?

AGAMEMNON:
He would have trod the cloths, I think, for certain.

CLYTEMNESTRA:
Then do not flinch before the blame of men.

AGAMEMNON:
The voice of the multitude is very strong.

CLYTEMNESTRA:
But the man none envy is not enviable.

AGAMEMNON:
It is not a woman's part to love disputing.

CLYTEMNESTRA:
But it is a conqueror's part to yield upon occasion.

AGAMEMNON:
You think such victory worth fighting for?

CLYTEMNESTRA:
Give way. Consent to let me have the mastery.

AGAMEMNON:
Well, if such is your wish, let someone quickly loose
My vassal sandals, underlings of my feet,
And stepping on these sea-purples may no god
Shoot me from far with the envy of his eye.
Great shame it is to ruin my house and spoil
The wealth of costly weavings with my feet.
But of this matter enough. This stranger woman here
Take in with kindness. The man who is a gentle master
God looks on from far off complacently.
For no one of his will bears the slave's yoke.
This woman, of many riches being the chosen
Flower, gift of the soldiers, has come with me.
But since I have been prevailed on by your words
I will go to my palace home, treading on purples.

> [*He dismounts from the chariot and begins to walk up the tapestried path. During the following speech he enters the palace.*

CLYTEMNESTRA:
There is the sea and who shall drain it dry? It breeds

Its wealth in silver of plenty of purple gushing
And ever-renewed, the dyeings of our garments.
The house has its store of these by God's grace, King.
This house is ignorant of poverty
And I would have vowed a pavement of many garments
Had the palace oracle enjoined that vow
Thereby to contrive a ransom for his life.
For while there is root, foliage comes to the house
Spreading a tent of shade against the Dog Star.
So now that you have reached your hearth and home
You prove a miracle—advent of warmth in winter;
And further this—even in the time of heat
When God is fermenting wine from the bitter grape,
Even then it is cool in the house if only
Its master walk at home, a grown man, ripe.
O Zeus the Ripener, ripen these my prayers;
Your part it is to make the ripe fruit fall.

                                    [*She enters the palace.*

CHORUS:
Why, why at the doors
Of my fore-seeing heart
Does this terror keep beating its wings?
And my song play the prophet
Unbidden, unhired—
Which I cannot spit out
Like the enigmas of dreams
Nor plausible confidence
Sit on the throne of my mind?
It is long time since
The cables let down from the stern
Were chafed by the sand when the seafaring army started
    for Troy.

And I learn with my eyes
And witness myself their return;
But the hymn without lyre goes up,
The dirge of the Avenging Fiend,
In the depths of my self-taught heart
Which has lost its dear

Possession of the strength of hope.
But my guts and my heart
Are not idle which seethe with the waves
Of trouble nearing its hour.
But I pray that these thoughts
May fall out not as I think
   And not be fulfilled in the end.

Truly when health grows much
It respects not limit; for disease,
Its neighbour in the next door room,
Presses upon it.
A man's life, crowding sail,
Strikes on the blind reef:
But if caution in advance
Jettison part of the cargo
With the derrick of due proportion,
The whole house does not sink,
Though crammed with a weight of woe
The hull does not go under.
The abundant bounty of God
And his gifts from the year's furrows
Drive the famine back.

But when upon the ground there has fallen once
The black blood of a man's death,
Who shall summon it back by incantations?
Even Asclepius who had the art
To fetch the dead to life, even to him
Zeus put a provident end.
But, if of the heaven-sent fates
One did not check the other,
Cancel the other's advantage,
My heart would outrun my tongue
In pouring out these fears.
But now it mutters in the dark,
Embittered, no way hoping
To unravel a scheme in time
   From a burning mind.

[CLYTEMNESTRA *appears in the door of the palace.*

CLYTEMNESTRA:
Go in too, you; I speak to you, Cassandra,
Since God in his clemency has put you in this house
To share our holy water, standing with many slaves
Beside the altar that protects the house,
Step down from the car there, do not be overproud.
Heracles himself they say was once
Sold, and endured to eat the bread of slavery.
But should such a chance inexorably fall,
There is much advantage in masters who have long been
   rich.
Those who have reaped a crop they never expected
Are in all things hard on their slaves and overstep the
   line.
From us you will have the treatment of tradition.

LEADER OF THE CHORUS:
You, it is you she has addressed, and clearly.
Caught as you are in these predestined toils
Obey her if you can. But should you disobey . . .

CLYTEMNESTRA:
If she has more than the gibberish of the swallow,
An unintelligible barbaric speech,
I hope to read her mind, persuade her reason.

LEADER OF THE CHORUS:
As things now stand for you, she says the best.
Obey her; leave that car and follow her.

CLYTEMNESTRA:
I have no leisure to waste out here, outside the door.
Before the hearth in the middle of my house
The victims stand already, wait the knife.
You, if you will obey me, waste no time.
But if you cannot understand my language—
                                    [*To* CHORUS LEADER
You make it plain to her with the brute and voiceless
   hand

LEADER OF THE CHORUS:

The stranger seems to need a clear interpreter.
She bears herself like a wild beast newly captured.

CLYTEMNESTRA:

The fact is she is mad, she listens to evil thoughts,
Who has come here leaving a city newly captured
Without experience how to bear the bridle
So as not to waste her strength in foam and blood.
I will not spend more words to be ignored.

[*She re-enters the palace.*

CHORUS:

But I, for I pity her, will not be angry.
Obey, unhappy woman. Leave this car.
Yield to your fate. Put on the untried yoke.

CASSANDRA:

Apollo! Apollo!

CHORUS:

Why do you cry like this upon Apollo?
He is not the kind of god that calls for dirges.

CASSANDRA:

Apollo! Apollo!

CHORUS:

Once more her funereal cries invoke the god
Who has no place at the scene of lamentation.

CASSANDRA:

Apollo! Apollo!
God of the Ways! My destroyer!
Destroyed again—and this time utterly!

CHORUS:

She seems about to predict her own misfortunes.
The gift of the god endures, even in a slave's mind.

CASSANDRA:

Apollo! Apollo!
God of the Ways! My destroyer!
Where? To what house? Where, where have you brought
    me?

CHORUS:

To the house of the sons of Atreus. If you do not know it,

I will tell you so. You will not find it false.

CASSANDRA:

No, no, but to a god-hated, but to an accomplice
In much kin-killing, murdering nooses,
Man-shambles, a floor asperged with blood.

CHORUS:

The stranger seems like a hound with a keen scent,
Is picking up a trail that leads to murder.

CASSANDRA:

Clues! I have clues! Look! They are these.
These wailing, these children, butchery of children;
Roasted flesh, a father sitting to dinner.

CHORUS:

Of your prophetic fame we have heard before
But in this matter prophets are not required.

CASSANDRA:

What is she doing? What is she planning?
What is this new great sorrow?
Great crime . . . within here . . . planning
Unendurable to his folk, impossible
Ever to be cured. For help
    Stands far distant.

CHORUS:

This reference I cannot catch. But the children
I recognized; that refrain is hackneyed.

CASSANDRA:

Damned, damned, bringing this work to completion—
Your husband who shared your bed
To bathe him, to cleanse him, and then—
How shall I tell of the end?
Soon, very soon, it will fall.
    The end comes hand over hand
Grasping in greed.

CHORUS:

Not yet do I understand. After her former riddles
Now I am baffled by these dim pronouncements.

CASSANDRA:

Ah God, the vision! God, God, the vision!
A net, is it? Net of Hell!

But herself is the net; shared bed; shares murder.
O let the pack ever-hungering after the family
Howl for the unholy ritual, howl for the victim.

CHORUS:

What black Spirit is this you call upon the house—
To raise aloft her cries? Your speech does not lighten me.
Into my heart runs back the blood
Yellow as when for men by the spear fallen
The blood ebbs out with the rays of the setting life
    And death strides quickly.

CASSANDRA:

Quick! Be on your guard! The bull—
Keep him clear of the cow.
Caught with a trick, the black horn's point,
She strikes. He falls; lies in the water.
Murder; a trick in a bath. I tell what I see.

CHORUS:

I would not claim to be expert in oracles
But these, as I deduce, portend disaster.
Do men ever get a good answer from oracles?
No. It is only through disaster
That their garrulous craft brings home
The meaning of the prophet's panic.

CASSANDRA:

And for me also, for me, chance ill-destined!
My own now I lament, pour into the cup my own.
Where is this you have brought me in my misery?
Unless to die as well. What else is meant?

CHORUS:

You are mad, mad, carried away by the god,
Raising the dirge, the tuneless
Tune, for yourself. Like the tawny
Unsatisfied singer from her luckless heart
Lamenting 'Itys, Itys', the nightingale
Lamenting a life luxuriant with grief.

CASSANDRA:

Oh the lot of the songful nightingale!
The gods enclosed her in a winged body,
Gave her a sweet and tearless passing.

But for me remains the two-edged cutting blade.

CHORUS:
From whence these rushing and God-inflicted
Profitless pains?
Why shape with your sinister crying
The piercing hymn—fear-piercing?
How can you know the evil-worded landmarks
  On the prophetic path?

CASSANDRA:
Oh the wedding, the wedding of Paris—death to his
  people!
O river Scamander, water drunk by my fathers!
When I was young, alas, upon your beaches
I was brought up and cared for.
But now it is the River of Wailing and the banks of Hell
  That shall hear my prophecy soon.

CHORUS:
What is this clear speech, too clear?
A child could understand it.
I am bitten with fangs that draw blood
By the misery of your cries,
Cries harrowing the heart.

CASSANDRA:
O trouble on trouble of a city lost, lost utterly!
My father's sacrifices before the towers,
Much killing of cattle and sheep,
No cure—availed not at all
To prevent the coming of what came to Troy,
And I, my brain on fire, shall soon enter the trap.

CHORUS:
This speech accords with the former.
What god, malicious, over-heavy, persistently pressing,
Drives you to chant of these lamentable
Griefs with death their burden?
But I cannot see the end.

                    [CASSANDRA *now steps down from the car.*

CASSANDRA:
The oracle now no longer from behind veils
Will be peeping forth like a newly-wedded bride;

But I can feel it like a fresh wind swoop
And rush in the face of the dawn and, wave-like, wash
Against the sun a vastly greater grief
Than this one. I shall speak no more conundrums.
And bear me witness, pacing me, that I
Am trailing on the scent of ancient wrongs.
For this house here a choir never deserts,
Chanting together ill. For they mean ill,
And to puff up their arrogance they have drunk
Men's blood, this band of revellers that haunts the house,
Hard to be rid of, fiends that attend the family.
Established in its rooms they hymn their hymn
Of that original sin, abhor in turn
The adultery that proved a brother's ruin.
A miss? Or do my arrows hit the mark?
Or am I a quack prophet who knocks at doors, a babbler?
Give me your oath, confess I have the facts,
The ancient history of this house's crimes.

LEADER OF THE CHORUS:
And how could an oath's assurance, however finely
    assured,
Turn out a remedy? I wonder, though, that you
Being brought up overseas, of another tongue,
Should hit on the whole tale as if you had been standing
    by.

CASSANDRA:
Apollo the prophet set me to prophesy.

LEADER OF THE CHORUS:
Was he, although a god, struck by desire?

CASSANDRA:
Till now I was ashamed to tell that story.

LEADER OF THE CHORUS:
Yes. Good fortune keeps us all fastidious.

CASSANDRA:
He wrestled hard upon me, panting love.

LEADER OF THE CHORUS:
And did you come, as they do, to child-getting?

CASSANDRA:
No. I agreed to him. And I cheated him.

LEADER OF THE CHORUS:
Were you already possessed by the mystic art?

CASSANDRA:
Already I was telling the townsmen all their future
suffering.

LEADER OF THE CHORUS:
Then how did you escape the doom of Apollo's anger?

CASSANDRA:
I did not escape. No one ever believed me.

LEADER OF THE CHORUS:
Yet to us your words seem worthy of belief.

CASSANDRA:
Oh misery, misery!
Again comes on me the terrible labour of true
Prophecy, dizzying prelude; distracts . . .
Do you see these who sit before the house,
Children, like the shapes of dreams?
Children who seem to have been killed by their kinsfolk,
Filling their hands with meat, flesh of themselves,
Guts and entrails, handfuls of lament—
Clear what they hold—the same their father tasted.
For this I declare someone is plotting vengeance—
A lion? Lion but coward, that lurks in bed,
Good watchdog truly against the lord's return—
My lord, for I must bear the yoke of serfdom.
Leader of the ships, overturner of Troy,
He does not know what plots the accursed hound
With the licking tongue and the pricked-up ear will plan
In the manner of a lurking doom, in an evil hour.
A daring criminal! Female murders male.
What monster could provide her with a title?
An amphisbaena or hag of the sea who dwells
In rocks to ruin sailors—
A raving mother of death who breathes against her folk
War to the finish. Listen to her shout of triumph,
Who shirks no horrors, like men in a rout of battle.
And yet she poses as glad at their return.
If you distrust my words, what does it matter?

That which will come will come. You too will soon stand
here
And admit with pity that I spoke too truly.

LEADER OF THE CHORUS:
Thyestes' dinner of his children's meat
I understood and shuddered, and fear grips me
To hear the truth, not framed in parables.
But hearing the rest I am thrown out of my course.

CASSANDRA:
It is Agamemnon's death I tell you you shall witness.

LEADER OF THE CHORUS:
Stop! Provoke no evil. Quiet your mouth!

CASSANDRA:
The god who gives me words is here no healer.

LEADER OF THE CHORUS:
Not if this shall be so. But may some chance avert it.

CASSANDRA:
You are praying. But others are busy with murder.

LEADER OF THE CHORUS:
What man is he promotes this terrible thing?

CASSANDRA:
Indeed you have missed my drift by a wide margin!

LEADER OF THE CHORUS:
But I do not understand the assassin's method.

CASSANDRA:
And yet too well I know the speech of Greece!

LEADER OF THE CHORUS:
So does Delphi but the replies are hard.

CASSANDRA:
Ah what a fire it is! It comes upon me.
Apollo, Wolf-Destroyer, pity, pity . . .
It is the two-foot lioness who beds
Beside a wolf, the noble lion away,
It is she will kill me. Brewing a poisoned cup
She will mix my punishment too in the angry draught
And boasts, sharpening the dagger for her husband,
To pay back murder for my bringing here.
Why then do I wear these mockeries of myself,
The wand and the prophet's garland round my neck?

My hour is coming—but you shall perish first.
Destruction! Scattered thus you give me my revenge;
Go and enrich some other woman with ruin.
See: Apollo himself is stripping me
Of my prophetic gear, who has looked on
When in this dress I have been a laughing-stock
To friends and foes alike, and to no purpose;
They called me crazy, like a fortune-teller,
A poor starved beggar-woman—and I bore it.
And now the prophet undoing his prophetess
Has brought me to this final darkness.
Instead of my father's altar the executioner's block
Waits me the victim, red with my hot blood.
But the gods will not ignore me as I die.
One will come after to avenge my death,
A matricide, a murdered father's champion.
Exile and tramp and outlaw he will come back
To gable the family house of fatal crime;
His father's outstretched corpse shall lead him home.
Why need I then lament so pitifully?
For now that I have seen the town of Troy
Treated as she was treated, while her captors
Come to their reckoning thus by the god's verdict,
I will go in and have the courage to die.
Look, these gates are the gates of Death. I greet them.
And I pray that I may meet a deft and mortal stroke
So that without a struggle I may close
My eyes and my blood ebb in easy death.

LEADER OF THE CHORUS:
Oh woman very unhappy and very wise,
Your speech was long. But if in sober truth
You know your fate, why like an ox that the gods
Drive, do you walk so bravely to the altar?

CASSANDRA:
There is no escape, strangers. No; not by postponement

LEADER OF THE CHORUS:
But the last moment has the privilege of hope.

CASSANDRA:
The day is here. Little should I gain by flight.

LEADER OF THE CHORUS:
This patience of yours comes from a brave soul.

CASSANDRA:
A happy man is never paid that compliment.

LEADER OF THE CHORUS:
But to die with credit graces a mortal man.

CASSANDRA:
Oh my father! You and your noble sons!
[*She approaches the door, then suddenly recoils.*

LEADER OF THE CHORUS:
What is it? What is the fear that drives you back?

CASSANDRA:
Faugh.

LEADER OF THE CHORUS:
Why faugh? Or is this some hallucination?

CASSANDRA:
These walls breathe out a death that drips with blood.

LEADER OF THE CHORUS:
Not so. It is only the smell of the sacrifice.

CASSANDRA:
It is like a breath out of a charnel-house.

LEADER OF THE CHORUS:
You think our palace burns odd incense then!

CASSANDRA:
But I will go to lament among the dead
My lot and Agamemnon's. Enough of life!
Strangers,
I am not afraid like a bird afraid of a bush
But witness you my words after my death
When a woman dies in return for me a woman
And a man falls for a man with a wicked wife.
I ask this service, being about to die.

LEADER OF THE CHORUS:
Alas, I pity you for the death you have foretold.

CASSANDRA:
One more speech I have; I do not wish to raise
The dirge for my own self. But to the sun I pray
In face of his last light that my avengers
May make my murderers pay for this my death,

Death of a woman slave, an easy victim.

[She enters the palace.

LEADER OF THE CHORUS:
    Ah the fortunes of men! When they go well
    A shadow sketch would match them, and in ill-fortune
    The dab of a wet sponge destroys the drawing.
    It is not myself but the life of man I pity.
CHORUS:
    Prosperity in all men cries
    For more prosperity. Even the owner
    Of the finger-pointed-at palace never shuts
    His door against her, saying 'Come no more'.
    So to our king the blessed gods had granted
    To take the town of Priam, and heaven-favoured
    He reaches home. But now if for former bloodshed
        He must pay blood
    And dying for the dead shall cause
        Other deaths in atonement
    What man could boast he was born
        Secure, who heard this story?

AGAMEMNON:

[Within

    Oh! I am struck a mortal blow—within!

LEADER OF THE CHORUS:
    Silence! Listen. Who calls out, wounded with a mortal
        stroke?

AGAMEMNON:
    Again—the second blow—I am struck again.

LEADER OF THE CHORUS:
    You heard the king cry out. I think the deed is done.
    Let us see if we can concert some sound proposal.
2ND OLD MAN:
    Well, I will tell you my opinion—
    Raise an alarm, summon the folk to the palace.

3RD OLD MAN:

    I say burst in with all speed possible,
    Convict them of the deed while still the sword is wet.

4TH OLD MAN:

    And I am partner to some such suggestion.
    I am for taking some course. No time to dawdle.

5TH OLD MAN:

    The case is plain. This is but the beginning.
    They are going to set up dictatorship in the state.

6TH OLD MAN:

    We are wasting time. The assassins tread to earth
    The decencies of delay and give their hands no sleep.

7TH OLD MAN:

    I do not know what plan I could hit on to propose.
    The man who acts is in the position to plan.

8TH OLD MAN:

    So I think, too, for I am at a loss
    To raise the dead man up again with words.

9TH OLD MAN:

    Then to stretch out our life shall we yield thus
    To the rule of these profaners of the house?

10TH OLD MAN:

    It is not to be endured. To die is better.
    Death is more comfortable than tyranny.

11TH OLD MAN:

    And are we on the evidence of groans
    Going to give oracle that the prince is dead?

12TH OLD MAN:

    We must know the facts for sure and *then* be angry.
    Guesswork is not the same as certain knowledge.

LEADER OF THE CHORUS:

    Then all of you back me and approve this plan—
    To ascertain how it is with Agamemnon.

> [*The doors of the palace open, revealing the
> bodies of* AGAMEMNON *and* CASSANDRA. CLYTEM·
> NESTRA *stands above them.*

CLYTEMNESTRA:
    Much having been said before to fit the moment,
    To say the opposite now will not outface me.
    How else could one serving hate upon the hated,
    Thought to be friends, hang high the nets of doom
    To preclude all leaping out?
    For me I have long been training for this match,
    I tried a fall and won—a victory overdue.
    I stand here where I struck, above my victims;
    So I contrived it—this I will not deny—
    That he could neither fly nor ward off death;
    Inextricable like a net for fishes
    I cast about him a vicious wealth of raiment
    And struck him twice and with two groans he loosed
    His limbs beneath him, and upon him fallen
    I deal him the third blow to the God beneath the earth,
    To the safe keeper of the dead a votive gift,
    And with that he spits his life out where he lies
    And smartly spouting blood he sprays me with
    The sombre drizzle of bloody dew and I
    Rejoice no less than in God's gift of rain
    The crops are glad when the ear of corn gives birth.
    These things being so, you, elders of Argos,
    Rejoice if rejoice you will. Mine is the glory.
    And if I could pay this corpse his due libation
    I should be right to pour it and more than right;
    With so many horrors this man mixed and filled
    The bowl—and, coming home, has drained the draught
        himself.
LEADER OF THE CHORUS:
    Your speech astonishes us. This brazen boast
    Above the man who was your king and husband!
CLYTEMNESTRA:
    You challenge me as a woman without foresight
    But I with unflinching heart to you who know
    Speak. And you, whether you will praise or blame,
    It makes no matter. Here lies Agamemnon,
    My husband, dead, the work of this right hand,
    An honest workman. There you have the facts.

CHORUS:
> Woman, what poisoned
> Herb of the earth have you tasted
> Or potion of the flowing sea
> To undertake this killing and the people's curses?
> You threw down, you cut off—The people will cast you
>   out,
> Black abomination to the town.

CLYTEMNESTRA:
> Now your verdict—in my case—is exile
> And to have the people's hatred, the public curses,
> Though then in no way you opposed this man
> Who carelessly, as if it were a head of sheep
> Out of the abundance of his fleecy flocks,
> Sacrificed his own daughter, to me the dearest
> Fruit of travail, charm for the Thracian winds.
> He was the one to have banished from this land,
> Pay off the pollution. But when you hear what I
> Have done, you judge severely. But I warn you—
> Threaten me on the understanding that I am ready
> For two alternatives—Win by force the right
> To rule me, but, if God brings about the contrary,
> Late in time you will have to learn self-discipline.

CHORUS:
> You are high in the thoughts,
> You speak extravagant things,
> After the soiling murder your crazy heart
> Fancies your forehead with a smear of blood.
> Unhonoured, unfriended, you must
> Pay for a blow with a blow.

CLYTEMNESTRA:
> Listen then to this—the sanction of my oaths:
> By the Justice totting up my child's atonement,
> By the Avenging Doom and Fiend to whom I killed this
>   man,
> For me hope walks not in the rooms of fear
> So long as my fire is lit upon my hearth
> By Aegisthus, loyal to me as he was before.
> The man who outraged me lies here,

The darling of each courtesan at Troy,
And here with him is the prisoner clairvoyante,
The fortune-teller that he took to bed,
Who shares his bed as once his bench on shipboard,
A loyal mistress. Both have their deserts.
He lies so; and she who like a swan
Sang her last dying lament
Lies his lover, and the sight contributes
An appetiser to my own bed's pleasure.

CHORUS:
Ah would some quick death come not overpainful,
Not overlong on the sickbed,
Establishing in us the ever-
Lasting unending sleep now that our guardian
Has fallen, the kindest of men,
Who suffering much for a woman
By a woman has lost his life.

   O Helen, insane, being one
   One to have destroyed so many
   And many souls under Troy,
   Now is your work complete, blossomed not for oblivion,
   Unfading stain of blood. Here now, if in any home,
   Is Discord, here is a man's deep-rooted ruin.

CLYTEMNESTRA:
Do not pray for the portion of death
Weighed down by these things, do not turn
Your anger on Helen as destroyer of men,
One woman destroyer of many
Lives of Greek men,
   A hurt that cannot be healed.

CHORUS:
O Evil Spirit, falling on the family,
On the two sons of Atreus and using
Two sisters in heart as your tools,
A power that bites to the heart—
See on the body
Perched like a raven he gloats
Harshly croaking his hymn.

CLYTEMNESTRA:

Ah, now you have amended your lips' opinion,
Calling upon this family's three times gorged
Genius—demon who breeds
Blood-hankering lust in the belly:
Before the old sore heals, new pus collects.

CHORUS:

It is a great spirit—great—
You tell of, harsh in anger,
A ghastly tale, alas,
Of unsatisfied disaster
Brought by Zeus, by Zeus,
Cause and worker of all.
For without Zeus what comes to pass among us?
Which of these things is outside Providence?
    O my king, my king,
    How shall I pay you in tears,
    Speak my affection in words?
    You lie in that spider's web,
    In a desecrating death breathe out your life,
    Lie ignominiously
    Defeated by a crooked death
    And the two-edged cleaver's stroke.

CLYTEMNESTRA:

You say this is *my* work—mine?
Do not cozen yourself that I am Agamemnon's wife.
Masquerading as the wife
Of the corpse there the old sharp-witted Genius
Of Atreus who gave the cruel banquet
Has paid with a grown man's life
The due for children dead.

CHORUS:

That you are not guilty of
This murder who will attest?
No, but you may have been abetted
By some ancestral Spirit of Revenge.
Wading a millrace of the family's blood
The black Manslayer forces a forward path
To make the requital at last

For the eaten children, the blood-clot cold with time.
  O my king, my king,
  How shall I pay you in tears,
  Speak my affection in words?
  You lie in that spider's web,
  In a desecrating death breathe out your life,
  Lie ignominiously
  Defeated by a crooked death
  And the two-edged cleaver's stroke.

CLYTEMNESTRA:
  Did he not, too, contrive a crooked
  Horror for the house? My child by him,
  Shoot that I raised, much-wept-for Iphigeneia,
  He treated her like this;
  So suffering like this he need not make
  Any great brag in Hell having paid with death
  Dealt by the sword for work of his own beginning.

CHORUS:
  I am at a loss for thought, I lack
  All nimble counsel as to where
  To turn when the house is falling.
  I fear the house-collapsing crashing
  Blizzard of blood—of which these drops are earnest.
  Now is Destiny sharpening her justice
  On other whetstones for a new infliction.
    O earth, earth, if only you had received me
    Before I saw this man lie here as if in bed
        In a bath lined with silver.
    Who will bury him? Who will keen him?
    Will you, having killed your own husband,
    Dare now to lament him
    And after great wickedness make
        Unamending amends to his ghost?
    And who above this godlike hero's grave
    Pouring praises and tears
        Will grieve with a genuine heart?

CLYTEMNESTRA:
  It is not your business to attend to that.
  By my hand he fell low, lies low and dead,

And I shall bury him low down in the earth,
And his household need not weep him
For Iphigeneia his daughter
Tenderly, as is right,
Will meet her father at the rapid ferry of sorrows,
Put her arms round him and kiss him!

CHORUS:
Reproach answers reproach,
It is hard to decide,
The catcher is caught, the killer pays for his kill.
But the law abides while Zeus abides enthroned
That the wrongdoer suffers. That is established.
Who could expel from the house the seed of the Curse?
The race is soldered in sockets of Doom and Vengeance.

CLYTEMNESTRA:
In this you say what is right and the will of God.
But for my part I am ready to make a contract
With the Evil Genius of the House of Atreus
To accept what has been till now, hard though it is,
But that for the future he shall leave this house
And wear away some other stock with deaths
Imposed among themselves. Of my possessions
A small part will suffice if only I
Can rid these walls of the mad exchange of murder.

[*Enter* AEGISTHUS, *followed by soldiers.*

AEGISTHUS:
O welcome light of a justice-dealing day!
From now on I will say that the gods, avenging men,
Look down from above on the crimes of earth,
Seeing as I do in woven robes of the Furies
This man lying here—a sight to warm my heart—
Paying for the crooked violence of his father.
For his father Atreus, when he ruled the country,
Because his power was challenged, hounded out
From state and home his own brother Thyestes.
My father—let me be plain—was this Thyestes,
Who later came back home a suppliant,

There, miserable, found so much asylum
As not to die on the spot, stain the ancestral floor.
But to show his hospitality godless Atreus
Gave him an eager if not a loving welcome,
Pretending a day of feasting and rich meats
Served my father with his children's flesh.
The hands and feet, fingers and toes, he hid
At the bottom of the dish. My father sitting apart
Took unknowing the unrecognizable portion
And ate of a dish that has proved, as you see, expensive.
But when he knew he had eaten worse than poison
He fell back groaning, vomiting their flesh,
And invoking a hopeless doom on the sons of Pelops
Kicked over the table to confirm his curse—
So may the whole race perish!
Result of this—you see this man lie here.
I stitched this murder together; it was my title.
Me the third son he left, an unweaned infant,
To share the bitterness of my father's exile.
But I grew up and Justice brought me back,
I grappled this man while still beyond his door,
Having pieced together the programme of his ruin.
So now would even death be beautiful to me
Having seen Agamemnon in the nets of Justice.

LEADER OF THE CHORUS:

Aegisthus. I cannot respect brutality in distress.
You claim that you deliberately killed this prince
And that you alone planned this pitiful murder.
Be sure that in your turn your head shall not escape
The people's volleyed curses mixed with stones.

AEGISTHUS:

Do you speak so who sit at the lower oar
While those on the upper bench control the ship?
Old as you are, you will find it is a heavy load
To go to school when old to learn the lesson of tact.
For old age, too, gaol and hunger are fine
Instructors in wisdom, second-sighted doctors.
You have eyes. Cannot you see?
Do not kick against the pricks. The blow will hurt you

LEADER OF THE CHORUS:

> You woman waiting in the house for those who return
>   from battle
> While you seduce their wives! Was it you devised
> The death of a master of armies?

AEGISTHUS:

> And these words, too, prepare the way for tears.
> Contrast your voice with the voice of Orpheus: he
> Led all things after him bewitched with joy, but you
> Having stung me with your silly yelps shall be
> Led off yourself, to prove more mild when mastered.

LEADER OF THE CHORUS:

> Indeed! So you are now to be king of Argos,
> You who, when you had plotted the king's death,
> Did not even dare to do that thing yourself!

AEGISTHUS:

> No. For the trick of it was clearly woman's work.
> I was suspect, an enemy of old.
> But now I shall try with Agamemnon's wealth
> To rule the people. Any who is disobedient
> I will harness in a heavy yoke, no tracehorse work for him
> Like barley-fed colt, but hateful hunger lodging
> Beside him in the dark will see his temper soften.

LEADER OF THE CHORUS:

> Why with your cowardly soul did you yourself
> Not strike this man but left that work to a woman
> Whose presence pollutes our country and its gods?
> But Orestes—does he somewhere see the light
> That he may come back here by favour of fortune
> And kill this pair and prove the final victor?

AEGISTHUS:

> [*Summoning his guards*
> Well, if such is your design in deeds and words, you will
>   quickly learn—
> Here my friends, here my guards, there is work for you
>   at hand.

LEADER OF THE CHORUS:

> Come then, hands on hilts, be each and all of us prepared.
>   [*The old men and the guards threaten each other.*

AEGISTHUS:

Very well! I too am ready to meet death with sword in hand.

LEADER OF THE CHORUS:

We are glad you speak of dying. We accept your words for luck.

CLYTEMNESTRA:

No, my dearest, do not so. Add no more to the train of wrong.

To reap these many present wrongs is harvest enough of misery.

Enough of misery. Start no more. Our hands are red.

But do you, and you old men, go home and yield to fate in time,

In time before you suffer. We have acted as we had to act.

If only our afflictions now could prove enough, we should agree—

We who have been so hardly mauled in the heavy claws of the evil god.

So stands my word, a woman's, if any man thinks fit to hear.

AEGISTHUS:

But to think that these should thus pluck the blooms of an idle tongue

And should throw out words like these, giving the evil god his chance,

And should miss the path of prudence and insult their master so!

LEADER OF THE CHORUS:

It is not the Argive way to fawn upon a cowardly man.

AEGISTHUS:

Perhaps. But I in later days will take further steps with you.

LEADER OF THE CHORUS:

Not if the god who rules the family guides Orestes to his home.

AEGISTHUS:

Yes. I know that men in exile feed themselves on barren hopes.

LEADER OF THE CHORUS:

Go on, grow fat defiling justice . . . while you have your
hour.

AEGISTHUS:

Do not think you will not pay me a price for your
stupidity.

LEADER OF THE CHORUS:

Boast on in your self-assurance, like a cock beside his hen.

CLYTEMNESTRA:

Pay no heed, Aegisthus, to these futile barkings. You and
I,

Masters of this house, from now shall order all things
well.

[*They enter the palace.*

NOTES

11   6   *The shining Masters*: The stars control the vicissi-
         tudes of time and the seasons. *Cf. Genesis* i. 16 *sq.*

12   20 *A great ox*: Proverbial; an ox (or, sometimes, a key) on
         the tongue signified keeping an uncomfortable secret.
         The Watchman, like his fellow citizens, is aware of
         the evil that has been done by Clytemnestra and
         Aegisthus during Agamemnon's absence at Troy.

12   24 CHORUS: The opening Chorus, an entry-song (*párodos*)
         passing without interruption into a long and elabo-
         rately constructed Ode (*stásimon*), is a complex mix-
         ture of narrative, philosophy, and theology. The nar-
         rative relates the circumstances attending the sailing
         of the Greek expedition for Troy. For a long time
         the fleet was held at the port of Aulis, the rendezvous,
         by adverse winds. The prophet Calchas, interpreting
         the omen of a pair of eagles destroying a pregnant
         hare, declared that the goddess Artemis had been
         offended and that the fleet could not sail until she
         had been propitiated by the ritual sacrifice of Aga-
         memnon's daughter, Iphigeneia. Agamemnon, in de-
         spair, consented to this necessary murder; the winds
         changed, the fleet sailed. Nevertheless the Chorus
         hints that in yielding to the demands of the prophet
         Agamemnon acted selfishly, and that his submission
         was, in effect, an act of *hybris,* a punishable arrogance.
         The theological point is delicate indeed; but there
         can be no doubt that it was the sacrifice of her
         daughter that Queen Clytemnestra made the pretext
         for her subsequent murder of Agamemnon.

13   35 *But you, daughter of Tyndareus*: Leda, wife of King
         Tyndareus of Sparta, was seduced by Zeus in the
         shape of a Swan. Of this union four children were
         born: the heroes Castor and Pollux; Clytemnestra, who
         married King Agamemnon of Argos; and Helen, who

became the wife of Agamemnon's brother Menelaus, and who later was carried off to Troy by Prince Paris Alexander. [Clytemnestra seems to have entered during the *párodos*. Certainly she is on the stage at this point; but she disdains the Chorus's questions, and may be supposed to make a silent exit at the end of this section.]

14   21   *Of the omen*: The Choral Ode begins.

15   31   *Zeus, whoever He is*: What shall we call God? 'Zeus' is a convention; but there is no certainty that the Name is right or acceptable. Man can only imperfectly apprehend God, through man-made symbols.

16   4   *Not He who formerly was great . . . And He who was next*: Uranus and Cronus, immediate ancestors of Zeus, both overthrown.

19   9   *In this very night*: The signal fires, starting with the beacon upon Mount Ida, have carried the news from Troy across the Aegean Sea. This fact is probable. The almost immediate entrance of Agamemnon, however, is a dramatic impossibility. The actualities of time, in these plays, are disregarded: each episode exists in its own time, and there is no attempt to bring about 'realistic' transitions.

23   10   *The grace of shapely statues*: The statues are hateful to Menelaus because they remind him of the beauty of his lost wife. Admetos, in the *Alcestis* of Euripides, makes a typically gross application of this idea (*cf.* p. 163:4).

32   35   *Long current among men*: Aeschylus, speaking through the Chorus, describes two theories of tragic action. According to the first, which is the more primitive, calamity is engendered by man's prosperity, whether the prosperity be innocent or guilty: 'His good luck breeds for his house/Distress'. The second theory, which the Chorus prefers, holds that the tragic downfall must be deserved, that it springs from some kind of 'unrighteous action'. It is interesting to reflect that the less rational of these ideas—there is a Némesis that punishes pre-eminence itself—was the one that reappeared in mediaeval thinking: so the definition of Tragedy in Chaucer's *Monk's Tale*:

> *Tragediës noon oother maner thyng*
> *Ne kan in synging crie ne biwaille*
> *But that Fortune alwey wole assaille*
> *With unwar strook the regnes that been proude;*
> *For whan men trusteth hire, thanne wol she faille,*
> *And covere hire brighte face with a clowde.*

Tragic art is wholly concerned, he says, with the unforeseen stroke of Fortune falling upon the haughty and the proud ('He hath put down the mighty from their seats': *Luke* i. 52) at the moment of their greatest self-confidence. The more philosophical idea, that the tragic hero coöperates in his own downfall, became an essential part of Aristotle's literary criticism.

36   6   *the giant in the legend*: Geryon, a three-headed, three-bodied monster killed by Heraklês.

38   23   *treading on purples*: Purple is the gods' color. Walking upon it, even without sandals, is a kind of profanation. It would be absurd to suppose that Agamemnon is 'punished' for this minor sacrilege. The act is important because it is symbolic, as Clytemnestra clearly intends it to be: Agamemnon's fall proceeds from the sum of his *hybris* before, during, and after the war at Troy. Iphigeneia, the murdered daughter, and Cassandra, the outraged priestess, are the two most obvious victims of his lack of control.

40   26   *Even Asclepius*: Cf. note to *Alcestis*, p. 149:4.

41   2   *Since God in his clemency*: The irony is bitter and spiteful. At the fall of Troy, Cassandra was ravished by the Lesser Ajax and taken into an exile of concubinage by Agamemnon. Clytemnestra has already planned to murder her.

42   18   *My destroyer!*: Apollo, attempting to win the love of the Princess Cassandra, gave her the gift of prophecy. She accepted the gift but tricked the god of his pleasure. Since Apollo could not retract what he had so solemnly given, he added, as an after-curse, that Cassandra's prophecies would never be believed. It was his continuing resentment that accounted for the calamitous treatment of her when Troy fell.

43   7   Cassandra. as prophetess, now experiences two visions

Page Line

of horror: 1], in retrospect, the ancestral curse of the house of Atreus; 2], in imminent prospect, the murder of Agamemnon. —Atreus, the father of Agamemnon and Menelaus, was adulterously offended by his brother Thyestes, the father of Aegisthus. Pretending a reconciliation, Atreus invited Thyestes to a feast, at which he served Thyestes the disguised flesh of the latter's infant sons. In a sense, then, Aegisthus's violent appropriation of Agamemnon's wife and throne is an act of retribution for the wrong done Thyestes by Atreus.

51 18 *I am struck a mortal blow—within!*: Something is clearly wrong with the text, but it is useless to try emendations. Naturally Agamemnon is being murdered 'within'—that is to say, off-stage, within the house; the absurdity lies in his being so specific.

51 19 *Silence! Listen.*: The Leader interrupts the Chorus at Agamemnon's first cry; after the second (which, again, is rather unnaturally specific) he opens a debate on the subject *What shall we old men do?* Each member of the Chorus proposes a two-line opinion, after which the Leader sums up: *We shall find out what has happened to the King.*—Here it is idle to try to find anything approaching probability of speech or action. It is almost as idle to try to avoid being amused. But what can the Chorus do? They can not leave the *orchêstra*; besides, if they were to burst into the house and interfere, they would spoil the drama. So they talk, helpless old men, absurdly. Unless Aeschylus is ironically commenting upon the usual reactions of the crowd at a moment of sudden public emergency—and this supposition is far from likely— we may as well conclude that the passage is a rare example of a great poet's being caught napping. In representation, the lines were better spoken all together in a noisy jumble. The opening of the palace door brings immediate silence.

55 31 *two sisters*: Helen and Clytemnestra.

60 27 *Come then, hands on hilts*: What hilts? Certainly the chorus is unarmed. Nor could they, in any circumstances, physically threaten Aegisthus.—The distribu-

tion of speeches is probably wrong, and a practical solution is to be found in George Thomson's translation (*The* Oresteia *of Aeschylus. Edited with Introduction, Translation, and a Commentary in which is included the work of the late Walter G. Headlam,* by George Thomson. Cambridge University Press, 1938):

CAPTAIN OF THE GUARD:
   Ho, let each man draw and hold his sword in readiness!
CHORUS:
   Be it so, we too are ready, unafraid to die.
AEGISTHUS:
   Die! Well-spoken, we shall gladly take you at your word.

The play ends abruptly, and it may be that some sort of concluding tag has been lost.

THE OEDIPUS REX
OF SOPHOCLES

TRANSLATED BY

DUDLEY FITTS AND
ROBERT FITZGERALD

INTRODUCTORY NOTE

The story of Oedipus attracted the attention of Sophocles at least three times in the course of his long life, and on each occasion he wrote a play that has withstood every assault of time and change. The first of these dramas, *Antigoné*, was produced between 442 and 440 B.C., the poet being then in his middle fifties. The second, *Oedipus Rex*, can not be dated with confidence; but the afflictions of Thebes described in the opening scenes suggest the great plague that swept Athens in 430, and the play was probably composed shortly after that event. The third treatment of the theme was *Oedipus at Colonus*, and we know that the poet completed this work shortly before his death in his ninety-first year. The plays are not a formal Trilogy, like the *Oresteia* of Aeschylus, since they were written at widely separated intervals; but if we place *Antigoné* last, exchanging the chronology of composition for the chronology of plot, we can turn them into a kind of accidental trilogy, a three-fold manipulation of a single tragic theme. Such a reading gives us the rise and fall of Oedipus; his wanderings, suffering, and final transfiguration; the self-destruction of his disloyal sons; the mystical and heroic martyrdom of his daughter Antigoné. Of this great action *Oedipus Rex* is the source, the point of departure, although it is also an independent drama, perfectly self-contained.

Any great play has a number of levels of significance. There are so many in *Oedipus Rex* that one is tempted to make arbitrary assertions, if only in self-defence. Thus, it is a detective story: an important person has been murdered, and there can be neither health nor peace in the state until the culprit has been discovered and punished. Here the play is considered at its lowest level, in terms of crude action. A more sensitive reading finds it a story of ironic self-revelation: an important person has been murdered, but it is the culprit himself, ignorant of his guilt, who brings about the discovery and the necessary self-condemnation. Here we have something that is on the way to being Aristotelian: a man is brought, by the best of intentions, to destroy himself. It is the irony, of course, that stiffens our rather elementary detective story; though the irony, like the action, is still of a rather raw cast. We may move to a yet higher level and regard the play as a study of human character, a symbolic representation of man's search for his own identity, a theological utterance on the subject of man's relationship to God, a pessimistic yet glorious paradigm of the limitations set by fate and time upon the aspiring drive of the human intellect. *Oedipus Rex* is all of these things, and all of them inextricably and at once. It is poetry, moreover, of the highest order; and it is spectacle, and song. Man has a body that acts, a mind that thinks, and a soul that knows and enjoys. So it is with drama, which is the delineation of man living: a level of action, a level of reflection, and a level of understanding.

In the commentary appended to his translation of *Oedipus at Colonus* Robert Fitzgerald writes:

It would be hard to imagine any tribulation more severe than that endured by Oedipus, king of Thebes. At the summit of his power he discovered himself damned, by his own pertinacity discovered that he had horribly offended against the decencies by which man must live. In one day he fell from sovereignty and fame to self-blinded degradation, and later he was driven into exile. He comes on the stage a blind beggar led by a girl. The Athenians had no romantic notions about vagabondage or exile; in their eyes Oedipus had been reduced to the worst extremity, barring slavery, that a noble man could suffer.

So we see the hero at Colonus on the last day of his life. In the present play we mark the first steps of his journey to the Furies' Grove; and what makes them horribly significant is the fact that they are self-willed, passionately and relentlessly determined by Oedipus himself. Each of these self-destructive steps, moreover, is an act of pride. However praiseworthy the motives—to save the City, to avoid criminal pollution, to establish his own identity, and so on—the decisions that the king makes are colored by his headstrong rejection of the situation in which the gods have miserably and incomprehensibly placed him. Certainly it is not idle to ask where the ultimate blame lies; but it is a dangerous question, and it would be better for the prudent man to avoid it.

There was a boy who mistakenly believed himself to be his father's son. Upon coming of age he learned that Fate had doomed him to kill his father and marry his mother. He tried to avoid these calamities, naturally, by leaving his parents forever and going somewhere else. ('Naturally,' we say; but if we were ancient Greeks we should add 'wrongly and uselessly': a man cannot circumvent Fate, and any attempt to do so is a setting of his will against that of the gods.) On his way to somewhere else—it is Thebes— our refugee encounters an irascible old man in a chariot and kills him in a dispute over the right of way. He does not know that the old gentleman is his real father, King Laïos of Thebes. It may be that he is too forceful in asserting his traffic rights, although the Greeks do not seem to have thought so; but there is no doubt that he has unwittingly obeyed the Oracle and committed the sin of patricide. Very well. He resumes his journey, but again stops by the wayside to match wits with a riddling Sphinx just outside Thebes. He destroys her by brilliantly answering her riddle, thus relieving the City of a suburban horror; but it was a kind of arrogance, however innocently intended, to assert the force of his human intelligence against the divine unreason embodied in the monster; and later, reflecting upon the miseries that have sprung from this encounter, we conclude that the victory was actually another defeat. However that may be, when Oedipus gets to Thebes he discovers that the reward for destroying the Sphinx is the hand of the recently widowed Queen, Iokastê. Naturally —again!—he marries her and ascends the royal throne. He does not know that the Queen is his real mother; but he has obeyed the Oracle once more, this time committing the most grievous form of incest. The marriage, naturally, entails children—a fact that is to madden him, years later, when he learns that his sons and daughters are his brothers and sisters as well. And all of these horrors, incurred in ignorance, are only the prelude to our play. The pattern is set, and Oedipus follows it faithfully to the intolerable end.

We are tempted to echo the terrible cry of Kreon, towards the close of *Antigonê*: 'The pains that men will take to come to pain!'* That is the point, that is the final ironic comment upon human striving and suffering. The Tragic Hero, says Aristotle, destroys himself. In tragic action it is his glory as well as his misfortune that he should do so—a human glory, frowned upon by the gods, but magnificent in its refusal to abandon a lost game. Even the consciously criminal, like Agamemnon and Clytemnestra, have this touch of splendor. What shall we say of Oedipus, who has never consciously sinned, whose whole endeavor has been to avoid the wrong and establish the right? Perhaps we shall say, with Thomas Hardy, that the President of the Immortals has been having his sport—a very Greek thought, though it is more like Euripides than Sophocles. More reasonably, though no more comfortably, we may assert the error of unconscious pride. This, too, is what the Greeks called *hybris*: the tendency in a great-souled man to forget his subordinate place in the natural order established by Zeus; to aspire, like Icarus and Phaëthon, or like Capaneus at the seige of Thebes, too high. Of all the conjectures about man, there is one that seems irrefutably true: in any mortal sense, he can not win. Nevertheless he must try. The god within him, perversely and fortunately placed there by the divine Antagonist, insists upon falling greatly in a falling world. It is useless, then, to ask whether it was right or wrong of Oedipus to pursue his quest. It was both right and wrong, and the one because of the other. Surely we, given the flights and aspirations of our own technological age, are no strangers to the riddle.

DF

* *Ant.* 1276: φεῦ, φεῦ, ἰὼ πόνοι βροτῶν δύσπονοι.

CONTENTS

PERSONS REPRESENTED:

OEDIPUS
A PRIEST
KREON
TEIRESIAS
IOKASTE
MESSENGER
SHEPHERD OF LAÏOS
SECOND MESSENGER
CHORUS OF THEBAN ELDERS

THE SCENE. *Before the palace of Oedipus, King of Thebes.*
A central door and two lateral doors open onto a plat-
form which runs the length of the façade. On the plat-
form, right and left, are altars; and three steps lead down
into the "orchêstra," or chorus-ground. At the beginning
of the action these steps are crowded by suppliants who
have brought branches and chaplets of olive leaves and
who sit in various attitudes of despair. OEDIPUS *enters.*

✿ PROLOGUE - backround info

OEDIPUS:
    My children, generations of the living
    In the line of Kadmos, nursed at his ancient hearth:
    Why have you strewn yourselves before these altars
    In supplication, with your boughs and garlands?
    The breath of incense rises from the city
    With a sound of prayer and lamentation.

Children,
I would not have you speak through messengers,
And therefore I have come myself to hear you—
I, Oedipus, who bear the famous name.

[*To a* PRIEST:
You, there, since you are eldest in the company,
Speak for them all, tell me what preys upon you,
Whether you come in dread, or crave some blessing:
Tell me, and never doubt that I will help you
In every way I can; I should be heartless
Were I not moved to find you suppliant here.

PRIEST:
Great Oedipus, O powerful King of Thebes!
You see how all the ages of our people
Cling to your altar steps: here are boys
Who can barely stand alone, and here are priests
By weight of age, as I am a priest of God,
And young men chosen from those yet unmarried;
As for the others, all that multitude,
They wait with olive chaplets in the squares,
At the two shrines of Pallas, and where Apollo
Speaks in the glowing embers.
                                Your own eyes
Must tell you: Thebes is tossed on a murdering sea ⟩ plague
And can not lift her head from the death surge.
A rust consumes the buds and fruits of the earth;   'nothing's
 The herds are sick; children die unborn,   growing
pregnant mothers dying —And labor is vain. The god of plague and pyre
Raids like detestable lightning through the city,   ~bursting in
And all the house of Kadmos is laid waste,   flames; a [?]
All emptied, and all darkened: Death alone   of sickness
Battens upon the misery of Thebes.

You are not one of the immortal gods, we know;
Yet we have come to you to make our prayer
As to the man surest in mortal ways
And wisest in the ways of God. You saved us
From the Sphinx, that flinty singer, and the tribute
We paid to her so long; yet you were never

J

Better informed than we, nor could we teach you: *the gods*
A god's touch, it seems, enabled you to help us. *aren't fair*

`IRONY :dramatic

Therefore, O mighty power, we turn to you:
Find us our safety, find us a remedy,
Whether by counsel of the gods or of men.
A king of wisdom tested in the past
Can act in a time of troubles, and act well.
Noblest of men, restore
Life to your city! Think how all men call you
Liberator for your boldness long ago;
Ah, when your years of kingship are remembered,
Let them not say *We rose, but later fell*—
Keep the State from going down in the storm!
Once, years ago, with happy augury,
You brought us fortune; be the same again!
No man questions your power to rule the land:
But rule over men, not over a dead city!
Ships are only hulls, high walls are nothing,
When no life moves in the empty passageways.

OEDIPUS:

Poor children! You may be sure I know
All that you longed for in your coming here.
I know that you are deathly sick; and yet,
Sick as you are, not one is as sick as I.
Each of you suffers in himself alone
His anguish, not another's; but my spirit
Groans for the city, for myself, for you.

I was not sleeping, you are not waking me.
No, I have been in tears for a long while
And in my restless thought walked many ways.
In all my search I found one remedy,
And I have adopted it: I have sent Kreon,
Son of Menoikeus, brother of the Queen,
To Delphi, Apollo's place of revelation,
To learn there, if he can,
What act or pledge of mine may save the city.
I have counted the days, and now, this very day,

I am troubled, for he has overstayed his time.
What is he doing? He has been gone too long.
Yet whenever he comes back, I should do ill
Not to take any action the god orders.

PRIEST:

It is a timely promise. At this instant
They tell me Kreon is here.

OEDIPUS:

O Lord Apollo!
May his news be fair as his face is radiant!

PRIEST:

Good news, I gather: he is crowned with bay,
The chaplet is thick with berries.

OEDIPUS:

We shall soon know;
He is near enough to hear us now.

[*Enter* KREON

O Prince:
Brother: son of Menoikeus:
What answer do you bring us from the God?

KREON:

A strong one. I can tell you, great afflictions
Will turn out well, if they are taken well.

OEDIPUS:

What was the oracle? These vague words
Leave me still hanging between hope and fear.

KREON:

Is it your pleasure to hear me with all these
Gathered around us? I am prepared to speak,
But should we not go in?

OEDIPUS:

Speak to them all.
It is for them I suffer, more than for myself.

KREON:

Then I will tell you what I heard at Delphi.

In plain words
The god commands us to expel from the land of Thebes
An old defilement we are sheltering.

It is a deathly thing, beyond cure;
We must not let it feed upon us longer.

OEDIPUS:

What defilement? How shall we rid ourselves of it?

KREON:

By exile or death, blood for blood. It was
Murder that brought the plague-wind on the city.

OEDIPUS:

Murder of whom? Surely the god has named him?

KREON:

My lord: Laïos once ruled this land,
Before you came to govern us.

OEDIPUS:

                              I know;
I learned of him from others; I never saw him.

KREON:

He was murdered; and Apollo commands us now
To take revenge upon whoever killed him.

OEDIPUS:

Upon whom? Where are they? Where shall we find a clue
To solve that crime, after so many years?

KREON:

Here in this land, he said. Search reveals
Things that escape an inattentive man.

OEDIPUS:

Tell me: Was Laïos murdered in his house,
Or in the fields, or in some foreign country?

KREON:

He said he planned to make a pilgrimage.
He did not come home again.

OEDIPUS:

                              And was there no one,
No witness, no companion, to tell what happened?

KREON:

They were all killed but one, and he got away
So frightened that he could remember one thing only.

OEDIPUS:

What was that one thing? One may be the key
To everything, if we resolve to use it.

KREON:

>He said that a band of highwaymen attacked them,
>Outnumbered them, and overwhelmed the King.

OEDIPUS:

>Strange, that a highwayman should be so daring—
>Unless some faction here bribed him to do it.

KREON:

>We thought of that. But after Laïos' death
>New troubles arose and we had no avenger.

OEDIPUS:

>What troubles could prevent your hunting down the
>   killers?

KREON:

>The riddling Sphinx's song
>Made us deaf to all mysteries but her own.

OEDIPUS:

>Then once more I must bring what is dark to light.
>It is most fitting that Apollo shows,
>As you do, this compunction for the dead.
>You shall see how I stand by you, as I should,
>Avenging this country and the god as well,
>And not as though it were for some distant friend,
>But for my own sake, to be rid of evil.
>Whoever killed King Laïos might—who knows?—
>Lay violent hands even on me—and soon.
>I act for the murdered king in my own interest.

>Come, then, my children: leave the altar steps,
>Lift up your olive boughs!
>   One of you go
>And summon the people of Kadmos to gather here.
>I will do all that I can; you may tell them that.

>   [*Exit a* PAGE

>So, with the help of God.
>We shall be saved—or else indeed we are lost.

PRIEST:

>Let us rise, children. It was for this we came,
>And now the King has promised it.
>Phoibos has sent us an oracle; may he descend

Himself to save us and drive out the plague.

[*Exeunt* OEDIPUS *and* KREON *into the palace by
the central door. The* PRIEST *and the* SUPPLIANTS
disperse R and L. After a short pause the
CHORUS *enters the* orchêstra.

❧ PÁRODOS

CHORUS:

What is God singing in his profound   [STROPHE 1
Delphi of gold and shadow?
What oracle for Thebes, the sunwhipped city?

Fear unjoints me, the roots of my heart tremble.

Now I remember, O Healer, your power and wonder:
Will you send doom like a sudden cloud, or weave it
Like nightfall of the past?

Speak to me, tell me, O
Child of golden Hope, immortal Voice.

                                          [ANTISTROPHE 1
Let me pray to Athenê, the immortal daughter of Zeus,
And to Artemis her sister
Who keeps her famous throne in the market ring,

And to Apollo, archer from distant heaven—

O gods, descend! Like three streams leap against
The fires of our grief, the fires of darkness;
Be swift to bring us rest!

As in the old time from the brilliant house
Of air you stepped to save us, come again!

Now our afflictions have no end,   [STROPHE 2

Now all our stricken host lies down
And no man fights off death with his mind;

The noble plowland bears no grain,
And groaning mothers can not bear—

See, how our lives like birds take wing,
Like sparks that fly when a fire soars,
To the shore of the god of evening.

The plague burns on, it is pitiless,   [ANTISTROPHE 2
Though pallid children laden with death
Lie unwept in the stony ways,

And old gray women by every path
Flock to the strand about the altars

There to strike their breasts and cry
Worship of Phoibos in wailing prayers:
Be kind, God's golden child!

There are no swords in this attack by fire,   [STROPHE 3
No shields, but we are ringed with cries.

Send the besieger plunging from our homes
Into the vast sea-room of the Atlantic
Or into the waves that foam eastward of Thrace—

For the day ravages what the night spares—

Destroy our enemy, lord of the thunder!
Let him be riven by lightning from heaven!

      [ANTISTROPHE 3
Phoibos Apollo, stretch the sun's bowstring,
That golden cord, until it sing for us,

Flashing arrows in heaven!
                    Artemis, Huntress,
Race with flaring lights upon our mountains!

O scarlet god, O golden-banded brow,
O Theban Bacchos in a storm of Maenads,
                         [*Enter* OEDIPUS, *C.*
Whirl upon Death, that all the Undying hate!
Come with blinding torches, come in joy!

✿ SCENE I - *condemns himself*

OEDIPUS:
    Is this your prayer? It may be answered. Come,
    Listen to me, act as the crisis demands,
    I And you shall have relief from all these evils.

    I Until now I was a stranger to this tale,
    As I had been a stranger to the crime.
    Could I track down the murderer without a clue?
    But now, friends,
    As one who became a citizen after the murder,
    I make this proclamation to all Thebans:

    If any man knows by whose hand Laïos, son of Labdakos,
    Met his death, I direct that man to tell me everything, *H*
    No matter what he fears for having so long withheld it.
    I Let it stand as promised that no further trouble
    Will come to him, but he may leave the land in safety.

    Moreover: If anyone knows the murderer to be foreign,
    Let him not keep silent: he shall have his reward from me.
    However, if he does conceal it; if any man
    Fearing for his friend or for himself disobeys this edict,
    Hear what I propose to do:

    I I solemnly forbid the people of this country,
    Where power and throne are mine, ever to receive that
        man

        *shun whomever did
            the deed*

Or speak to him, no matter who he is, or let him
Join in sacrifice, lustration, or in prayer.
I decree that he be driven from every house,
Being, as he is, corruption itself to us: the Delphic
Voice of Apollo has pronounced this revelation.
Thus I associate myself with the oracle. *F - already assossiated*
And take the side of the murdered king.

I/F - As for the criminal, I pray to God—
Whether it be a lurking thief, or one of a number—
I pray that that man's life be consumed in evil and
    wretchedness.
And as for me, this curse applies no less
If it should turn out that the culprit is my guest here,
himself- Sharing my hearth.
                            You have heard the penalty.

I lay it on you now to attend to this
For my sake, for Apollo's, for the sick
Sterile city that heaven has abandoned.
Suppose the oracle had given you no command:
Should this defilement go uncleansed for ever?
You should have found the murderer: your king,
A noble king, had been destroyed!
                            Now I,
Having the power that he held before me, *they are!*
Having his bed, begetting children there
Upon his wife, as he would have, had he lived—
ew! Their son would have been my children's brother,
I If Laïos had had luck in fatherhood!
(And now his bad fortune has struck him down)—
I say I take the son's part, just as though
I were his son, to press the fight for him
And see it won! I'll find the hand that brought
Death to Labdakos' and Polydoros' child,
Heir of Kadmos' and Agenor's line.
And as for those who fail me,
May the gods deny them the fruit of the earth,
Fruit of the womb, and may they rot utterly!

Let them be wretched as we are wretched, and worse!

For you, for loyal Thebans, and for all
Who find my actions right, I pray the favor
Of justice, and of all the immortal gods.

— He doesn't have their favor

CHORAGOS:

Since I am under oath, my lord, I swear
I did not do the murder, I can not name
The murderer. Phoibos ordained the search;
Why did he not say who the culprit was?

OEDIPUS:

An honest question. But no man in the world
Can make the gods do more than the gods will.

CHORAGOS:

There is an alternative, I think—

OEDIPUS:

                              Tell me.
Any or all, you must not fail to tell me.

CHORAGOS:

A lord clairvoyant to the lord Apollo,
As we all know, is the skilled Teiresias.
One might learn much about this from him, Oedipus.

OEDIPUS:

H   I am not wasting time:
Kreon spoke of this, and I have sent for him—
Twice, in fact; it is strange that he is not here.

CHORAGOS:

The other matter—that old report—seems useless.

OEDIPUS:

What was that? I am interested in all reports.

CHORAGOS:

The King was said to have been killed by highwaymen.

OEDIPUS:

I know. But we have no witnesses to that.

CHORAGOS:

If the killer can feel a particle of dread,   I
Your curse will bring him out of hiding!

OEDIPUS:

                              No.

The man who dared that act will fear no curse.
[*Enter the blind seer* TEIRESIAS, *led by a* PAGE

CHORAGOS:
But there is one man who may detect the criminal.
This is Teiresias, this is the holy prophet
In whom, alone of all men, truth was born.

OEDIPUS:
Teiresias: seer: student of mysteries,
Of all that's taught and all that no man tells,
Secrets of Heaven and secrets of the earth:
Blind though you are, you know the city lies
Sick with plague; and from this plague, my lord,
We find that you alone can guard or save us.

Possibly you did not hear the messengers?
Apollo, when we sent to him,
Sent us back word that this great pestilence
Would lift, but only if we established clearly
The identity of those who murdered Laïos.
They must be killed or exiled.
                          Can you use
Birdflight or any art of divination
To purify yourself, and Thebes, and me
From this contagion? We are in your hands.
There is no fairer duty
Than that of helping others in distress.

TEIRESIAS:
How dreadful knowledge of the truth can be
When there's no help in truth! I knew this well,
But did not act on it: else I should not have come.

OEDIPUS:
What is troubling you? Why are your eyes so cold?

TEIRESIAS:
Let me go home. Bear your own fate, and I'll
Bear mine. It is better so: trust what I say.

OEDIPUS:
What you say is ungracious and unhelpful
To your native country. Do not refuse to speak.

TEIRESIAS:
When it comes to speech, your own is neither temperate
Nor opportune. I wish to be more prudent.
OEDIPUS:
In God's name, we all beg you—
TEIRESIAS:
You are all ignorant.
No; I will never tell you what I know.
Now it is my misery; then, it would be yours.
OEDIPUS:
What! You do know something, and will not tell us?
You would betray us all and wreck the State?
TEIRESIAS:
I do not intend to torture myself, or you.
Why persist in asking? You will not persuade me.
OEDIPUS:
What a wicked old man you are! You'd try a stone's
Patience! Out with it! Have you no feeling at all?
TEIRESIAS:
You call me unfeeling. If you could only see
The nature of your own feelings . . .
OEDIPUS:
Why,
Who would not feel as I do? Who could endure
Your arrogance toward the city?
TEIRESIAS:
What does it matter?
Whether I speak or not, it is bound to come.
OEDIPUS:
Then, if 'it' is bound to come, you are bound to tell me.
TEIRESIAS:
No, I will not go on. Rage as you please.
OEDIPUS:
Rage? Why not!
And I'll tell you what I think:
You planned it, you had it done, you all but
Killed him with your own hands: if you had eyes,
I'd say the crime was yours, and yours alone.

TEIRESIAS:

So? I charge you, then,
Abide by the proclamation you have made:
From this day forth
Never speak again to these men or to me;
You yourself are the pollution of this country.

dun dun dun

OEDIPUS:

You dare say that! Can you possibly think you have
Some way of going free, after such insolence?

TEIRESIAS:

I have gone free. It is the truth sustains me.

OEDIPUS:

Who taught you shamelessness? It was not your craft.

TEIRESIAS:

You did. You made me speak. I did not want to.

OEDIPUS:

Speak what? Let me hear it again more clearly.

TEIRESIAS:

Was it not clear before? Are you tempting me?

OEDIPUS:

I did not understand it. Say it again.

TEIRESIAS:

Ha! — I say that you are the murderer whom you seek.

OEDIPUS:

Now twice you have spat out infamy. You'll pay for it!

TEIRESIAS:

Would you care for more? Do you wish to be really angry?

OEDIPUS:

Say what you will. Whatever you say is worthless.

TEIRESIAS:

I say you live in hideous shame with those
Most dear to you. You can not see the evil.

OEDIPUS:

Can you go on babbling like this for ever?

TEIRESIAS:

I can, if there is power in truth.

OEDIPUS:

There is:
But not for you, not for you,

You sightless, witless, senseless, mad old man!

TEIRESIAS:

You are the madman. There is no one here
Who will not curse you soon, as you curse me.

OEDIPUS:

You child of total night! I would not touch you,
Neither would any man who sees the sun.

TEIRESIAS:

True: it is not from you my fate will come. 〉 **Greek value**
That lies within Apollo's competence, 〉 **system**
As it is his concern.

OEDIPUS:

Tell me, who made
These fine discoveries? Kreon? or someone else?

TEIRESIAS:

Kreon is no threat. You weave your own doom.

OEDIPUS:

Wealth, power, craft of statesmanship!
H - Kingly position, everywhere admired!
What savage envy is stored up against these,
If Kreon, whom I trusted, Kreon my friend,
For this great office which the city once
Put in my hands unsought—if for this power
Kreon desires in secret to destroy me!

He has bought this decrepit fortune-teller, this
Collector of dirty pennies, this prophet fraud—
Why, he is no more clairvoyant than I am!

Tell us:
Has your mystic mummery ever approached the truth?
When that hellcat the Sphinx was performing here,
What help were you to these people?
Her magic was not for the first man who came along:
It demanded a real exorcist. Your birds—
What good were they? or the gods, for the matter of that?
But I came by,
H Oedipus, the simple man, who knows nothing—
I thought it out for myself, no birds helped me!
And this is the man you think you can destroy,

That you may be close to Kreon when he's king!
Well, you and your friend Kreon, it seems to me,
Will suffer most. If you were not an old man,
You would have paid already for your plot.

no they won't

CHORAGOS:
We can not see that his words or yours
Have been spoken except in anger, Oedipus,
And of anger we have no need. How to accomplish
The god's will best: that is what most concerns us.

TEIRESIAS:
You are a king. But where argument's concerned
I am your man, as much a king as you.
I am not your servant, but Apollo's.
I have no need of Kreon's name.

Listen to me. You mock my blindness, do you?
But I say that you, with both your eyes, are blind:
You can not see the wretchedness of your life,
Nor in whose house you live, no, nor with whom.
Who are your father and mother? Can you tell me?
You do not even know the blind wrongs
That you have done them, on earth and in the world
      below.
But the double lash of your parents' curse will whip you
Out of this land some day, with only night
Upon your precious eyes.
Your cries then—where will they not be heard?
What fastness of Kithairon will not echo them?
And that bridal-descant of yours—you'll know it then,
The song they sang when you came here to Thebes
And found your misguided berthing.
All this, and more, that you can not guess at now,
Will bring you to yourself among your children.

Be angry, then. Curse Kreon. Curse my words.
I tell you, no man that walks upon the earth
Shall be rooted out more horribly than you.

OEDIPUS:
Am I to bear this from him?—Damnation

Take you! Out of this place! Out of my sight!

TEIRESIAS:

I would not have come at all if you had not asked me.

OEDIPUS:

Could I have told that you'd talk nonsense, that
You'd come here to make a fool of yourself, and of me?

TEIRESIAS:

A fool? Your parents thought me sane enough.

OEDIPUS:

My parents again!—Wait: who were my parents?

TEIRESIAS:

This day will give you a father, and break your heart.

OEDIPUS:

Your infantile riddles! Your damned abracadabra!

TEIRESIAS:

You were a great man once at solving riddles.

OEDIPUS:

Mock me with that if you like; you will find it true.

TEIRESIAS:

It was true enough. It brought about your ruin.

OEDIPUS:

But if it saved this town?

TEIRESIAS:

[*To the* PAGE:
Boy, give me your hand.

OEDIPUS:

Yes, boy; lead him away.

—While you are here
We can do nothing. Go; leave us in peace.

TEIRESIAS:

I will go when I have said what I have to say.
How can you hurt me? And I tell you again:
The man you have been looking for all this time,
The damned man, the murderer of Laïos,
That man is in Thebes. To your mind he is foreign-born,
But it will soon be shown that he is a Theban,
A revelation that will fail to please.

A blind man,
Who has his eyes now; a penniless man, who is rich now:

And he will go tapping the strange earth with his staff.
To the children with whom he lives now he will be
Brother and father—the very same; to her
Who bore him, son and husband—the very same
Who came to his father's bed, wet with his father's blood.

Enough. Go think that over.
If later you find error in what I have said,
You may say that I have no skill in prophecy.

[*Exit* TEIRESIAS, *led by his* PAGE. OEDIPUS *goes into
the palace.*

ODE I

CHORUS:

The Delphic stone of prophecies   [STROPHE 1
Remembers ancient regicide – killing a king
And a still bloody hand.
That killer's hour of flight has come.
He must be stronger than riderless
Coursers of untiring wind,
spirits of revenge — For the son of Zeus armed with his father's thunder
Leaps in lightning after him;
And the Furies hold his track, the sad Furies.

mount For poets — Holy Parnassos' peak of snow   [ANTISTROPHE 1
Flashes and blinds that secret man,
That all shall hunt him down:
Though he may roam the forest shade
Like a bull gone wild from pasture
To rage through glooms of stone.
Doom comes down on him; flight will not avail him;
For the world's heart calls him desolate,
And the immortal voices follow, for ever follow.

But now a wilder thing is heard   [STROPHE 2
From the old man skilled at hearing Fate in the wing-
beat of a bird.

Bewildered as a blown bird, my soul hovers and can not
    find
Foothold in this debate, or any reason or rest of mind.
But no man ever brought—none can bring
Proof of strife between Thebes' royal house,
Labdakos' line, and the son of Polybos;
And never until now has any man brought word
Of Laïos' dark death staining Oedipus the King.

Divine Zeus and Apollo hold   [ANTISTROPHE 2
Perfect intelligence alone of all tales ever told;
And well though this diviner works, he works in his own
    night;
No man can judge that rough unknown or trust in second
    sight,
For wisdom changes hands among the wise.
Shall I believe my great lord criminal
At a raging word that a blind old man let fall?
I saw him, when the carrion woman faced him of old,
Prove his heroic mind. These evil words are lies.

carrion—dead/decaying (flesh)

SCENE II

KREON:
Men of Thebes:
I am told that heavy accusations
Have been brought against me by King Oedipus.

I am not the kind of man to bear this tamely.

If in these present difficulties
He holds me accountable for any harm to him
Through anything I have said or done—why, then,
I do not value life in this dishonor.

It is not as though this rumor touched upon
Some private indiscretion. The matter is grave.
The fact is that I am being called disloyal

To the State, to my fellow citizens, to my friends.

CHORAGOS:
He may have spoken in anger, not from his mind.

KREON:
{ But did you not hear him say I was the one
Who seduced the old prophet into lying?

CHORAGOS:
The thing was said; I do not know how seriously.

KREON:
But you were watching him! Were his eyes steady?
Did he look like a man in his right mind?

CHORAGOS:
                              I do not know.
I can not judge the behavior of great men.
But here is the King himself.

                              [Enter OEDIPUS

OEDIPUS:
                    So you dared come back.
Why? How brazen of you to come to my house,
You murderer!
              Do you think I do not know
That you plotted to kill me, plotted to steal my throne?
Tell me, in God's name: am I coward, a fool,
That you should dream you could accomplish this?
A fool who could not see your slippery game?
A coward, not to fight back when I saw it?
You are the fool, Kreon, are you not? hoping
Without support or friends to get a throne?
Thrones may be won or bought: you could do neither.

KREON:
Now listen to me. You have talked; let me talk, too.
You can not judge unless you know the facts.

OEDIPUS:
You speak well: there is one fact; but I find it hard
To learn from the deadliest enemy I have.

KREON:
That above all I must dispute with you.

OEDIPUS:
That above all I will not hear you deny.

KREON:

If you think there is anything good in being stubborn
Against all reason, then I say you are wrong.

OEDIPUS:

If you think a man can sin against his own kind
And not be punished for it, I say you are mad.

KREON:

I agree. But tell me: what have I done to you?

OEDIPUS:

You advised me to send for that wizard, did you not?

KREON:

I did. I should do it again.

OEDIPUS:

Very well. Now tell me:
How long has it been since Laïos—

KREON:

What of Laïos?

OEDIPUS:

Since he vanished in that onset by the road?

KREON:

It was long ago, a long time.

OEDIPUS:

And this prophet,
Was he practicing here then?

KREON:

He was; and with honor, as now

OEDIPUS:

Did he speak of me at that time?

KREON:

He never did;
At least, not when I was present.

OEDIPUS:

But . . . the enquiry?
I suppose you held one?

KREON:

We did, but we learned nothing.

OEDIPUS:

Why did the prophet not speak against me then?

KREON:

> I do not know; and I am the kind of man
> Who holds his tongue when he has no facts to go on.

OEDIPUS:

> There's one fact that you know, and you could tell it.

KREON:

> What fact is that? If I know it, you shall have it.

OEDIPUS:

> If he were not involved with you, he could not say
> That it was I who murdered Laïos.

KREON:

> If he says that, you are the one that knows it!—
> But now it is my turn to question you.

OEDIPUS:

> Put your questions. I am no murderer.

KREON:

> First, then: You married my sister?

OEDIPUS:

> I married your sister.

KREON:

> And you rule the kingdom equally with her?

OEDIPUS:

> Everything that she wants she has from me.

KREON:

> And I am the third, equal to both of you?

OEDIPUS:

> That is why I call you a bad friend.

KREON:

> No. Reason it out, as I have done.
> Think of this first: Would any sane man prefer
> Power, with all a king's anxieties,
> To that same power and the grace of sleep?
> Certainly not I.
> I have never longed for the king's power—only his rights.
> Would any wise man differ from me in this?
> As matters stand, I have my way in everything
> With your consent, and no responsibilities.
> If I were king, I should be a slave to policy.

How could I desire a sceptre more
Than what is now mine—untroubled influence?
No, I have not gone mad; I need no honors,
Except those with the perquisites I have now.
I am welcome everywhere; every man salutes me,
And those who want your favor seek my ear,
Since I know how to manage what they ask.
Should I exchange this ease for that anxiety?
Besides, no sober mind is treasonable.
I hate anarchy
And never would deal with any man who likes it.

Test what I have said. Go to the priestess
At Delphi, ask if I quoted her correctly.
And as for this other thing: if I am found
Guilty of treason with Teiresias,
Then sentence me to death. You have my word
It is a sentence I should cast my vote for—
But not without evidence!
                        You do wrong
When you take good men for bad, bad men for good.
A true friend thrown aside—why, life itself
Is not more precious!
                    In time you will know this well:
For time, and time alone, will show the just man,
Though scoundrels are discovered in a day.

CHORAGOS:
This is well said, and a prudent man would ponder it.
Judgments too quickly formed are dangerous.

OEDIPUS:
But is he not quick in his duplicity?
And shall I not be quick to parry him?
Would you have me stand still, hold my peace, and let
This man win everything, through my inaction?

KREON:
And you want—what is it, then? To banish me?

OEDIPUS:
No, not exile. It is your death I want,
So that all the world may see what treason means.

KREON:
  You will persist, then? You will not believe me?
OEDIPUS:
  How can I believe you?
KREON:
                  Then you are a fool.
OEDIPUS:
  To save myself?
KREON:
                  In justice, think of me.
OEDIPUS:
  You are evil incarnate.
KREON:
                  But suppose that you are wrong?
OEDIPUS:
  Still I must rule.
KREON:
                  But not if you rule badly.
OEDIPUS:
  O city, city!
KREON:
                  It is my city, too!
CHORAGOS:
  Now, my lords, be still. I see the Queen,
  Iokastê, coming from her palace chambers;
  And it is time she came, for the sake of you both.
  This dreadful quarrel can be resolved through her.
                                    [*Enter* IOKASTE
IOKASTE:
  Poor foolish men, what wicked din is this?
  With Thebes sick to death, is it not shameful
  That you should rake some private quarrel up?
                                    [*To* OEDIPUS
  Come into the house.
                  —And you, Kreon, go now:
  Let us have no more of this tumult over nothing.
KREON:
  Nothing? No, sister: what your husband plans for me
  Is one of two great evils: exile or death.

OEDIPUS:

He is right.

Why, woman I have caught him squarely
Plotting against my life.

KREON:

No! Let me die
Accurst if ever I have wished you harm!

IOKASTE:

Ah, believe it, Oedipus!
In the name of the gods, respect this oath of his
For my sake, for the sake of these people here!

CHORAGOS: [STROPHE 1

Open your mind to her, my lord. Be ruled by her, I beg
    you!

OEDIPUS:

What would you have me do?

CHORAGOS:

Respect Kreon's word. He has never spoken like a fool,
And now he has sworn an oath.

OEDIPUS:

You know what you ask?

CHORAGOS:

I do.

OEDIPUS:

Speak on, then.

CHORAGOS:

A friend so sworn should not be baited so,
In blind malice, and without final proof.

OEDIPUS:

You are aware, I hope, that what you say
Means death for me, or exile at the least.

CHORAGOS:

No, I swear by Helios, first in Heaven!   [STROPHE 2
    May I die friendless and accurst,
The worst of deaths, if ever I meant that!
        It is the withering fields

That hurt my sick heart:
Must we bear all these ills,
And now your bad blood as well?

OEDIPUS:
Then let him go. And let me die, if I must,
Or be driven by him in shame from the land of Thebes.
It is your unhappiness, and not his talk,
That touches me.
                    As for him—
Wherever he goes, hatred will follow him.

KREON:
Ugly in yielding, as you were ugly in rage!
Natures like yours chiefly torment themselves.

OEDIPUS:
Can you not go? Can you not leave me?

KREON:
                                        I can.
You do not know me; but the city knows me,
And in its eyes I am just, if not in yours.

                                        [*Exit* KREON

CHORAGOS: [ANTISTROPHE 1
Lady Iokastê, did you not ask the King to go to his
    chambers?

IOKASTE:
First tell me what has happened.

CHORAGOS:
There was suspicion without evidence; yet it rankled
As even false charges will.

IOKASTE:
                On both sides?

CHORAGOS:
                        On both.

IOKASTE:
                                But what was said?

CHORAGOS:
Oh let it rest, let it be done with!

Have we not suffered enough?
OEDIPUS:
You see to what your decency has brought you:
You have made difficulties where my heart saw none.

CHORAGOS: [ANTISTROPHE 2
Oedipus, it is not once only I have told you—
    You must know I should count myself unwise
To the point of madness, should I now forsake you—
        You, under whose hand,
            In the storm of another time,
        Our dear land sailed out free.
            But now stand fast at the helm!

IOKASTE:
In God's name, Oedipus, inform your wife as well:
Why are you so set in this hard anger?
OEDIPUS:
I will tell you, for none of these men deserves
My confidence as you do. It is Kreon's work,
His treachery, his plotting against me.
IOKASTE:
Go on, if you can make this clear to me.
OEDIPUS:
He charges me with the murder of Laïos.
IOKASTE:
Has he some knowledge? Or does he speak from hearsay?
OEDIPUS:
He would not commit himself to such a charge,
But he has brought in that damnable soothsayer
To tell his story.
IOKASTE:
                    Set your mind at rest.
If it is a question of soothsayers, I tell you
That you will find no man whose craft gives knowledge
Of the unknowable.

                    Here is my proof:

An oracle was reported to Laïos once
(I will not say from Phoibos himself, but from
His appointed ministers, at any rate)
That his doom would be death at the hands of his **own**
     son—
His son, born of his flesh and of mine!

{ Now, you remember the story: Laïos was killed
  By marauding strangers where three highways meet;
  But his child had not been three days in this world
  Before the King had pierced the baby's ankles
  And left him to die on a lonely mountainside.

Thus, Apollo never caused that child
To kill his father, and it was not Laïos' fate
To die at the hands of his son, as he had feared.
This is what prophets and prophecies are worth!
Have no dread of them.
                        It is God himself
Who can show us what he wills, in his own way.

OEDIPUS:

{ How strange a shadowy memory crossed my mind,
  Just now while you were speaking; it chilled my heart.

IOKASTE:

What do you mean? What memory do you speak of?

OEDIPUS:

If I understand you, Laïos was killed
At a place where three roads meet.

IOKASTE:

                        So it was said;
We have no later story.

OEDIPUS:

                  Where did it happen?

IOKASTE:

Phokis, it is called: at a place where the Theban Way
Divides into the roads toward Delphi and Daulia.

OEDIPUS:

When?

IOKASTE:

      We had the news not long before you came
And proved the right to your succession here.

OEDIPUS:

Ah, what net has God been weaving for me?

IOKASTE:

Oedipus! Why does this trouble you?

OEDIPUS:

                       Do not ask me yet.
First, tell me how Laïos looked, and tell me
How old he was.

IOKASTE:

            He was tall, his hair just touched
With white; his form was not unlike your own.

OEDIPUS:

I think that I myself may be accurst
By my own ignorant edict.

IOKASTE:

               You speak strangely.
It makes me tremble to look at you, my King.

OEDIPUS:

I am not sure that the blind man can not see.
But I should know better if you were to tell me—

IOKASTE:

Anything—though I dread to hear you ask it.

OEDIPUS:

Was the King lightly escorted, or did he ride
With a large company, as a ruler should?

IOKASTE:

There were five men with him in all: one was a herald;
And a single chariot, which he was driving.

OEDIPUS:

Alas, that makes it plain enough!
                  But who—
Who told you how it happened?

IOKASTE:

              A household servant,
The only one to escape.

OEDIPUS:

                    And is he still

A servant of ours?

IOKASTE:

                 No; for when he came back at last
And found you enthroned in the place of the dead king,
He came to me, touched my hand with his, and begged
That I would send him away to the frontier district
Where only the shepherds go—
As far away from the city as I could send him.
I granted his prayer; for although the man was a slave,
He had earned more than this favor at my hands.

OEDIPUS:

Can he be called back quickly?

IOKASTE:

                    Easily.

But why?

OEDIPUS:

             I have taken too much upon myself
Without enquiry; therefore I wish to consult him.

IOKASTE:

Then he shall come.

               But am I not one also
To whom you might confide these fears of yours?

OEDIPUS:

That is your right; it will not be denied you,
Now least of all; for I have reached a pitch
Of wild foreboding. Is there anyone
To whom I should sooner speak?

Polybos of Corinth is my father.
My mother is a Dorian: Meropê.
I grew up chief among the men of Corinth
Until a strange thing happened—
Not worth my passion, it may be, but strange.

At a feast, a drunken man maundering in his cups
Cries out that I am not my father's son!

I contained myself that night, though I felt anger
And a sinking heart. The next day I visited
My father and mother, and questioned them. They
    stormed,
Calling it all the slanderous rant of a fool;
And this relieved me. Yet the suspicion
Remained always aching in my mind;
I knew there was talk; I could not rest;
And finally, saying nothing to my parents,
I went to the shrine at Delphi.

The god dismissed my question without reply;
He spoke of other things.
                            Some were clear,
Full of wretchedness, dreadful, unbearable:
As, that I should lie with my own mother, breed
Children from whom all men would turn their eyes;
And that I should be my father's murderer.

He did!

I heard all this, and fled. And from that day
Corinth to me was only in the stars
Descending in that quarter of the sky,
As I wandered farther and farther on my way
To a land where I should never see the evil
Sung by the oracle. And I came to this country
Where, so you say, King Laïos was killed.

I will tell you all that happened there, my lady.

There were three highways
Coming together at a place I passed;
And there a herald came towards me, and a chariot
Drawn by horses, with a man such as you describe
Seated in it. The groom leading the horses
Forced me off the road at his lord's command;
But as this charioteer lurched over towards me
I struck him in my rage. The old man saw me
And brought his double goad down upon my head

As I came abreast.

                        He was paid back, and more!
Swinging my club in this right hand I knocked him
Out of his car, and he rolled on the ground.

                                        I killed him.

I killed them all.
Now if that stranger and Laïos were—kin,
Where is a man more miserable than I?
More hated by the gods? Citizen and alien alike
Must never shelter me or speak to me—
I must be shunned by all.

                        And I myself
Pronounced this malediction upon myself!

Think of it: I have touched you with these hands,
These hands that killed your husband. What defilement!

Am I all evil, then? It must be so,
Since I must flee from Thebes, yet never again
See my own countrymen, my own country,
For fear of joining my mother in marriage
And killing Polybos, my father.

                        Ah,
If I was created so, born to this fate,
Who could deny the savagery of God?

O holy majesty of heavenly powers!
May I never see that day! Never!
Rather let me vanish from the race of men
Than know the abomination destined me!

CHORAGOS:
We too, my lord, have felt dismay at this.
But there is hope: you have yet to hear the shepherd.

OEDIPUS:
Indeed, I fear no other hope is left me.

IOKASTE:
What do you hope from him when he comes?

OEDIPUS:

                                        This much:

If his account of the murder tallies with yours,
Then I am cleared.
IOKASTE:
                    What was it that I said
Of such importance?
OEDIPUS:
                    Why, 'marauders', you said,
Killed the King, according to this man's story.
If he maintains that still, if there were several,
Clearly the guilt is not mine: I was alone.
But if he says one man, singlehanded, did it,
Then the evidence all points to me.
IOKASTE:
You may be sure that he said there were several;
And can he call back that story now? He cán not.
The whole city heard it as plainly as I.
But suppose he alters some detail of it:
He can not ever show that Laïos' death
Fulfilled the oracle: for Apollo said
My child was doomed to kill him; and my child—
Poor baby!—it was my child that died first.

No. From now on, where oracles are concerned,
I would not waste a second thought on any.
OEDIPUS:
You may be right.
                    But come: let someone go
For the shepherd at once. This matter must be settled.
IOKASTE:
I will send for him.
I would not wish to cross you in anything,
And surely not in this.—Let us go in.
                    [*Exeunt into the palace*

🎕 ODE II

CHORUS:
Let me be reverent in the ways of right,   [STROPHE 1

Lowly the paths I journey on;
Let all my words and actions keep
The laws of the pure universe
From highest Heaven handed down.
For Heaven is their bright nurse,
Those generations of the realms of light;
Ah, never of mortal kind were they begot,
Nor are they slaves of memory, lost in sleep:
Their Father is greater than Time, and ages not.

The tyrant is a child of Pride   [ANTISTROPHE 1
Who drinks from his great sickening cup
Recklessness and vanity,
Until from his high crest headlong
He plummets to the dust of hope.
That strong man is not strong.
But let no fair ambition be denied;
May God protect the wrestler for the State
In government, in comely policy,
Who will fear God, and on His ordinance wait.

Haughtiness and the high hand of disdain   [STROPHE 2
Tempt and outrage God's holy law;
And any mortal who dares hold
No immortal Power in awe
Will be caught up in a net of pain:
The price for which his levity is sold.
Let each man take due earnings, then,
And keep his hands from holy things,
And from blasphemy stand apart—
Else the crackling blast of heaven
Blows on his head, and on his desperate heart.
Though fools will honor impious men,
In their cities no tragic poet sings.

[ANTISTROPHE 2

Shall we lose faith in Delphi's obscurities,
We who have heard the world's core
Discredited, and the sacred wood

Of Zeus at Elis praised no more?
The deeds and the strange prophecies
Must make a pattern yet to be understood.
Zeus, if indeed you are lord of all,
Throned in light over night and day,
Mirror this in your endless mind:
Our masters call the oracle
Words on the wind, and the Delphic vision blind!
Their hearts no longer know Apollo,
And reverence for the gods has died away.

✿ SCENE III

[*Enter* IOKASTE

IOKASTE:
Princes of Thebes, it has occurred to me
To visit the altars of the gods, bearing
These branches as a suppliant, and this incense.
Our King is not himself: his noble soul
Is overwrought with fantasies of dread,
Else he would consider
The new prophecies in the light of the old.
He will listen to any voice that speaks disaster,
And my advice goes for nothing.
                    [*She approaches the altar, R.*
                    To you, then, Apollo,
Lycéan lord, since you are nearest, I turn in prayer.

Receive these offerings, and grant us deliverance
From defilement. Our hearts are heavy with fear
When we see our leader distracted, as helpless sailors
Are terrified by the confusion of their helmsman.
                    [*Enter* MESSENGER

MESSENGER:
Friends, no doubt you can direct me:
Where shall I find the house of Oedipus,
Or, better still, where is the King himself?

CHORAGOS:
  It is this very place, stranger; he is inside.
  This is his wife and mother of his children.

MESSENGER:
  I wish her happiness in a happy house,
  Blest in all the fulfillment of her marriage.

IOKASTE:
  I wish as much for you: your courtesy
  Deserves a like good fortune. But now, tell me:
  Why have you come? What have you to say to us?

MESSENGER:
  Good news, my lady, for your house and your husband.

IOKASTE:
  What news? Who sent you here?

MESSENGER:
                                    I am from Corinth.
  The news I bring ought to mean joy for you,
  Though it may be you will find some grief in it.

IOKASTE:
  What is it? How can it touch us in both ways?

MESSENGER:
  The word is that the people of the Isthmus
  Intend to call Oedipus to be their king.

IOKASTE:
  But old King Polybos—is he not reigning still?

MESSENGER:
  No. Death holds him in his sepulchre.

IOKASTE:
  What are you saying? Polybos is dead?

MESSENGER:
  If I am not telling the truth, may I die myself.

IOKASTE: [*To a* MAIDSERVANT:
  Go in, go quickly; tell this to your master.

  O riddlers of God's will, where are you now!
  This was the man whom Oedipus, long ago,
  Feared so, fled so, in dread of destroying him—
  But it was another fate by which he died.

                              [*Enter* OEPIDUS, *C.*

OEDIPUS:
Dearest Iokastê, why have you sent for me?

IOKASTE:
Listen to what this man says, and then tell me
What has become of the solemn prophecies.

OEDIPUS:
Who is this man? What is his news for me?

IOKASTE:
He has come from Corinth to announce your father's
death!

OEDIPUS:
Is it true, stranger? Tell me in your own words.

MESSENGER:
I can not say it more clearly: the King is dead.

OEDIPUS:
Was it by treason? Or by an attack of illness?

MESSENGER:
A little thing brings old men to their rest.

OEDIPUS:
It was sickness, then?

MESSENGER:
Yes, and his many years.

OEDIPUS:
Ah!
Why should a man respect the Pythian hearth, or
Give heed to the birds that jangle above his head?
They prophesied that I should kill Polybos,
Kill my own father; but he is dead and buried,
And I am here—I never touched him, never,
Unless he died of grief for my departure,
And thus, in a sense, through me. No. Polybos
Has packed the oracles off with him underground.
They are empty words.

IOKASTE:
Had I not told you so?

OEDIPUS:
You had; it was my faint heart that betrayed me.

IOKASTE:
From now on never think of those things again.

OEDIPUS:
> And yet—must I not fear my mother's bed?

IOKASTE:
> Why should anyone in this world be afraid,
> Since Fate rules us and nothing can be foreseen?
> A man should live only for the present day.
>
> Have no more fear of sleeping with your mother:
> How many men, in dreams, have lain with their mothers!
> No reasonable man is troubled by such things.

OEDIPUS:
> That is true; only—
> If only my mother were not still alive!
> But she is alive. I can not help my dread.

IOKASTE:
> Yet this news of your father's death is wonderful.

OEDIPUS:
> Wonderful. But I fear the living woman.

MESSENGER:
> Tell me, who is this woman that you fear?

OEDIPUS:
> It is Meropê, man; the wife of King Polybos.

MESSENGER:
> Meropê? Why should you be afraid of her?

OEDIPUS:
> An oracle of the gods, a dreadful saying.

MESSENGER:
> Can you tell me about it or are you sworn to silence?

OEDIPUS:
> I can tell you, and I will.
> Apollo said through his prophet that I was the man
> Who should marry his own mother, shed his father's blood
> With his own hands. And so, for all these years
> I have kept clear of Corinth, and no harm has come—
> Though it would have been sweet to see my parents again.

MESSENGER:
> And is this the fear that drove you out of Corinth?

OEDIPUS:
> Would you have me kill my father?

MESSENGER:
                                  As for that
You must be reassured by the news I gave you.

OEDIPUS:
If you could reassure me, I would reward you.

MESSENGER:
I had that in mind, I will confess: I thought
I could count on you when you returned to Corinth.

OEDIPUS:
No: I will never go near my parents again.

MESSENGER:
Ah, son, you still do not know what you are doing—

OEDIPUS:
What do you mean? In the name of God tell me!

MESSENGER:
—If these are your reasons for not going home.

OEDIPUS:
I tell you, I fear the oracle may come true.

MESSENGER:
And guilt may come upon you through your parents?

OEDIPUS:
That is the dread that is always in my heart.

MESSENGER:
Can you not see that all your fears are groundless?

OEDIPUS:
Groundless? Am I not my parents' son?

MESSENGER:
Polybos was not your father.

OEDIPUS:
                                  Not my father?

MESSENGER:
No more your father than the man speaking to you.

OEDIPUS:
But you are nothing to me!

MESSENGER:
                                  Neither was he.

OEDIPUS:
Then why did he call me son?

MESSENGER:

                                      I will tell you:
Long ago he had you from my hands, as a gift.

OEDIPUS:
Then how could he love me so, if I was not his?

MESSENGER:
He had no children, and his heart turned to you.

OEDIPUS:
What of you? Did you buy me? Did you find me by
    chance?

MESSENGER:
I came upon you in the woody vales of Kithairon.

OEDIPUS:
And what were you doing there?

MESSENGER:

                                Tending my flocks.

OEDIPUS:
A wandering shepherd?

MESSENGER:
                        But your savior, son, that day.

OEDIPUS:
From what did you save me?

MESSENGER:
                       Your ankles should tell you that.

OEDIPUS:
Ah, stranger, why do you speak of that childhood pain?

MESSENGER:
I pulled the skewer that pinned your feet together.

OEDIPUS:
I have had the mark as long as I can remember.

MESSENGER:
That was why you were given the name you bear.

OEDIPUS:
God! Was it my father or my mother who did it?
Tell me!

MESSENGER:
        I do not know. The man who gave you to me
Can tell you better than I.

OEDIPUS:
It was not you that found me, but another?
MESSENGER:
It was another shepherd gave you to me.
OEDIPUS:
Who was he? Can you tell me who he was?
MESSENGER:
I think he was said to be one of Laïos' people.
OEDIPUS:
You mean the Laïos who was king here years ago?
MESSENGER:
Yes; King Laïos; and the man was one of his herdsmen.
OEDIPUS:
Is he still alive? Can I see him?
MESSENGER:
These men here
Know best about such things.
OEDIPUS:
Does anyone here
Know this shepherd that he is talking about?
Have you seen him in the fields, or in the town?
If you have, tell me. It is time things were made plain.
CHORAGOS:
I think the man he means is that same shepherd
You have already asked to see. Iokastê perhaps
Could tell you something.
OEDIPUS:
Do you know anything
About him, Lady? Is he the man we have summoned?
Is that the man this shepherd means?
IOKASTE:
Why think of him?
Forget this herdsman. Forget it all.
This talk is a waste of time.
OEDIPUS:
How can you say that,
When the clues to my true birth are in my hands?
IOKASTE:
For God's love, let us have no more questioning!

Is your life nothing to you?
My own is pain enough for me to bear.

OEDIPUS:
You need not worry. Suppose my mother a slave,
And born of slaves: no baseness can touch you.

IOKASTE:
Listen to me, I beg you: do not do this thing!

OEDIPUS:
I will not listen; the truth must be made known.

IOKASTE:
Everything that I say is for your own good!

OEDIPUS:
                                        My own good
Snaps my patience, then; I want none of it.

IOKASTE:
You are fatally wrong! May you never learn who you are!

OEDIPUS:
Go, one of you, and bring the shepherd here.
Let us leave this woman to brag of her royal name.

IOKASTE:
Ah, miserable!
That is the only word I have for you now.
That is the only word I can ever have.

                              [*Exit into the palace*

CHORAGOS:
Why has she left us, Oedipus? Why has she gone
In such a passion of sorrow? I fear this silence:
Something dreadful may come of it.

OEDIPUS:
                                  Let it come!
However base my birth, I must know about it.
The Queen, like a woman, is perhaps ashamed
To think of my low origin. But I
Am a child of Luck; I can not be dishonored.
Luck is my mother; the passing months, my brothers,
Have seen me rich and poor.
                              If this is so,
How could I wish that I were someone else?
How could I not be glad to know my birth?

🎚 ODE III

CHORUS:

If ever the coming time were known   [STROPHE
To my heart's pondering,
Kithairon, now by Heaven I see the torches
At the festival of the next full moon,
And see the dance, and hear the choir sing
A grace to your gentle shade:
Mountain where Oedipus was found,
O mountain guard of a noble race!
May the god who heals us lend his aid,
And let that glory come to pass
For our king's cradling-ground.

[handwritten: talking to the mountain]

                                        [ANTISTROPHE

Of the nymphs that flower beyond the years,
Who bore you, royal child,
To Pan of the hills or the timberline Apollo,
Cold in delight where the upland clears,
Or Hermês for whom Kyllenê's heights are piled?
Or flushed as evening cloud,
Great Dionysos, roamer of mountains,
He—was it he who found you there,
And caught you up in his own proud
Arms from the sweet god-ravisher
Who laughed by the Muses' fountains?

🎚 SCENE IV

OEDIPUS:

Sirs: though I do not know the man,
I think I see him coming, this shepherd we **want**:
He is old, like our friend here, and the men
Bringing him seem to be servants of my house.
But you can tell, if you have ever seen him.
                    [*Enter* SHEPHERD *escorted by servants*

CHORAGOS:
I know him, he was Laïos' man. You can trust him.

OEDIPUS:
Tell me first, you from Corinth: is this the shepherd
We were discussing?

MESSENGER:
This is the very man.

OEDIPUS: [*To* SHEPHERD:
Come here. No, look at me. You must answer
Everything I ask.—You belonged to Laïos?

SHEPHERD:
Yes: born his slave, brought up in his house.

OEDIPUS:
Tell me: what kind of work did you do for him?

SHEPHERD:
I was a shepherd of his, most of my life.

OEDIPUS:
Where mainly did you go for pasturage?

SHEPHERD:
Sometimes Kithairon, sometimes the hills near-by.

OEDIPUS:
Do you remember ever seeing this man out there?

SHEPHERD:
What would he be doing there? This man?

OEDIPUS:
This man standing here. Have you ever seen him before?

SHEPHERD:
No. At least, not to my recollection. — Lying

MESSENGER:
And that is not strange, my lord. But I'll refresh
His memory: he must remember when we two
Spent three whole seasons together, March to September,
On Kithairon or thereabouts. He had two flocks;
I had one. Each autumn I'd drive mine home
And he would go back with his to Laïos' sheepfold.—
Is this not true, just as I have described it?

SHEPHERD:
True, yes; but it was all so long ago.

MESSENGER:
   Well, then: do you remember, back in those days,
   That you gave me a baby boy to bring up as my own?
SHEPHERD:
   What if I did? What are you trying to say?
MESSENGER:
   King Oedipus was once that little child.
SHEPHERD:
   Damn you, hold your tongue!
OEDIPUS:
                              No more of that!
   It is your tongue needs watching, not this man's.
SHEPHERD:
   My King, my Master, what is it I have done wrong?
OEDIPUS:
   You have not answered his question about the boy.
SHEPHERD:
   He does not know . . . He is only making trouble . . .
OEDIPUS:
   Come, speak plainly, or it will go hard with you.
SHEPHERD:
   In God's name, do not torture an old man!
OEDIPUS:
   Come here, one of you; bind his arms behind him.
SHEPHERD:
   Unhappy king! What more do you wish to learn?
OEDIPUS:
   Did you give this man the child he speaks of?
SHEPHERD:
                                        I did.
   And I would to God I had died that very day.
OEDIPUS:
   You will die now unless you speak the truth.
SHEPHERD:
   Yet if I speak the truth, I am worse than dead.
OEDIPUS: [To Attendant:
   He intends to draw it out, apparently—
SHEPHERD:
   No! I have told you already that I gave him the boy.

OEDIPUS:
Where did you get him? From your house? From somewhere else?

SHEPHERD:
Not from mine, no. A man gave him to me.

OEPIDUS:
Is that man here? Whose house did he belong to?

SHEPHERD:
For God's love, my King, do not ask me any more!

OEDIPUS:
You are a dead man if I have to ask you again.

SHEPHERD:
Then . . . Then the child was from the palace of Laïos.

OEPIDUS:
A slave child? or a child of his own line?

SHEPHERD:
Ah, I am on the brink of dreadful speech!

OEDIPUS:
And I of dreadful hearing. Yet I must hear.

SHEPHERD:
If you must be told, then . . .

They said it was Laïos' child;
But it is your wife who can tell you about that.

OEDIPUS:
My wife!—Did she give it to you?

SHEPHERD:

My lord, she did.

OEDIPUS:
Do you know why?

SHEPHERD:

I was told to get rid of it.

OEDIPUS:
Oh heartless mother!

SHEPHERD:

But in dread of prophecies . . .

OEDIPUS:
Tell me.

SHEPHERD:
It was said that the boy would kill his own father.

OEDIPUS:
   Then why did you give him over to this old man?
SHEPHERD:
   I pitied the baby, my King,
   And I thought that this man would take him far away
   To his own country.
                              He saved him—but for what a fate!
   For if you are what this man says you are,
   No man living is more wretched than Oedipus.
OEDIPUS:
   Ah God!
   It was true!
              All the prophecies!
                              —Now,
   O Light, may I look on you for the last time!
   I, Oedipus,
   Oedipus, damned in his birth, in his marriage damned,
   Damned in the blood he shed with his own hand!

off to gouge his eyes out!   [He rushes into the palace

ODE IV

CHORUS:
   Alas for the seed of men.   [STROPHE 1

   What measure shall I give these generations
   That breathe on the void and are void
   And exist and do not exist?

   Who bears more weight of joy
   Than mass of sunlight shifting in images,
   Or who shall make his thought stay on
   That down time drifts away?

1. poetic beauty
2. recap
3.

   Your splendor is all fallen.

   O naked brow of wrath and tears,
   O change of Oedipus!

I who saw your days call no man blest—
Your great days like ghósts góne.

That mind was a strong bow.   [ANTISTROPHE 1

Deep, how deep you drew it then, hard archer,
At a dim fearful range,

And brought dear glory down!

You overcame the stranger—
The virgin with her hooking lion claws—
And though death sang, stood like a tower
To make pale Thebes take heart.

3. recap
4. pleading to go
5. what ppl think (of Oedipus)

Fortress against our sorrow!

True king, giver of laws,
Majestic Oedipus!
No prince in Thebes had ever such renown,
No prince won such grace of power.

And now of all men ever known   [STROPHE 2
Most pitiful is this man's story:
His fortunes are most changed, his state
Fallen to a low slave's
Ground under bitter fate.

6. forshadowing

O Oedipus, most royal one!
The great door that expelled you to the light
Gave at night—ah, gave night to your glory:
As to the father, to the fathering son.

> blindness

All understood too late.

How could that queen whom Laïos won,
The garden that he harrowed at his height,
Be silent when that act was done?

because she will be dead

But all eyes fail before time's eye,   [ANTISTROPHE 2
All actions come to justice there.
Though never willed, though far down the deep past,
Your bed, your dread sirings,
Are brought to book at last.   7. common
                                                  towns people

Child by Laïos doomed to die,
Then doomed to lose that fortunate little death,
Would God you never took breath in this air
That with my wailing lips I take to cry:

For I weep the world's outcast.

I was blind, and now I can tell why:
Asleep, for you had given ease of breath
To Thebes, while the false years went by.

ÉXODOS

                    [*Enter, from the palace,* SECOND MESSENGER
SECOND MESSENGER: UPSET
    Elders of Thebes, most honored in this land,
    What horrors are yours to see and hear, what weight
    Of sorrow to be endured, if, true to your birth,
    You venerate the line of Labdakos!
    I think neither Istros nor Phasis, those great rivers,
    Could purify this place of all the evil
    It shelters now, or soon must bring to light—
    Evil not done unconsciously, but willed.

    The greatest griefs are those we cause ourselves.
CHORAGOS:
    Surely, friend, we have grief enough already;
    What new sorrow do you mean?
SECOND MESSENGER:
                        The Queen is dead.

CHORAGOS:
  O miserable Queen! But at whose hand?
SECOND MESSENGER:

                                    Her own.
  The full horror of what happened you can not know,
  For you did not see it; but I, who did, will tell you
  As clearly as I can how she met her death.

  When she had left us,
  In passionate silence, passing through the court,
  She ran to her apartment in the house,
  Her hair clutched by the fingers of both hands.
  She closed the doors behind her; then, by that bed
  Where long ago the fatal son was conceived—
  That son who should bring about his father's death—
  We heard her call upon Laïos, dead so many years,
  And heard her wail for the double fruit of her marriage,
  A husband by her husband, children by her child.

  Exactly how she died I do not know:
  For Oedipus burst in moaning and would not let us
  Keep vigil to the end: it was by him
  As he stormed about the room that our eyes were caught.
  From one to another of us he went, begging a sword,
  Hunting the wife who was not his wife, the mother
  Whose womb had carried his own children and himself.
  I do not know: it was none of us aided him,
  But surely one of the gods was in control!
  For with a dreadful cry
  He hurled his weight, as though wrenched out of himself,
  At the twin doors: the bolts gave, and he rushed in.
  And there we saw her hanging, her body swaying
  From the cruel cord she had noosed about her neck.
  A great sob broke from him, heartbreaking to hear,
  As he loosed the rope and lowered her to the ground.

  I would blot out from my mind what happened next!
  For the King ripped from her gown the golden brooches

That were her ornament, and raised them, and plunged
    them down
Straight into his own eyeballs, crying, 'No more,
No more shall you look on the misery about me,
The horrors of my own doing! Too long you have known
The faces of those whom I should never have seen,
Too long been blind to those for whom I was searching!
From this hour, go in darkness!' And as he spoke,
He struck at his eyes—not once, but many times;
And the blood spattered his beard,
Bursting from his ruined sockets like red hail.

So from the unhappiness of two this evil has sprung,
A curse on the man and woman alike. The old
Happiness of the house of Labdakos
Was happiness enough: where is it today?
It is all wailing and ruin, disgrace, death—all
The misery of mankind that has a name—
And it is wholly and for ever theirs.

CHORAGOS:
    Is he in agony still? Is there no rest for him?

SECOND MESSENGER:
    He is calling for someone to open the doors wide
    So that all the children of Kadmos may look upon
    His father's murderer, his mother's—no,
    I can not say it!
                And then he will leave Thebes,
    Self-exiled, in order that the curse
    Which he himself pronounced may depart from the house.
    He is weak, and there is none to lead him,
    So terrible is his suffering.
                    But you will see:
    Look, the doors are opening; in a moment
    You will see a thing that would crush a heart of stone.

        [*The central door is opened;* OEDIPUS, *blinded,
        is led in*

CHORAGOS:
    Dreadful indeed for men to see.
    Never have my own eyes

Looked on a sight so full of fear.

Oedipus!
What madness came upon you, what daemon
Leaped on your life with heavier
Punishment than a mortal man can bear?
No: I can not even
Look at you, poor ruined one.
And I would speak, question, ponder,
If I were able. No.
You make me shudder.

OEDIPUS:
God.   God.
Is there a sorrow greater?
Where shall I find harbor in this world?
My voice is hurled far on a dark wind.
What has God done to me?

CHORAGOS:
Too terrible to think of, or to see.

OEDIPUS:
O cloud of night,   [STROPHE 1
Never to be turned away: night coming on,
I can not tell how: night like a shroud!

My fair winds brought me here.
                    O God. Again
The pain of the spikes where I had sight,
The flooding pain
Of memory, never to be gouged out.

CHORAGOS:
This is not strange.
You suffer it all twice over, remorse in pain,
Pain in remorse.

OEDIPUS:
Ah dear friend   [ANTISTROPHE 1
Are you faithful even yet, you alone?

Are you still standing near me, will you stay here,
Patient, to care for the blind?
                                        The blind man!
Yet even blind I know who it is attends me,
By the voice's tone—
Though my new darkness hide the comforter.

CHORAGOS:
  Oh fearful act!
  What god was it drove you to rake black
  Night across your eyes?

OEDIPUS:
  Apollo. Apollo. Dear   [STROPHE 2
  Children, the god was Apollo.
  He brought my sick, sick fate upon me.
  But the blinding hand was my own!
  How could I bear to see
  When all my sight was horror everywhere?

CHORAGOS:
  Everywhere; that is true.

OEDIPUS:
  And now what is left?
  Images? Love? A greeting even,
  Sweet to the senses? Is there anything?
  Ah, no, friends: lead me away.
  Lead me away from Thebes.
                                        Lead the great wreck
  And hell of Oedipus, whom the gods hate.

CHORAGOS:
  Your misery, you are not blind to that.
  Would God you had never found it out!

OEDIPUS:
  Death take the man who unbound   [ANTISTROPHE 2
  My feet on that hillside

And delivered me from death to life! What life?
If only I had died,
This weight of monstrous doom
Could not have dragged me and my darlings down.

CHORAGOS:
  I would have wished the same.

OEDIPUS:
  Oh never to have come here
  With my father's blood upon me! Never
  To have been the man they call his mother's husband!
  Oh accurst! Oh child of evil,
  To have entered that wretched bed—
                          the selfsame one!
  More primal than sin itself, this fell to me.

CHORAGOS:
  I do not know what words to offer you.
  You were better dead than alive and blind.

OEDIPUS:
  Do not counsel me any more. This punishment
  That I have laid upon myself is just.
  If I had eyes,
  I do not know how I could bear the sight
  Of my father, when I came to the house of Death,
  Or my mother: for I have sinned against them both
  So vilely that I could not make my peace
  By strangling my own life.
                          Or do you think my children,
  Born as they were born, would be sweet to my eyes?
  Ah never, never! Nor this town with its high walls,
  Nor the holy images of the gods.
                          For I,
  Thrice miserable!—Oedipus, noblest of all the line
  Of Kadmos, have condemned myself to enjoy
  These things no more, by my own malediction
  Expelling that man whom the gods declared

To be a defilement in the house of Laïos.
After exposing the rankness of my own guilt,
How could I look men frankly in the eyes?
No, I swear it,
If I could have stifled my hearing at its source,
I would have done it and made all this body
A tight cell of misery, blank to light and sound:
So I should have been safe in my dark mind
Beyond external evil.
                        Ah Kithairon!
Why did you shelter me? When I was cast upon you,
Why did I not die? Then I should never
Have shown the world my execrable birth.

Ah Polybos! Corinth, city that I believed
The ancient seat of my ancestors: how fair
I seemed, your child! And all the while this evil
Was cancerous within me!
                        For I am sick
In my own being, sick in my origin.

O three roads, dark ravine, woodland and way
Where three roads met: you, drinking my father's blood,
My own blood, spilled by my own hand: can you remem-
        ber
The unspeakable things I did there, and the things
I went on from there to do?
                        O marriage, marriage!
The act that engendered me, and again the act
Performed by the son in the same bed--
                        Ah, the net
Of incest, mingling fathers, brothers, sons,
With brides, wives, mothers: the last evil
That can be known by men: no tongue can say
How evil!
        No. For the love of God, conceal me
Somewhere far from Thebes; or kill me; or hurl me
Into the sea, away from men's eyes for ever.

Come, lead me. You need not fear to touch me.
Of all men, I alone can bear this guilt.

[*Enter* KREON

CHORAGOS:
Kreon is here now. As to what you ask,
He may decide the course to take. He only
Is left to protect the city in your place.

OEDIPUS:
Alas, how can I speak to him? What right have I
To beg his courtesy whom I have deeply wronged?

KREON:
I have not come to mock you, Oedipus,
Or to reproach you, either.

[*To* ATTENDANTS:
—You, standing there:
If you have lost all respect for man's dignity,
At least respect the flame of Lord Helios:
Do not allow this pollution to show itself
Openly here, an affront to the earth
And Heaven's rain and the light of day. No, take him
Into the house as quickly as you can.
For it is proper
That only the close kindred see his grief.

OEDIPUS:
I pray you in God's name, since your courtesy
Ignores my dark expectation, visiting
With mercy this man of all men most execrable:
Give me what I ask—for your good, not for mine.

KREON:
And what is it that you turn to me begging for?

OEDIPUS:
Drive me out of this country as quickly as may be
To a place where no human voice can ever greet me.

KREON:
I should have done that before now—only,
God's will had not been wholly revealed to me.

OEDIPUS:
But his command is plain: the parricide
Must be destroyed. I am that evil man.

KREON:

That is the sense of it, yes; but as things are,
We had best discover clearly what is to be done.

OEDIPUS:

You would learn more about a man like me?

KREON:

You are ready now to listen to the god.

OEDIPUS:

I will listen. But it is to you
That I must turn for help. I beg you, hear me.

The woman in there—
Give her whatever funeral you think proper:
She is your sister.
                    —But let me go, Kreon!
Let me purge my father's Thebes of the pollution
Of my living here, and go out to the wild hills,
To Kithairon, that has won such fame with me,
The tomb my mother and father appointed for me,
And let me die there, as they willed I should.
And yet I know
Death will not ever come to me through sickness
Or in any natural way: I have been preserved
For some unthinkable fate. But let that be.

As for my sons, you need not care for them.
They are men, they will find some way to live.
But my poor daughters, who have shared my table,
Who never before have been parted from their father—
Take care of them, Kreon; do this for me.
And will you let me touch them with my hands
A last time, and let us weep together?
Be kind, my lord,
Great prince, be kind!
                    Could I but touch them,
They would be mine again, as when I had my eyes.
                    [*Enter* ANTIGONE *and* ISMENE, *attended*
Ah, God!
Is it my dearest children I hear weeping?

Has Kreon pitied me and sent my daughters?

KREON:

Yes, Oedipus: I knew that they were dear to you
In the old days, and know you must love them still.

OEDIPUS:

May God bless you for this—and be a friendlier
Guardian to you than he has been to me!

Children, where are you?
Come quickly to my hands: they are your brother's—
Hands that have brought your father's once clear eyes
To this way of seeing—

                Ah dearest ones,
I had neither sight nor knowledge then, your father
By the woman who was the source of his own life!
And I weep for you—having no strength to see you—,
I weep for you when I think of the bitterness
That men will visit upon you all your lives.
What homes, what festivals can you attend
Without being forced to depart again in tears?
And when you come to marriageable age,
Where is the man, my daughters, who would dare
Risk the bane that lies on all my children?
Is there any evil wanting? Your father killed
His father; sowed the womb of her who bore him;
Engendered you at the fount of his own existence!

That is what they will say of you.

                        Then, whom
Can you ever marry? There are no bridegrooms for you,
And your lives must wither away in sterile dreaming.

O Kreon, son of Menoikeus!
You are the only father my daughters have,
Since we, their parents, are both of us gone for ever.
They are your own blood: you will not let them
Fall into beggary and loneliness;
You will keep them from the miseries that are mine!

Take pity on them; see, they are only children,
Friendless except for you. Promise me this,
Great Prince, and give me your hand in token of it.

[KREON *clasps his right hand*

Children:
I could say much, if you could understand me,
But as it is, I have only this prayer for you:
Live where you can, be as happy as you can—
Happier, please God, than God has made your father.

KREON:
Enough. You have wept enough. Now go within.

OEDIPUS:
I must; but it is hard.

KREON:
                              Time eases all things.

OEDIPUS:
You know my mind, then?

KREON:
                                 Say what you desire.

OEDIPUS:
Send me from Thebes!

KREON:
                              God grant that I may!

OEDIPUS:
But since God hates me . . .

KREON:
                         No, he will grant your wish.

OEDIPUS:
You promise?

KREON:
             I can not speak beyond my knowledge.

OEDIPUS:
Then lead me in.

KREON:
                    Come now, and leave your children.

OEDIPUS:
No! Do not take them from me!

KREON:
                              Think no longer
That you are in command here, but rather think
How, when you were, you served your own destruction.

> [*Exeunt into the house all but the* CHORUS; *the*
> CHORAGOS *chants directly to the audience:*

CHORAGOS:
Men of Thebes: look upon Oedipus.

This is the king who solved the famous riddle
And towered up, most powerful of men.
No mortal eyes but looked on him with envy,
Yet in the end ruin swept over him.

Let every man in mankind's frailty
Consider his last day; and let none
Presume on his good fortune until he find
Life, at his death, a memory without pain.

NOTES

78   33 *the Sphinx*: This monster, a manifestation of the goddess Hêra's hatred for the royal house of Thebes,
has been infesting the city's environs, propounding a
riddle and devouring those unable to guess the answer.
The riddle: 'What animal goes on four legs in the
morning, two legs at noon, and three legs in the
evening?' Oedipus, passing by on his way from
Corinth, promptly gives the solution: 'Man; for he
creeps in infancy, walks erect in maturity, and uses
a staff in old age.' Hearing this answer, the Sphinx
destroys herself.

81   16 *Was Laïos murdered in his house?*: It is idle to speculate as to why Oedipus during all the years of his reign
has not troubled to inform himself as to the details
of the death of his predecessor. Ancient drama was
unconcerned with realistic probability, either of action
or of time; what mattered was the grand design of the
plot. In this instance, as elsewhere, we encounter an
improbability, but not an inconsistency, of plotting

83   2 *Párodos*: The suppliants in the Prologue have been
silent supernumeraries. Now the Chorus enters, to
remain until the end of the play. The chanted Odes—
stásima—are its reflections upon the action; when it intervenes in the dialogue, it does so in the person of its
leader (*Choragos*), who is to be understood as uttering
the sentiments of the group.

89   10 *What a wicked old man*: It is the quick rage of Oedipus, the unreflecting violence, that is the tragic flaw
in a noble nature. So he killed Laïos at the cross-
roads; so he condemns Teiresias, and will condemn
Kreon; so, even his last words to Iokastê are to spring
from impulsive misunderstanding. The 'probabilities'
of behavior are less important here than the symbolic
exposition of character.

137

Page	Line	
91	25	*Your birds*: Teiresias, as official seer, uses the method of augury. This involves the observation of the flight and behavior of birds in order to foretell the future or recover the hidden past.

91   25   *Your birds*: Teiresias, as official seer, uses the method of augury. This involves the observation of the flight and behavior of birds in order to foretell the future or recover the hidden past.

93   9   *You were a great man once at solving riddles*: Oedipus's solving the Sphinx's riddle was not in itself an act of *hybris*; but his success has clearly gone to his head, and his intemperate language, in this scene and later, verges upon *hybris* and helps precipitate his downfall.

94   9   The Chorus reflects rather confusedly upon what they have heard. On the one hand, Teiresias, as a professional interpreter of the Delphic Oracle, can not be wrong when he proclaims the eventual discovery and punishment of the murderer of Laïos; on the other hand, it seems unbelievable that their King, a stranger to Thebes and to the line of Lábdakos, could be the guilty man described. Their impulsive conclusion is that Teiresias, being mortal and blind, must somehow be mistaken. This is echoed later by Iokastê in her genuinely blasphemous dismissal of oracles and soothsayers.

94   9   *The Delphic stone*: A large ceremonial stone in the shrine of Apollo at Delphi. It was called, from its shape, Earth's Navel.

96   11   *You murderer!*: Whatever he may be in the two other plays dealing with the Oedipus theme, *Oedipus Coloneus* and *Antigonê*, the Creon of *Oedipus Rex* is temperate, sensible, coöperative, and just. The headstrong fatal fury of Oedipus, based upon a wild conjecture, is made all the more striking by its being directed against this unoffending bystander. Naturally there is no conspiracy—no human conspiracy, at any rate—to harm Oedipus. Kreon's refutation of the King's charges is unanswerable.

100   6   *O city, city!*: Yeats has it, excellently: 'Hear him, O Thebes!' Moving because of its very wrongheadedness, the appeal to the City marks the emotional crisis of the first part of this scene. With the entrance of Iokastê a different accumulation of passions is begun.

Page   Line

102   18   *Oh let it rest, let it be done with!*: This is the sensible
            counsel of the man in the street; it was also the idea
            behind Teiresias's initial unwillingness to tell what
            he knew. Unhappily, the situation is now so far out
            of hand that there is no possibility of saving it by
            ordinary good sense.

104   14   *This is what prophets and prophecies are worth!*:
            Iokastê is careful to distinguish between the fallible
            utterances of seers like Teiresias and the hidden de-
            signs of the gods; but her statement, in any circum-
            stances, would be reckless to the point of blasphemy.
            She, too, is self-destructive.

104   17   *How strange a shadowy memory*: The beginning of
            recognition. In this scene Oedipus gradually becomes
            aware of himself as the killer of Laïos, but the total
            revelation does not come until he has questioned the
            Shepherd.

109   24   *Let me be reverent*: The stress is on the pronoun. In
            this *stásimon* the Chorus retracts the mild scepticism
            that it had expressed earlier (see note to 94:9) and
            asserts the conservative saving value of orthodox faith.
            Human pride, manifest in the hybristic utterances of
            the King and Queen, will always bring down Némesis,
            the wrath of the offended gods. The social order, the
            Chorus says, is threatened by rationalistic doubts; man-
            kind is sick, infected here by its own rulers.

117   20   *no more questioning!*: Iokastê now sees everything;
            Oedipus, however, is not fully enlightened. The
            Queen's exit—she is going to her chamber to kill
            herself—is made the more tragic by her husband-son's
            misunderstanding her motives and behavior. He thinks
            that her despair springs from social vanity, that she
            wants to cut off the investigation because she fears
            that Oedipus will be revealed as of ignoble birth.

119   1   CHORUS: The third *stásimon* is a rapid dance-poem
            (*hypórchêma*), blindly optimistic in tone. Oedipus,
            surely, will turn out to be not only of noble birth,
            but of divine birth! The ironic device of placing an
            exuberantly hopeful Ode directly before the catas-
            trophe is employed again by Sophocles in *Antigonê*.

124   22   *The great door*: Like 'the garden' (line 27), the womb of Iokastê.

125   4   *your dread sirings*: Oedipus and Iokastê had two sons, Polyneikês and Eteoklês, and two daughters, Antigonê and Ismenê. The sons killed each other during the assault of the Seven against Thebes, shortly after Oedipus's death. At the same time Antigonê was condemned to death by Kreon on a charge of treason, and committed suicide. Ismenê drifts insignificantly out of the story.

127   23   *Self-exiled*: He must live to expiate his sin; he is not yet worthy of the release of death.

128   17   STROPHE: Here the strophic system is a *kommós*, a lyric dialogue between the actor on the stage and the Chorus in the *orchêstra*.

132   12   *this pollution*: Not a brutality, or no more brutal than the situation demands. Apollo, as god of health and light, must not be offended by the sight of Oedipus, sick, blinded, lamentably streaming blood and tears. As Regent of Thebes, since Polyneikês and Eteoklês are too young to rule, Kreon sets about restoring order and reëstablishing the proprieties.

135   11   *God grant that I may*: Thebes has already suffered from too much purely human initiative. Kreon will not promise to let Oedipus leave the city until he has determined, presumably from Teiresias, the further will of Heaven.

136   3   *Men of Thebes*: Metre and diction suggest that the concluding lines are spurious, though they must date back to the time of the play. It may be that they are an actor's interpolation. In any event, some such epilogue is necessary: it would be awkward to end the play with Kreon's last line.

THE ALCESTIS
OF EURIPIDES
TRANSLATED BY
DUDLEY FITTS AND
ROBERT FITZGERALD

INTRODUCTORY NOTE

Alcestis was first performed in Athens, probably at the annual festival of the Great Dionysia, in 483 B.C. Euripides was then in his middle forties, a successful dramatist of some fifteen years' experience, and his contribution on this occasion was a series of four unrelated plays. Of these only *Alcestis*, which was acted fourth, has come down to us; but the titles of the three lost plays are enough to suggest that what the poet submitted was not the more or less usual Trilogy with Satyr Play appended, but four separate dramas. The point seems worth making because critics, even in ancient times, have been troubled by the paradox of a happy ending in Tragedy, and because later commentators have tried to account for it by taking the hint of the fourth position and reading *Alcestis* as a kind of undecisive Satyr Play, half comic and half tragic. It is true that Aristotle laid out the tragic line of action: the Hero passes from happiness to adversity; but it is also true that Euripides had never read Aristotle on the subject. In several of his plays, notably the *Iôn* and the *Helen*, he brings about a happy ending, although the happiness is usually of an ambiguous nature.

In *Alcestis*, to be sure, there are scenes of an earthy coarseness that we do not generally associate with classical tragedy —the Admetos-Pherês *agôn*, for instance, and the alcoholic revelry of Heraklês—but we have no reason to assume that Euripides did not know what he was doing, or that what he was doing was unacceptable to his audience. Admittedly, he did not take the first prize in 483: that went to his older rival Sophocles; but it seems excessive to find a reason for this in the structure of his *Alcestis*.

At the same time, we must confess that the twist of this particular happy ending is provocative—too provocative, it may be, for a wholly comfortable response. We do not know

143

enough about earlier handlings of the Alcestis myth to be
able to tell how much Euripides has added or subtracted,
but it seems safe to say that his analysis of character and
motive represents something new in the history of drama.
We should guess that the original story, surely a very primitive one, contained elements of the resurrection myth (Persephonê comes to mind, who rises from the dead at the end
of each winter*) and of ideas connected with the sacred
obligations of hospitality. If so, Euripides has not concerned
himself with the religious implications of deliverance from
the dead; but it is not too much to say that the whole of his
plot turns upon the theme of hospitality. It was *because*
Admetos had been hospitable to Apollo that Apollo saved
him from death; and it was *because* of his almost fanatical
hospitality to Heraklês that his wife was finally returned
to him. The theme is conventional enough; what is really
unusual, and characteristically Euripidean, is the wry ap-
proach to the theme. Are the virtues of Admetos all that
they seem to be? Is this a story of piety rewarded?

Here the danger is that we may read too much of ourselves
into an ancient play. Our prejudices and preoccupations are
not those of Euripides. For a variety of reasons, many of
them creditable, we find it outrageous that a man should
accept such a sacrifice as Alcestis makes for her husband.
To Admetos it is a painful state of affairs, but a necessary
one: a woman, after all, is only a woman; a wife is her
husband's chattel, existing only for his welfare; and besides, this husband happens to be a king as well. The
Athenian play-goer would not find these ideas outrageous,
or even strange. It is the unworthiness, the ignobility, of
this particular husband that Euripides is concerned with.
The unlovely debate between father and son is only the
most striking of the many instances that illumine the
equivocal nature of Admetos. It is his selfish sensuality that
offends us most. 'No other woman, however beautiful,' he
says, will sleep in his dead wife's bed; he will acquire an

---

* It is interesting to find that Apollodoros, a mythographer writing
some 300 years later than Euripides, asserts that it was Persephonê,
not Heraklês, who restored Alcestis to the world of the living.

ivory image of Alcestis, he says, for that same bed; he will temporarily discontinue the music, and the dancing girls, and the flowing hair; he will even stay away from parties in town because there are mean souls, he says, who might look at him queerly, and that would make him uncomfortable. He has asked his wife to die for him; yet suddenly, in a burst of unusually beautiful poetry, he sees himself as a romantic hero, another Orpheus, charming the dark houses of the Dead and bringing his Eurydicê back into the world of light. Even at his moments of greatest insight—at the end of the *kommós* and in his final argument with Heraklês —it is his social reputation, what other gentlemen will be thinking about him, that concerns him most.

It is a bleakly ironic stroke, pure Euripides, to make this infatuated gentleman violate his word as a gentleman. Surely this is the meaning of the *éxodos*: that a man who has solemnly engaged himself never to do *x* finds himself, though with becoming reluctance, doing *x* on the very day that he has sworn not to. He has promised never to take another woman into his house; but now he yields to Heraklês and takes another woman—his own wife, to be sure, but he does not know that it is Alcestis, and we must judge him on his own grounds. But if we elaborate this oddly bitter 'happy ending' and go on to speculate as to just what Alcestis' first words will be when she has completed her three days of ritual silence, we are in danger of reading Euripides too curiously. Even so, the conjecture seems forgivable. Though it is wrong to think of Euripides as though he were Ibsen, with all the questions unanswered as the final curtain falls, we should be even more wrong to ignore his acid questioning of motives, the tone of disillusionment that runs through every scene of this domestic comedy.

DF

CONTENTS

PERSONS REPRESENTED:

APOLLO
DEATH
CHORUS OF PHERAIAN CITIZENS
A MAIDSERVANT
ALCESTIS
ADMETOS
A CHILD [EUMELOS]
HERAKLES
PHERES
A SERVANT

SCENE: *Before the palace of* ADMETOS, *in Pherai.*

🎝 PROLOGUE

> [*Enter from the palace* APOLLO, *clothed in white,
> masked, armed with golden bow. He faces the
> house, and apostrophizes it in a declamatory
> tone:*

APOLLO:
House of Admetos, where I brought myself
to share the food of slaves—and I a god!

> [*To the audience:*

Zeus's providence. He had stabbed my son,
Asklêpios, with lightning, and I, raging,
cut down his fire-forgers, the Wheeleyes;
and for penalty the Father of Heaven bound me
servant to death-bound man.

149

So I came here
to be a cowherd in a stranger's country.
His house I have cared for to this day. Returning
good for good, I saved him even from death
when I tricked the three fatal Sisters, forcing
their word for it that he need not go down
into the dark land if he found a friend
to take his place among the Dead.

A friend?
Admetos went to all his friends in turn,
to his father and his mother also; and he found
none but his wife who dared to die for him,
dared to give up the sweet sunlight for him!
None but his wife: and now
in the house they are comforting her, for she is fainting;
this is the day appointed for her death;
and I must leave the dear shelter of this place,
not to be stained with it.

For see: already
Thánatos, priest of the dying, has come
to lead her down to the sad world under ground.

[*Enter the figure of* DEATH, *shrouded in black,
masked, holding a naked sword.*

So you have come, Death. You have remembered her day.

DEATH:

Prince of Light,
have you come to quarrel with me in this house again?
Will you assume again those rights
that only Hell should use?
That you charmed the Sisters, that your twisting
slippery tricks delayed Admetos' death,
I know; but why you stand
armed at the door, bright guardian of Alcestis,
I do not know. Has she not promised—
to save her husband's life, Apollo—
has she not promised to die? And on this day?

APOLLO:

You need not fear. I have my own rights; and my reasons.

DEATH:
Yet you go armed, Apollo.

APOLLO:
                              I go armed always.

DEATH:
And are always over-kind to Admetos' house.

APOLLO:
I only sympathize with a friend in trouble.

DEATH:
And you would rob me of this second death?

APOLLO:
Did I take Admetos from you by force?

DEATH:
                                        He walks
above ground: why is he not beneath it?

APOLLO:
He has given you his wife—

DEATH:
                      And I have come for her.

APOLLO:
Then take her, and go!
                  —Not that I imagine
that any words of mine could move you—

DEATH:
                                    To what?
To take a life that is forfeit? I should say
that I know my office.

APOLLO:
                    No, no. I would have you
postpone her death.

DEATH:
                  Your proposal is duly noted.

APOLLO:
Allow Alcestis to reach her old age!

DEATH:
                              Never.
My honor is mine, Apollo, as yours is yours.

APOLLO:
Honor?

What honor do you find in taking one life?

DEATH:
A young life; more glory.

APOLLO:
Let her die old,
and her grave will bring you riches.

DEATH:
How like you!
You have the interests of the rich at heart.

APOLLO:
Who would ever have thought Death had a sense of
humor?

DEATH:
Your rich men could all buy up length of days.

APOLLO:
Then you will not grant me this?

DEATH:
I will not. You
have measured me, you know what I am.

APOLLO:
I know you:
the hatred of men, the loathing of the gods!

DEATH:
For once, you may not have what is not yours.

APOLLO:
Death, Death, I swear to you,
cruel as you are, your cruelty is too weak!
Listen: a man is coming,
here, to Pherês' house: a man is coming
on his way to the Thracian snowfields, sent
by Eurystheus to steal the famous horses.
In this very house
Admetos will receive him and honor him.
And it is he, Death, who will wrestle you and take
Alcestis from you. You will get no thanks from us
when you yield her, Death; and I will hate you still!

[*Exit* APOLLO.

DEATH:
This was a god of many words; but words
are not enough, Apollo.
> [DEATH *moves to the central door and touches it
> with the point of his sword. The door slowly
> opens while he addresses the audience directly:*

Today this woman must go down to Death.
My sword is ready.
The lock of hair, the sign of sacrifice
to the dark gods under ground,
now it is mine to take.
> [*Exit slowly into the house. The door closes*

🎜 PÁRODOS

> [*The* CHORUS, *composed of fifteen men of Pherai,
> enters the* orchêstra *during the opening speech of the*
> CHORAGOS.

CHORAGOS:
I wonder what the silence means.
Why is the whole house so silent?
There is no one here to tell us
If we must mourn for our Queen,
Or if she is alive still—
Alcestis, Pelias' daughter,
surely the best of women, best
of wives to her husband.

CHORUS:
Can anyone hear them weeping?   [STROPHE 1
Is there beating of hands, or lamentation,
Or any cry of death inside? No, nothing,
There is nothing. No sound.
No servant stands at the door. —O Paian,
God of Healing, come,
Use this lull in the storm!

A VOICE:
Would they be so quiet if she were dead?

A VOICE:
  She is surely dead.
A VOICE:
  One thing is sure: she has not been taken away.
A VOICE:
  I would not say for sure. How do you know?
A VOICE:
  How could Admetos have given private burial
  To a wife so loyal?

CHORUS:
  I can not see the urn at the door   [ANTISTROPHE 1
  With water in it, which is usual
  When a person is dead; nor any lock of hair
  Fallen, the sign of mourning, at the threshold.
  There is no sound at all
  Of young breasts beaten—
  Grief of her maids about her.
A VOICE:
  And yet, this is her day—
A VOICE:
  What are you murmuring?
A VOICE:
  Today she must go under ground.
A VOICE:
  You have touched my heart, you have touched my soul.
A VOICE:
  It must be so: when goodness dies,
  All good men suffer, too.

CHORUS:
  There is no power in the world   [STROPHE 2
  To whom we could send to save her,
  Neither in Lykia, nor in the dry land
  Where the temples of Ammon are.
  Strong death comes down upon her.
  I do not know what altars
  We could make sacrifices on.

Only if Apollo's son were here,   [ANTISTROPHE 2
If his eyes opened on the light again,
He yet might save her from the night,
From Death's dark corridor. That god
Made men stand up whom death had overthrown.
But Heaven's thunder consumed him,
Him also. Where then is our hope?

CHORAGOS:
The King has exhausted every ritual.
The black blood
Glows on the altars of the gods, a hopeless
Sacrifice against evil.

EPEISODION I

[*A* MAIDSERVANT *enters from the palace.*

CHORAGOS:
But look: here is one of her servants from the house,
and in tears. What can she tell us?
                                    —You grieve
for your lord and lady, girl; and that's reasonable.
But Alcestis? Tell us, is she alive, or dead?

MAIDSERVANT:
She is alive. And dead.

CHORAGOS:
                         How can that be?

MAIDSERVANT:
Her breath is failing. Her soul stands on the brink.

CHORAGOS:
Oh lost, Admetos!

MAIDSERVANT:
                    Let the King be.
He will not understand, until she is gone.

CHORAGOS:
Can nothing be done to save her?

MAIDSERVANT:
                                 Nothing.
The fatal day takes her.

CHORAGOS:
                    And the arrangements of custom,
    have they been made?
MAIDSERVANT:
                    Her fine things are set out
    for her adornment at burial.
CHORAGOS:
    She is beyond praise in her death. No wife,
    no other under the great sun is her equal!
MAIDSERVANT:
    Not in all the world. Who will deny it?
    Is there a higher excellence
    than this, that a wife should die her husband's death?
    The entire city knows it, and affirms it.

    But you will marvel when you hear what she has been
        doing.

    This morning, when she knew her day had come,
    she bathed her white body in fresh water from the stream,
    took her prettiest things from the cedar rooms
    and dressed herself becomingly; then stood
    before the Flame upon the hearth and prayed:
    'Goddess, now I am going into earth.
    'I shall not ever pray to you again.
    'Watch over my children when I am dead.
    'Give the boy a wife who will be dear to him,
    'and give the girl a good husband.
    'Do not let them die, like their mother, while they are
        young,
    'but grant that they may be fortunate.
    'Let them live happy lives in the land of their people.'

    Then she went from altar to altar in the house,
    praying, making wreaths for every shrine,
    shearing off the leaves of young myrtle branches,
    quietly, without a word, so still, so lovely,
    you would have said no threat of evil had touched her.
    But in her chamber,

then there were tears: 'Dear bed,'
she cried, 'dear bridal bed, where first I lay
'naked for him, and now I die for him . . .
'You are no longer mine. I do not hate you:
'you have destroyed me, only me. I would not
'betray you and my husband by denials,
'and so I die. Another wife
'will lie here, it may be, no more faithful than I—
'but oh, let her be more fortunate!'
                                         She knelt
and kissed the bed, weeping until
she could cry no more. Then rose
and left the chamber, slowly, returning often,
faltering.
          Her children
clung sobbing to her robe; she took them up
and embraced them in farewell; seeing her servants' tears,
she gave her right hand sweetly to each in turn:
even the meanest blessed her, and was blessed.

These are the sorrows of Admetos' house.

If he had died, why then he would have died;
but now his grief is so bitter that all his life
he never will escape it, never forget.

CHORAGOS:
He shows his grief, then? Knows what he must lose,
and the sorrows of his house?

MAIDSERVANT:
                        Weeping.
Holding her in his arms, his dearest wife,
begging her not to leave him now. All madness . . .
For she has only a little time to breathe,
and always her eyes are upon the moving sunlight,
as though she would never see the sun again
and now must say good-bye to it for ever . . .

Well. I will say to Admetos that you have come.
Not everyone is fond enough of princes

to have stood by in bitter times like these.
But you are a good friend, and have been always.
You are welcome here.

[Exit.

🎜 STÁSIMON I

A VOICE:
    Is there no escape, O God?   [STROPHE 1
    Must this evil come upon us?
A VOICE:
    Is there no help? Must my locks
    Be shorn? Must I go in mourning?
CHORAGOS:
    Clearly we must. Even so,
    Pray to the gods: they have great power.
CHORUS:
    Lord Apollo, Lord of Healing,
    Find a remedy for Admetos.
    Grant it, oh grant it!
    Save him, save him, as once before,
    From angry Death:
    Beat back murderous Hadês!

A VOICE:
    My tears are for you, Admetos.   [ANTISTROPHE 1
    How will you live, once she is gone?
A VOICE:
    A man could cut his own throat
    Or hang himself against heaven for this.
CHORAGOS:
    She is not dear, but dearest of all,
    This woman whose death you will see today.
CHORUS:
    Ah, she is coming from her house,
    And he is with her. Cry out,
    Let all Pherai mourn,
    Let earth itself cry out for her

Who passes now, fainting, sick,
To the house of Hadês.

Never say that marriage has more of joy than pain.
I have seen marriages. I have seen
The fortune of my king.
Lost is the loveliest, lost the dear wife.
What now can his days bring,
What pleasure to his life that is no life?

✸ EPEISODION II

> [*Enter* ALCESTIS *from the house, supported by*
> ADMETOS, *leading the child* EUMELOS *by the hand.*
> *She speaks remotely, as if entranced, disregard-*
> *ing at first the prosaic interruptions of her hus-*
> *band.*

ALCESTIS:

O Sun! O shining clear day,   [STROPHE 1
And white clouds wheeling in the clear of heaven!

ADMETOS:

He looks down and sees that we are both unhappy.
How have we harmed him, or the other gods?
Why should you die?

ALCESTIS:

O Iôlkos, and the dear roof   [ANTISTROPHE 1
That sheltered me the day that I was married!

ADMETOS:

Try to stand up, poor darling. Do not fail me.
Only pray to the almighty gods; it may be
they will have mercy on us both.

ALCESTIS:

I see the dark lake,   [STROPHE 2
The skiff in shore,
And Charôn holding the double oar, calling,
'Why are you waiting, Alcestis? Come,

'You are keeping us back . . .'
Can you not hear him? Listen!
He is angry.

ADMETOS:

To me it is a bitter voyage that you speak of . . .
What a terrible thing this is for both of us!

ALCESTIS:

Something is touching me—   [ANTISTROPHE 2
Do you see *any*one?—
Someone drawing me, drawing me down to death . . .
Ah the great black brows of Death!
                                   Frowning! Wings!
Let me alone!— Strange journey,
And I am afraid.

ADMETOS:

This is a terrible thing for those who love you,
terrible for your husband and your children.

ALCESTIS:

You need not hold me any more. Please,
let me lie down. I have no strength to stand,
so near to death, and the dark
creeps on my eyes like night.
                              Children,
no more. You have no mother any more.
Be happy in the sweet sunlight.

ADMETOS:

Oh God, I'd rather die than hear you say these things!
For my sake, for your children's sake, do not leave me now.
Come, make an effort, rise.
With you gone, how could I live? You, only you,
mean life or death to us, blest by your love.

ALCESTIS:

Admetos, Admetos . . .
You see what is happening to me now; but before I die,
I must tell you what I have in mind to ask you.

In deference to you, laying down my life

to let you see the sunlight in this country,
I come to die. Yet I need not have died.
I could have married any man in Thessaly,
lived with some great prince in his splendid house;
but without you, with my children fatherless,
I would not live. Yet I am young, and these years
have been pleasant.
     Your father and mother failed you in
  their age,
When, death being near, they might have died with
  honor
and saved their son with honor. You were all
they had, nor had they hope of other children.
You and I could have lived out all our days,
and you would not be abandoned, left alone
with these poor children.
     But I suppose some god
managed all this to turn out as it has,
and so let it be.
     —But now, Admetos,
I ask a favor in return: not so great a thing
(for nothing is more precious than a life),
but a favor that I deserve, surely. You love
these children just as I do—oh, you must!
Make them the masters of this house, my house,
and do not set another wife above them.
Whoever she might be, sometimes she'd strike them—
and they are our children!

I beg you, never that!
     A second wife
is hateful to the children of the first,
a viper is not more hateful.

     The boy here
has a strong defending tower in his father.
But, dearest daughter! . . .
     How will it be with you,
growing up, if your father marries again?

Will she be kind to you? If only
she will bring no scandal upon you in your girlhood
and spoil your wedding day!
Dearest, your mother will never see your wedding,
never hold your hand in childbirth, at that time
when there's no comfort greater than having her near you.
No. I must die, And it comes
not tomorrow, not the day after tomorrow, but now,
in only a moment: and I must take my place
with those who are not.

                    Good-bye. Be happy.

Admetos, you can be proud of a good wife.
Children, you can say that your mother was good.

CHORAGOS:

Be confident. I will speak for Admetos.
He is a man of sense, he will do this for you.

ADMETOS:

It shall be as you ask, believe me, it shall be so.
You only I have loved in life, love now you are dying.
You are my only Queen.
There is no other woman in all Thessaly
shall ever take your place beside me here;
no other woman, however beautiful, however
noble she may be. These are my life,
these children—and I pray the gods I may
live in them, since I am denied you.

Oh, grief for me to bear as long as I live!

But I shall hate my father and my mother:
friends in words, but enemies in deed,
while you gave up your dear life for my life.

Mourning?
I'll have mourning! I'll stop the dancing.
There will be no more feasts in my house, no garlands,
no laughter, no music.
I'll never touch the strings of a lyre again

or bring myself to sing to the Libyan flute.
You take my happiness away with you.

And listen:
I'll have wise carvers make your body's image
in ivory, for our own bed; and I'll lie against it,
dreaming
that when I clasp it and whisper your name
you are with me there . . .
                              Cold comfort, surely! Yet
it may relieve the weight around my heart.
And often, I think, in sleep you'll come to me:
a sweet thing, for whatever time,
to revisit in dreams the dear dead we have lost.

Oh, if I had Orpheus' voice and poetry
with which to move the Dark Maid and her Lord,
I'd call you back, dear love, from the world below.
I'd go down there for you. Charôn or the grim
King's dog could not prevent me then
from carrying you up into the fields of light.

But you, down there, be patient: I am coming.
Make a place for me, that we may be together.
In the same cedar boards with you I shall command
that these bones of mine be laid down with your own:
for not in death would I be far from you,
my dearest, my only faithful friend!

CHORAGOS:
    Your grief is my grief, Admetos, bitter and strong,
    as friend to friend. She is worthy of it.

ALCESTIS:
    Children, you have heard your father promise.
    He will not marry another woman to rule you.
    He will not dishonor my memory.

ADMETOS:
                              I swear it.

ALCESTIS:
    Then I leave you my children. Take them, love them.

ADMETOS:

A dear gift, from a dear hand!

ALCESTIS:

You must be their mother, too, now I am gone.

ADMETOS:

No question, since they have lost you.

ADMETOS:

Oh, my children,

to die so, with you needing me!

ADMETOS:

Tell me, tell me,

what shall I do, alone?

ALCESTIS:

Why, time will tell.

Time will take care of that. The dead are nothing at all.

ADMETOS:

For God's love, take me, take me with you below!

ALCESTIS:

This death is death enough I die for you.

ADMETOS:

Detestable Death, to steal a wife so dear!

ALCESTIS:

It is quite dark now. My eyes are heavy.

ADMETOS:

If you do really leave me, I am lost!

ALCESTIS:

I am nothing. Speak of me as nothing.

ADMETOS:

Turn your face. You can not leave your children!

ALCESTIS:

I must. It is not what I wish. Good-bye, children.

ADMETOS:

Look at them, look at them!

ALCESTIS:

No more.

ADMETOS:

What are you doing?

What has happened?

ALCESTIS:
Ah . . .

[*She dies. A long pause.*

ADMETOS:
Oh, I am the most unhappy man that ever lived!
CHORAGOS:
She has gone. The King's wife is dead.

CHILD:
Now I am lost. Dearest   [STROPHE
Mother has left us, Father,
Gone from the bright day.
I am forsaken.
            Father, look:
Her strange eyes, her fingers
Cold and stiff.
            Oh, Mother,
Can you listen? Here's your little one,
Bending, calling,
Trying to kiss your mouth.

ADMETOS:
She is deaf to us, she is blind. Children,
you and I are struck by the same disaster.

CHILD
Young to be bereft so,   [ANTISTROPHE
How can I play now, Father?
Hurt by the whole world.
Oh little sister,
            lonely, too!
And you—your marriage, Father,
All in vain.
            In vain all
Hope of growing old with Mother.
Death came first. Our house is dying,
Desolate in her death.

        [ADMETOS *moves slowly towards the central door.*
        The CHORAGOS *addresses him with remote stern-*
        ness:

CHORAGOS:
Admetos, you are not the first man to lose a dear wife,
nor will you be the last. Have patience, then, **and**
    remember
that death comes to all of us.

ADMETOS:
                                     I know it well . . .
This blow fell
not without warning. Long ago I had
foreknowledge, waited anxiously.
                                     And now
I must arrange for her funeral.
                                     Thessalians:
I command your attendance upon her, I command
that you raise a paean to the deaf King of the Dead.
Every man subject to me
shall share in my mourning. Let every man
crop his head and clothe himself in black.
Let horsemen and charioteers
clip their horses' manes. For twelve full months
I forbid the sound of lyre or flute in the city.

For never again shall I bury one more dear to me,
or one more generous. She is worthy of all honor,
since she alone has taken my place in death.
            [*He goes into the house. During the singing of*
            the Funeral Ode the servants raise the litter and
            slowly carry ALCESTIS *within. The door closes*
            after them. Near the end of the Ode, the MAID-
            SERVANT *comes out, places an urn beside the*
            door, and retires within.

🏵 STÁSIMON II

CHORUS:
Daughter of Pelias, our love goes with you   [STROPHE 1
Under dark earth where you must enter now,
Along the ways of death, the sunless houses.

Even that ancient and gloombearded god,
The Guide of Death, bent to his sad oar,
Let him remember well: no braver woman
Crossed with him ever to the silent shore.

[ANTISTROPHE 1

Singers whom the Muse haunts, haunting music
Often shall make to praise you on their strings
Or in bare singing to no instrument,
At Sparta in late summer when the moon
Glows all night long on nights of festival,
Or at rich Athens in the shining noon—
Such loveliness you leave them for their songs.

Would I could save you from the black water,   [STROPHE 2
Bring you to sunlight from that breathless dark!
Dearest of wives, daring alone
To yield your spirit up to death for him,
Light be the earth upon you, lightly rest.
If ever Admetos takes a bride again,
He shall be hateful to me and to your children.

[ANTISTROPHE 2

The old ones grudged old bodies to the earth,
Mother and father feared to save their son,
Hugging their lives, hoary and brief.
But you precede your lord; and you are young.
So dear a wife I wish might be my fortune,
So rare a thing, rarest in the world:
Then I would pray she might stay with me ever.

🕮 EPEISODION III

[*Enter* HERAKLES.

HERAKLES:
    My good people of Pherai,
    is Admetos in his house, and may I see him?

CHORAGOS:

He is at home, Heraklês. But tell us,
what brings you to Thessaly and our city here?

HERAKLES:

One of those labors of mine for King Eurystheus.

CHORAGOS:

Where must you go this time?

HERAKLES:

To Thrace.
Diomed's four horses are what I'm after.

CHORAGOS:

How will you get them? You don't know him, do you?

HERAKLES:

I do not. I have never been in his country.

CHORAGOS:

Then you've a fight on your hands to take those horses.

HERAKLES:

Maybe. But I've never yet run away from a fight.

CHORAGOS:

It's either kill Diomed or get killed yourself.

HERAKLES:

That kind of problem's nothing new to me.

CHORAGOS:

Suppose you win: what do you get out of it?

HERAKLES:

Only the horses to drive back to Tiryns.

CHORAGOS:

Not easy, even to get the bit into their mouths.

HERAKLES:

Why not? —unless you mean they snort fire?

CHORAGOS:

No, but they snap and tear men apart with their jaws.

HERAKLES:

You're thinking of mountain lions, friend, not horses.

CHORAGOS:

Wait till you see the blood stamped in their stalls.

HERAKLES:

What does he call himself who reared these beauties?

CHORAGOS:

The son of Arês. Lord of the Golden Shield.

HERAKLES:

Then this labor fits my destiny, always heavy.
A sheer cliff I keep climbing.
It seems that I must fight all the sons of Arês:
first Lykaôn, then the Swan, so-called,
and now I go to wrestle with the third,
the master of these horses. But I
am Alkmêna's son: no enemy
shall ever see my hand tremble in battle.

[Enter ADMETOS *from the house.*

ADMETOS:

Heraklês, son of Zeus, of Perseus' line,
you are welcome to my house.

HERAKLES:

Admetos, Prince
of Thessaly, I hope that I find you well.

ADMETOS:

I wish . . . But thank you for your kind concern.

HERAKLES:

Why have you shorn your head? Are you in mourning?

ADMETOS:

I have a burial to make today.

HERAKLES:

God keep all harm away from your children!

ADMETOS:

My children are alive here in my house.

HERAKLES:

If it is your father, why, his time had come,
he dies in death's season.

ADMETOS:

He and my mother
are both still living, Heraklês.

HERAKLES:

The Queen—?
But surely not Alcestis, not your wife?

ADMETOS:

There are two answers I might make to that.

HERAKLES:
  Are you saying she is alive, or she is dead?
ADMETOS:
  She is, and she is not. It tortures me.
HERAKLES:
  What is that supposed to mean? A riddle!
ADMETOS:
  You know the destiny in store for her.
HERAKLES:
  I certainly know that she promised to die for you.
ADMETOS:
  Then how can I say that she is really alive?
HERAKLES:
  Ah. Don't grieve now, man; wait till the time comes.
ADMETOS:
  Whoever is doomed to death is already dead.
HERAKLES:
  Being and not-being are thought to be different things.
ADMETOS:
  Make the distinction if you like. I can not.
HERAKLES:
  Still, why are you mourning? Who is this dead friend?
ADMETOS:
  A woman. Were we not talking about a woman?
HERAKLES:
  One of your family?
ADMETOS:
                    No; but there were ties between us.
HERAKLES:
  How did she come to die here in your house?
ADMETOS:
  When her father died she came here to live.
HERAKLES:
  A pity!
  I wish I had come when you were not so troubled.
                              [HERAKLES *turns to go*.
ADMETOS:
  What do you mean? What are you planning to do?

HERAKLES:
I must find lodging with some other friend.

ADMETOS:
No, no, Lord Heraklês, that must never happen!

HERAKLES:
A guest is a burden in a house of mourning.

ADMETOS:
The dead are dead. Come now into my house.

HERAKLES:
No. It would be painful.

ADMETOS:
                    The guest rooms are apart.

HERAKLES:
Let me go, and a thousand blessings.

ADMETOS:
                              No,
you must not go to another house tonight.

                              [*to a servant:*
Boy, you will show our guest to his rooms.
Open the private ones. Have the servants bring
plenty of food, and shut the main hall doors.
He must not be troubled by the sound of our weeping.

                              [*Exit* HERAKLES.

CHORAGOS:
What are you thinking of, Admetos? How can you
entertain a guest, after what has happened here?

ADMETOS:
If I turned this traveler away from my house,
would you think better of me? Surely not.
What good would it have done?
My sorrow would be no less, and I should have
one friend less;
and this would have been one more calamity,
to have my house called inhospitable.
This man is my good friend when I go to Argos.

CHORAGOS:
If he is really as much a friend as that,
how could you keep from telling him your sorrow?

ADMETOS:
He would not have wished to stay, if he had known . . .

I am aware that what I have done will be
misunderstood.
                    Nevertheless, my house
will always welcome guests and honor them.

                                        [*Exit* ADMETOS

🎇 STÁSIMON III

CHORUS:
It is a gracious house and ever was,   [STROPHE 1
Friendly to strangers, and a home to friends;
The god of Heaven's music loved this place:
Apollo—yet content to be a shepherd,
Down gentle mountains piping
After his flock the bridal songs of the hills.

                                        [ANTISTROPHE 1
Joy in that music brought the dappled lynxes
And tawny lions from the Othrys valley,
Following where he led them, without harm;
O Phoibos! from tall pines a spotted doe
Ventured on light hooves, dancing
To the cool tracing of your upland flute.

Along the clear reach of this inland water [STROPHE 2
Our king has rich lands whitened by his flocks:
Plowland and plain he has: far off his borders,
Westward, where the sun goes down in cloud,
Where Hêlios reins his horses in bright air;
And on the east the sea: no harbors there.

                                        [ANTISTROPHE 2
Now he has thrown his doors wide for the stranger,
Weeping, his eyes wet, weeping the new dead.
Here noble courtesy knows no restraining.

I marvel and take heart. Such wisdom guides
The good man that his very recklessness
Becomes high prudence, ordering distress.

❧ EPEISODION IV

> [*Enter* ADMETOS *from the house, followed by
> servants bearing the corpse of* ALCESTIS *on a
> litter. This is placed facing the audience, with
> the head slightly higher than the feet, so that
> the face is clearly visible.*

ADMETOS:
Friends, kindly company: There is only a
little left for us to do now: my servants have prepared her
for her funeral, for the tomb. But before
we take her away, I would have you salute her as is
     customary
for one setting out on this last journey.

CHORAGOS:
But look: here is your father coming in,
and slaves bringing burial ornaments for her.
How old he seems, and how feeble!

> [*Enter* PHERES, *slowly, leaning on his staff,
> followed by two slaves carrying small gifts.*

PHERES:
I have come to share your grief, son. No denying,
she was a good wife, and a wise one, and you have lost her
Nevertheless, man was born to suffer, to endure,
be the burden never so cruel.
                    Take then from me
these gifts that I have brought for her adorning,
and let her go in peace to the world below.
So, it is right to honor her, son:
she gave her life to save yours, she did not leave me
childless to drag out my dying day to its close.

Honor of womankind!
Dear audacious girl!

Alcestis, daughter, savior of my son
      (and of me also):
even in the house of Death, fare well!

Believe me, son: a marriage like your own
is a blessed thing, a most profitable thing.
Why else should a man take a wife?

ADMETOS:
Were you invited here?
You were not. There is no room for you
here, among her friends.
                       You dare to bring
gifts for her? Take your gifts! She needs
no gifts of yours to be lovely under ground.
You mourn for her?
Did I hear you groan for me when I faced danger?
Then, when I needed you, then—why, then
you stood by and let a stranger die, a young stranger!
And now you squeak for her at the grave's door!

My father!
Or were you my father?
And she, reputed by herself and by
other authorities to be my mother—
was she? Or perhaps I was the brat of a slave girl,
and you graciously gave me your wife's pap to suck at!
No, you have shown what you are;
I am no son of yours, and I disown you—
you, old, palsied at death's gate, afraid to die,
and with so little life left in you!
                          Coward! not to
Die for your own son!
Coward! to let a woman die instead!
Well; let her—and her alone—be all
the father and the mother I'll have for ever.

How great you might have been in this, how noble,
dying for your son when your own days were few!

Then we might have lived out all our days,
she and I: I should not now be mourning.

What have you not had that a man might have?
Power in your prime as King, and I to succeed you,
your own son, in your own house: you had in store
no childless death, no partition of your kingdom.

Or was I perhaps a bad son?
You will not say that I was a bad son, either.
I gave you all respect in your old age,
and here is my reward from both of you.
                                        Go,
time is short, go, get more children!
Someone to sit at your death-bed, shroud your corpse!
You get no burial from me, this hand of mine
shall be no comfort to you. I am dead,
so far as you could make me dead; and if I live
by grace of another savior—there, I say,
my obligation lies.
                        God, these old men!
How they pray for death! How heavy
they find this life in the slow drag of days!
And yet, when Death comes near them,
you will not find one who will rise and walk with him,
not one whose years are still a burden to him.
CHORAGOS:
  Let your father alone, Admetos.
  There is sorrow enough in this place.
PHERES:
  Am I a Lydian slave, or a Phrygian slave, son,
  that you should abuse me so? Or am I your father,
  a Thessalian Thessalian-born, a king, and a free man?
  This talk of yours is something worse
  than a young man's insolence. You will pay for it.
  Is it I, who made you heir to my house,
  who gave you everything—is it I whose duty it is
  to die for you as well? Does your father owe you that debt?

That is no law of the Greeks, my father
told me of no such law.

For happiness or unhappiness,
every man is born for himself. I gave you all
you deserved, slaves, subjects, money,
and you'll soon have my lands, as I had them from my
　　　father.
Then how have I hurt you? How have I cheated you?
Die for you—?
Don't you die for me, and I'll not die for you.
You love the daylight: do you think your father does not?
Our stay in the world below will be long enough.
Life, I take it, is short: it is none the less agreeable.

And as for dying—
Well, you put up a shameless kind of fight
against death, did you not? Are you dead now?
Have you not found a victim to take your place?
'Coward'! You call me a coward? You,
less brave than a woman? What a pretty-boy hero you are!

But you know best.
A gallant road you've found to Immortality!
Marry wife after wife, make sure they'll die for you—
that's all.
　　　　How do you dare insult
your own kin for declining to serve you so?
Hold your tongue, but put your mind on this: You love
your own sweet life, but so does every man
on the face of the earth; and if you rail at me,
I'll give you some home truths that will cost you dear.
CHORAGOS:
Say no more to your son, old Pherês.
There has been too much bitterness on both sides.
ADMETOS:
Say whatever you like, as I have. If the truth
hurts you, that's your fault for blundering here.

PHERES:
The real blunder would have been to die for you.

ADMETOS:
Is dying the same thing for a young man and an old?

PHERES:
There is one way of breath; there are not two.

ADMETOS:
Live on then; live a longer life than God!

PHERES:
You curse your parents so, with no cause for it?

ADMETOS:
I thought you expressed a wish to go on living.

PHERES:
I see Death in this place: but you are alive.

ADMETOS:
Proof of your cowardice, you wretched old man!

PHERES:
Surely you will not say that she died for me?

ADMETOS:
Ah,
if only you turn to me for help some day!

PHERES:
Take a dozen wives, let a dozen die for you!

ADMETOS:
A double-edged rebuke. You feared to die.

PHERES:
This daylight of God is sweet, I tell you, sweet!

ADMETOS:
And rotten that unmanly soul of yours!

PHERES:
Grim, wasn't it, not to cart off the old man's corpse?

ADMETOS:
Oh, you will die some day, and not with honor.

PHERES:
Dishonor will not trouble me, once I am dead.

ADMETOS:
God, God, how shameless these old men are!

PHERES:
This girl was not shameless, was she? Only demented.

ADMETOS:
Leave my house, go! Let me bury my dead wife.

PHERES:
Yes, I will go.
You, being her murderer, should know the best way to
    bury her.
But you will also be hearing from her family.
Akástos, I think, is not the man
to let his sister's blood go unavenged.

[*Exit* PHERES

ADMETOS:
Go back to your woman!
Back, you childless ancestor, and grow older!
You'll not come into my house again.

If heralds and trumpets could cut me off from you,
By God, I'd do it!

                    —But, friends: our present grief:
come, let us bring her body to burial.
            [*During the funeral song the litter is taken up
            by the servants and* ALCESTIS *is carried off. Exit*
            ADMETOS.

CHORAGOS:
Daughter of Pelias, Alcestis, Queen, farewell.

CHORUS:
Daughter of Pelias, incomparable, O heart
So daring, and broken in daring: fare well
Even to Hadês' gate!
There, may Hermês greet you, a kindly Angel;
There, may Death be gentle; and if great
Souls, and good, and generous, find favor
Beneath the ground, you shall sit throned beside
The Bride of the Dark King.
            [*The stage is empty. Enter a* MANSERVANT *angrily
            from the house.*

MANSERVANT:
In my time I've seen plenty of guests entertained here in
Admetos' house, people from all over Greece, but I'll take

my oath that I never had to look after a worse fellow
than this one, whoever he is! Why, as soon as he got here
he could see that the King was in mourning; but he had
to stay, just the same; and as if this weren't enough, he
felt he must insist upon all the details of hospitality, ordering us about. I can still see him hoisting that wine-bowl
up in both hands and pouring the stuff into himself, not
a drop of water in it, until he was flaming drunk; and
then he had to crown himself with myrtle and belch out
silly songs. A pretty bit of counterpoint *that* was! This
man in there bellowing, with never a thought for all
Admetos was suffering, and we in the next room mourning
for our Queen . . . But we had been told not to let him
see us with our eyes wet . . . And so here I am, waiting
on this guest, this blackguard, this bloated burglar, this
house-breaker— And she is gone. The Queen has left her
house. I could not reach out my hand to her, or even say
good-bye to her. She was my dear Lady, my mother, the
mother of all of us. How often she saved us from punishment when Admetos was angry! —Ah, this wine-stinking
stranger, bursting in on all our trouble!

> [*Enter* HERAKLES, *drunk, crowned with myrtle,*
> *holding a huge cup in both hands.*

HERAKLES:

Hello there. Why so
solemn? Why do you look so
grim?
Is this the correct way for a servant to act,
staring at the guests he serves? It
is not.
You ought to be trotting around with a
smile, like a good
fellow.
       Friend,
you behold in me your master's dearest friend.
And what do you do? You look, to say the least,
bilious.
And all for the death of a woman you hardly knew!

Come over here, and grow in wisdom.

[SERVANT *turns away.*

Do you understand the facts of this mortal life?
You do not. Of course not. Then listen to me:

[*Chanting tunelessly:*

All men have to die, and that's plain fax.
There isn't one knows when he'll get the axe.
Death isn't visible before he comes:
You can't predict your death by doing sums.

There you have it, friend, straight from a first-class authority. Ponder, rejoice, and have a drink.

Today's today. Tomorrow, we may be
Ourselves gone down the drain of Eternity.

And one other thing:
Aphroditê. Of all your gods and goddesses, your
greater and lesser di-
vinities, Kypris is the sweetest for mortal man.
Honor her, friend. She means well. And
forget whatever it is that's gnawing at you.
Remember what I've been telling you. You
believe me, I hope? I think so. Here, have a
garland, have a drink, have another drink, have
a drink,
          and grief
good-bye!

O mortal man, think mortal thoughts!

Seriously, friend, this wine will surprise you.
And as for all these sour-faced sigh-blasting bellyache
    fellows,
what's life to them? Nothing but a catastrophe.

MANSERVANT:

I know all about that. But what we are doing today
leaves no room in the house for feasting and laughter.

HERAKLES:

Whoever it is that's dead, she's a
stranger, isn't she?
I see no reason for inordinate mourning
since your master and mistress are both well.

MANSERVANT:

Both well? Is it possible that even now—

HERAKLES:

Has Admetos lied to me?

MANSERVANT:

                    Lied to you? No.
He has been too good to you.

HERAKLES:

                    Must I go without my dinner
because a stranger has died?

MANSERVANT:

                A stranger . . .
Ah, she was all too close to us!

HERAKLES:

                Is it possible
that Admetos has hidden a real sorrow from me?

MANSERVANT:

Go back to your drinking. Leave the suffering to us.

HERAKLES:

This is not the way one speaks of a casual grief.

MANSERVANT:

If it were that, we should not have minded your revelry.

HERAKLES:

Can it be that my friend has made a fool of me?

MANSERVANT:

You came at the wrong time, that's all.
The house is in mourning. You can see for yourself.

HERAKLES:

Who is it? One of the children? The old father?

MANSERVANT:

It is Alcestis, man. The Queen is dead.

        [*Long pause.* HERAKLES *throws down his cup and
        slowly removes the garland from his head.*

HERAKLES:
  The Queen. —And you entertained me in spite of that?
MANSERVANT:
  He would have been ashamed to turn you away.
HERAKLES:
  Admetos, what a companion you have lost!
MANSERVANT:
  It's the end of us all, not of the Queen alone.
HERAKLES:
  I knew it. I felt it. I saw his eyes red with weeping,
  his hair clipped short, his heavy motion.
  But he told me it was all for a stranger, a simple death!
  And I, blundering my way
  into the house of this admirable host, and he
  suffering so! Drinking, bawling,
  crowning my head with myrtle— But it is not
  wholly my fault: you might have told me.

  But let that be.
                    Where is he now? Where
  shall I find him burying her?
MANSERVANT:
                          Go straight out
  the Lárissa road, and there,
  not far from the town, you'll find the new-cut stone.
                          [*Exit* MANSERVANT
HERAKLES:
  Now, my brave heart, my good hands scarred strong
  by many labors,
  now you must prove that Alkmêna, Elektryon's daughter,
  bore Zeus a son indeed.
                    For Admetos' sake
  we must bring Alcestis back to her house from the dead.
  I will follow the blackrobed god,
  old Thánatos, to her tomb: for there, I think,
  I shall find him drinking the blood of the new victims.
  If I can take him
  from ambush, I will wrestle with death,

I will crack his charnel ribs between my hands
until he lets her go.
                    But if I miss him,
If he leaves the blood of offering untasted,
I will go down into the sad streets of the Dead,
to Persephonê and the dim Lord of Hell, and there
beg for her life.
                    And I
will bring Alcestis back to the good sunlight,
back to my friend who welcomed me in his house
in spite of his hard loss. Oh generous heart!
Where in all Thessaly, where in the whole of Greece,
should there be a kindlier, friendlier house than his?
And he must never say
that his effort was wasted upon a scoundrel.

                              [*Exit* HERAKLES

❦ KOMMÓS

> [*Enter* ADMETOS, *from R, accompanied by serv-
> ants. He walks slowly towards the central door,
> stopping at the chanting of strophe and anti-
> strophe.*

ADMETOS:
  God, the way home is hateful to me,
  the sight of the empty house is hateful.
  Where shall I turn? Where can I rest?
  What shall I say? What not! Die, and be done with it!

  My mother was accurst the night she bore me,
  and I am faint with envy of all the dead.
  How clean they are, who are out of life for ever!
  They are beautiful, and I would be with them.

  For I shall never be warm in the thick sunlight,
  nor walk again as other men walk the earth.
  She who was my life has been taken from me,
  stolen by Death for his still kingdom.

CHORUS: [STROPHE 1

Go deep into your house, Admetos: you must go in,
Though you are right to weep. We know,
You have walked through bitterness today,
But all your urgency can not move the dead:
You will not see her face again.

ADMETOS:

When you say that, my heart splits with the spearhead.
So true a wife lost! What is worse?
Better if she and I had never married,
never lived together in this house.
Men who do not marry, men who have no children,
each of them has one life to live, his own;
and a man can bear the pain of a single life.
He will not see his children sick,
his marriage empty, cold with death;
all his life long he will be safe from this.

CHORUS: [ANTISTROPHE 1

Fate, Fate is a grim wrestler; it is Fate's fall,
and yet you will not yield the match to Fate.
More grief than you can bear, and yet you must.
Men have lost their wives before.
Varying shapes of disaster crush us all.

ADMETOS:

Mourning without end, and heartbreak here,
and the earth heavy upon the ones we loved!
Why did you hold me back when I would have thrown
    myself
into her grave? I would have lain dead with her,
and now the King of Darkness would have two
instead of one alone.
Together we should have crossed the strange water.

CHORUS: [STROPHE 2

  A relation of mine had a son who died, a young man
Full of promise. It was his only son.
Yet he endured this bravely:
Sorrow enough, yet he endured it bravely.
A childless old man, white-haired, and bent towards
    death.

ADMETOS:

  My strange house! How can I go into it,
how live there, now the evil day has come?
How huge the gap is!
                I can see,
as if from a great distance,
the evening I came in under the torches,
holding her by the hand, and the music around us,
the singing, and the revel following
to wish her, who is now dead, happiness;
and happiness to me: they said our marriage
joined the magnificence of two lines of kings.
But now instead of songs there is only weeping;
where there were white robes, these in black
beckon me in to sleep in an empty bed.

CHORUS: [ANTISTROPHE 2

  You were a stranger to sorrow: therefore Fate
Has cursed you. Nevertheless, you have saved your life.
The wife you loved is dead;
But is this new, that a wife should leave her love?
Death has dissolved many marriages before this.

ADMETOS:

  Friends, Alcestis is happier than I,
whoever may think differently.
Now she will feel no distress, no sorrow ever,
but happiness and peace; and her name is blessed.

But as for me,
I have no right to be living. I've learned that at last.
I have begged off dying: now my life is dead.

How can I pass the doorway of this house?
Who will be there to greet me? Who will say
farewell to my going? Going where? —driven
out by the emptiness where once she was:
the bed, and the chairs that were hers, and the floor
covered with dust; and at my knees her children
crying, coming to me day after day, crying,
asking for her . . . And her servants in tears,
remembering what a sweet mistress they have lost.
And in the city there will be weddings, gatherings
with women: How can I bear to meet her friends?
This one who hates me will whisper to another,
'There is the man whose life is a daily shame,
'the man who dared not die, whose cowardice
'let his own wife lay down her life for him.
'What kind of man is he who hates his father
'because he himself is base?' What fame I'll have,
with all my sorrows!
                         I have saved my life?
I have lost my honor. I have lost everything.

🎜 STÁSIMON IV

CHORUS: [STROPHE 1]
I have found power in the mysteries of thought,
Exaltation in the chanting of the Muses;
I have been versed in the reasonings of men;
But Fate is stronger than anything I have known:
Nothing in mortal wisdom can subdue her,
Neither Orphic riddles on Thracian tablets,
Nor the Asklepiad skill that Phoibos taught.

[ANTISTROPHE 1

Fate has neither altar nor image, that we may kneel to;
She has no bloodstained stone where we can pray.
But let us pray to her now: 'O Goddess, Lady,
'Be never more cruel than you have been this day:
'Though all that God wills you must bring to pass,
'Pitiless and abrupt your ways for ever;
'Though your hand would crumple Chalybéan steel.'

Caught by her now, Admetos,   [STROPHE 2
Do you think to escape that grasp? —Rest there, friend.
The dead will not hear you crying, you in the daylight.
The children of the gods, all the loud heroes,
Where is their bravery now? Thin, drained in night.
But she who was dearest among us when she lived,
She shall be dearest still among the dead.

And not as one dead for ever: [ANTISTROPHE 2
Her tomb is no mere mound above the dead,
But a holy shrine that travelers shall love,
Where, turning from the road, a man may say:
'This woman died for her husband in the old days
'And now lives here, a gracious influence. Lady,
'Your blessing on mine!' So will they pray, and pass.

🎐 ÉXODOS

CHORAGOS:
   But what is this, Admetos? For some reason
   Alkmêna's son is coming back to your house.

>   [*Enter* HERAKLES *with* ALCESTIS, *veiled. During
>   the ensuing dialogue she is motionless, as though
>   in a trance, until the moment when her face is
>   disclosed.*

HERAKLES:
   Admetos, a man with a grievance against his friend
   should speak plainly.
   When I came to your house, you were in trouble.

I would have helped you, as a friend should; but you,
instead of telling me it was your wife that was dead,
hid the truth from me and made me welcome
here in your sad house.
And I? I crowned myself with myrtle, of course,
and made the usual libations to the gods—
and all the while I was in a house of mourning!
It was wrong of you, Admetos, wrong of you! But I
will not add my reproach to your suffering.

I have come back, and I will tell you why.

You see this woman here: take her, keep her for me
until I come again.
               For I must kill
the Thracian king and bring his horses back . . .
But if I fail—God forbid
that I should fail, though!—, keep her here,
let her serve you in your house.
                      These hands of mine
worked hard to win her. On my way from here
I happened on an athletic contest for all comers
and she was the prize I took. Horses
were awarded to the best runners and jumpers,
herds of oxen for the boxing and wrestling champions,
and then this woman. There I was,
and it would have been silly to pass by such a prize.

So, as I've said, here is the woman for you.
Take her. I came by her honestly,
and a time will come when you will thank me for her.
ADMETOS:
I had no thought of wronging you, friend,
when I hid my wife's unhappy fate from you.
Only, if you had gone to another's house
I should have been hurt twice over. It seemed enough
that I should mourn for her.
                  But as for this woman—
Oh, Heraklês, my friend and my lord! if you can do so

take her to some other man who has not suffered
and let him keep her for you. Pherai
is full of your friends; you will find someone.

Do not remind me of what I have to bear!
Seeing her here, in my own house,
how could I keep back my tears? I beg you,
do not add grief to grief: I have suffered enough.

A young woman?
Where is there a place here for a young woman?
(For she is young: one can tell by her dress and bearing.)
Here, living among men,
do you think she would ever be safe? I tell you,
youth is hot-blooded, youth is hard to restrain!

It is for your own good that I am saying these things.

Or perhaps you would have me lead her
to my dead wife's chamber, and install her there?
Could I do that? give her that bed—!
Who would hate me more, the people of my own house—
because by tumbling into a new girl's bed
I'd betrayed the memory of her who died for me—
or Alcestis herself? No. It is Alcestis that I
must remember always. She deserves nothing less.

Yet you, woman, whoever you are, you are like Alcestis—
did you know it?—the same body, the same—
                                        Heraklês,
Heraklês, for the love of God, take her away!
I am beaten: do not press me any more.
I look at her, and it is Alcestis that I see!
She turns my heart, my eyes
burst with tears.
                    What unspeakable misery!
I taste this torment now for the first time.
CHORAGOS:
    I could not call it a happy chance, myself.

Nevertheless a man must take what God gives.

HERAKLES:

If only I had a bit of your influence
with Death! Then I could do you the favor
of bringing your wife back to you from the grave.

ADMETOS:

I know you would. But why speak of it? The dead
never come back into the sunlight again.

HERAKLES:

You must not be excessive. Try to be brave.

ADMETOS:

Easy enough, to say 'be brave'. It is harder to do.

HERAKLES:

There is no future in perpetual mourning.

ADMETOS:

No future; but my grief is like a passion.

HERAKLES:

Love for the dead is strong, I know, and bitter.

ADMETOS:

It has destroyed me, more utterly than I can say.

HERAKLES:

No man will deny that you have lost a devoted wife.

ADMETOS:

And there is no more pleasure for me in anything.

HERAKLES:

Time cancels young pain.

ADMETOS:

Yes, if Time is Death.

HERAKLES:

A new wife will comfort you, a new marriage—

ADMETOS:

Not another word! I would not have thought this of you.

HERAKLES:

Never take a wife? A cold bed for ever?

ADMETOS:

No woman in this world will sleep by my side!

HERAKLES:

Do you think this attitude of yours will help the dead?

ADMETOS:

I will show her this much honor, wherever she is.

HERAKLES:

Good, very good. But some would say you're a fool.

ADMETOS:

Let them. They shall never call me a bridegroom.

HERAKLES:

I approve of this faithfulness to a dead wife.

ADMETOS:

If I betray her, dead, let me die too!

HERAKLES:

And now, friend,
take this woman and keep her in your good house.

ADMETOS:

By the great god who is your father, I say No!

HERAKLES:

You would be terribly wrong to deny me this.

ADMETOS:

The shame of it would eat out my heart!

HERAKLES:

Come, come,
in a little while you might begin to enjoy it.

ADMETOS:

Ah Heraklês,
why did you have to win *her* at the games?

HERAKLES:

And yet my victory was a victory for you.

ADMETOS:

Very kind of you. But now let the woman go.

HERAKLES:

She will go if she must. But must she? Think again.

ADMETOS:

She must . . .
Although I would not have you angry with me . . .

HERAKLES:

This request of mine has a solid reason behind it.

ADMETOS:

Very well, then.

You have won again. But you know what it is costing me.

HERAKLES:

Believe me, you'll thank me for this some day.

ADMETOS:

Take her in,
some one of you, since she's to live in our house.

HERAKLES:

No. I'll not turn her over to your slaves.

ADMETOS:

Then take her in yourself, if you feel that way.

HERAKLES:

No. I have given her to you. Here, take her hand.

ADMETOS:

I will not touch that woman! She can go in herself.

HERAKLES:

I have entrusted her to your hands alone.

ADMETOS:

Lord Heraklês, you force me against my will.

HERAKLES:

Your hand, then. Stretch out your hand and touch the
woman.

ADMETOS:

Here it is.

HERAKLES:

Looking away, as though you were killing
the Gorgon!
—There: you have her hand?

ADMETOS:

I have.

HERAKLES:

So I see. Then hold it tight! Some day
you will praise the son of Zeus as a good guest.

Look at her, Admetos. Do you not see
a resemblance to your wife? Forget your troubles!

[ALCESTIS *slowly removes her veil.*

ADMETOS:

Oh God, God, God,
what can I say? A miracle, beyond hope!

I see my wife! Is it really she?
or is this a cruel trick that God has played?

HERAKLES:

No trick. This lady before you is your own.

ADMETOS:

Wait. How do I know she's not a ghost from Hell?

HERAKLES:

The guest you honored is not a pimp of ghosts.

ADMETOS:

And this is my wife that I laid in her tomb myself?

HERAKLES:

Your wife. I understand your finding it strange.

ADMETOS:

And I can touch her? Speak to her as though she were
    alive?

HERAKLES:

Speak to her. Everything has come out as you wished.

ADMETOS:

Alcestis, Alcestis, my dear, my dearest wife!
You are mine again, and I thought you were lost for ever!

HERAKLES:

Yours. And I pray that your happiness bring down
no envious curse from the gods, Admetos.

ADMETOS:

                                        Friend,
great-hearted son of mighty Zeus! May God
keep you and guard you for ever! You alone,
Heraklês, have saved me and my house.
—But tell me: How did you bring her back from the
    dead?

HERAKLES:

Wrestling. I fought the spirit who possessed her.

ADMETOS:

Where did you meet this Spirit? Where did you fight him?

HERAKLES:

I hid near her tomb, and sprang out and threw him.

ADMETOS:

But why is she silent? Can she not speak again?

HERAKLES:

It is not permitted you to hear her voice
for three days longer; then she will have washed away
the stain of death and memory of Hell.

So take her in, Admetos, my good friend,
and be a generous host from this time on.
Be happy.
      —As for me, my duty lies
before me, thanks to Sthénelos' royal son.

ADMETOS:

Stay with us, Heraklês. All my house is yours.

HERAKLES:

Another day, perhaps. Now I must go.

                              [*Exit* HERACLES.

ADMETOS:

May every kind of happiness go with you,
and may you soon come back to us.
                  —Friends,
I command these things to the whole city, and
the Assembly of the Four Quarters: let groups of dancers
be formed to celebrate the glory of this day;
let the flesh of oxen smoke on every altar
to propitiate the gods. For now
the old life has changed for the new: and I say
that I am the happiest of all men.

CHORAGOS:

Destiny has many forms, and Heaven
Works in the dark with riddles and confusion.
      What seemed must be is not.
      What could not be, here's brought
            To pass: it is God's way.
This is the meaning of all you have watched today.

NOTES

149   1   The scene is Pherai, a town in Thessaly founded by Pherês, the father of Admetos. Here Apollo, exiled from Heaven for killing the Cyclopês, has spent nine years *incognito* as a common herdsman in the employ of the King. Within the last year Admetos has learned from an oracle that he is fated shortly to die. Apollo, grateful for the kindly treatment he has received as herdsman, has persuaded the Three Fates to alter their decree: Admetos need not die if he can find someone to die in his place.

149   4   Asklêpios, a physician, son of Apollo, was killed by Zeus for presuming to push his skill too far: he had succeeded in reviving patients from death. In revenge Apollo killed the Cyclopês, the one-eyed armorers of Zeus who had fashioned the thunderbolt that struck Asklêpios down.

150   6   We do not know how Apollo persuaded the Fates to change their decree, and the event itself seems almost without parallel. Not unnaturally, interested opponents of the deal attributed the god's success to the trickery of eloquence, or of wine, or of both.

150   18   Thánatos, 'Death', is not to be confused with Hadês, the Infernal King, but is here a subsidiary god representing physical death itself. As such, his presence is especially hateful to Apollo, who represents the principle of life.

152   13   *a man is coming*: The outcome of the plot is stated in the Prologue. This is an admirable illustration of the unimportance, to the Greek mind, of the element of suspense in building a plot. The material is given (as usually in Shakspere); the audience is interested not in the novelty of the dramatist's situations, but in his handling of them.

Page	Line	
153	5	The cutting off of a lock of hair at the nape of a dying person's neck was supposed to expedite the passage of the soul from the body.
153	8	The *Párodos* is the scene, both in Tragedy and in Comedy, where the Chorus enters, takes its position in the *orchêstra*, and chants its first song. The Chorus in this play is composed of fifteen men, representing the ruling class of Pherai.
155	1	'Apollo's son' is Asklêpios. See Note 149:4.
155	12	The play is divided into dramatic scenes (*epeisodia*, 'episodes') separated from each other by choric songs (*stásima*).
156	15	*the Flame*: The goddess is Hestía (*cf* the Roman *Vesta*), for whom a votive fire was kept burning on a hearth in every house.
158	7	Cropping one's hair was a sign of mourning.
158	13	Apollo had 'saved' Admetos the first time when he bargained with the Fates (*cf* Note 149:1).
159	14	*O Iôlkos*: Alcestis was a daughter of King Pelias of Iôlkos, a city in Magnesia.
161	13	*but I suppose some god*: It is Euripides, not Alcestis, who is being ironical. Apparently Admetos has not told his wife about Apollo's deal with the Fates (*cf* Note 149:1).
163	16	The 'grim King's dog' is Cerberus, a three-headed beast of inordinate savagery.
165	4	Both children are present, and at this point Eumêlos, Alcestis' little son, sings a brief monody upon his mother's death. The aria itself almost defies translation, since, except for one or two pathetic touches, it makes no concessions to the tender years and presumably unsophisticated mind of the child. To translate it into baby-talk would be a betrayal of Euripides; to render it as it stands would be to bring an infantile monstrosity upon the stage. In our first version of this play we cut Small Eumêlos's remarks entirely, substituting a stage direction: 'EUMELOS *throws himself*

across ALCESTIS' *body;* ADMETOS *tries to comfort him.'*
We are still of the opinion that this is the best way
of handling an awkward situation.

168   3   The eighth of the Twelve Labors that Heraklês was
obliged to perform for Eurystheus was the capture of
the man-eating mares of Diomedês, a Thracian king.
Heraklês not only stole the mares, but fed their
master Diomedês to them; after which he drove them
back as an uncomfortable gift to Eurystheus.

169   5   *the Swan*: Kyknos, a son of Arês; the name means
'Swan'.

170   13   It is worth noting that none of Admetos' answers is,
strictly speaking, a lie. For example, a wife is not
really 'related' to her husband. The obtuseness of
Heraklês is also notable, but there are at least two
possible explanations of it. The easy one is, that
Heraklês is, more often than not, represented as an
amiable, gluttonous, heroic lout; the more subtle one,
that he quite understands Admetos' embarrassed
evasions and is amusing himself—rather heavily, one
must confess—by watching his friend squirm.

171   14   *my house*: Hospitality was a sacred obligation. Indeed,
one might say that the basic, unwritten command-
ments were three: Honor the gods, Honor your parents,
Honor the stranger.

174   6   *Why else should a man take a wife?*: This is not
Euripidean cynicism; the old man is perfectly sincere,
and any right-minded Greek gentleman would accept the sentiment as a matter of course. It is only at
the end of this *agôn*, when he has thoroughly lost his
temper, that Pherês permits himself the kind of abusive
irony that a modern audience would expect throughout.

176   6   *and you'll soon have my lands*: Pherês is in semi-re-
tirement: he has delegated the administrative power
in the kingdom to Admetos, and apparently has deeded
to him the greater part of his goods; he retains his
lands, however, and will do so until his death.

Page   Line

177   5   *You curse*: It is a blasphemy, and hence a curse, to
             wish that any man outlive the gods. There may also
             be an allusion to the myth of Tithonos, who prayed
             for immortality—and was granted it—but who forgot
             to pray for eternal health and strength as well, and
             consequently became the first grasshopper.

178   21   'The Bride of the Dark King' is Persephonê, Queen
             of Hadês.

180   4   These doggerel verses are notable, in the original, for
             their employment of rime—a very rare thing:

> βροτοῖς ἅπασι κατθανεῖν ὀφείλεται,
> κοὐκ ἔστι θνητῶν ὅστις ἐξεπίσταται
> τὴν αὔριον μέλλουσαν εἰ βιώσεται·
> τὸ τῆς τύχης γὰρ ἀφανὲς οἷ προβήσεται,
> κἄστ᾿ οὐ διδακτὸν οὐδ᾿ ἁλίσκεται τέχνῃ.

183   14   The Fifth *Epeisodion* is replaced by a *Kommós,* a
             lyric lamentation divided between the Protagonist
             and the Chorus.

185   1   *A relation of mine*: The remark is curiously personal,
             and it may be that Euripides is alluding to a bereaved
             friend whose situation would be familiar enough to
             the audience. In any case the reference is now lost.

185   19   *You were a stranger to sorrow*: Not only because of
             his good fortune in escaping death, but because of
             the whole happy tenor of his life up to this time. The
             thought, here expressed with crushing simplicity, is
             a commonplace of Greek religion: too high a pitch
             of human happiness invites the jealous anger of the
             gods.

186   23   *I have found power*: The 'I' of this first strophe would
             appear to be the poet himself. Beginning with the
             antistrophe, the thought reverts to the Chorus.

186   28   *Orphic riddles*: The legendary poet Orpheus was re-
             puted to have left a collection of mystic writings,
             some of them of a medical nature, engraved on tablets
             and deposited in a shrine of Dionysos, in Thrace.
             The 'Asklepiad skill' is the medicine that Phoibos
             Apollo taught his son Asklêpios (*cf* Note 149:4).

187   24   *a man with a grievance*: Heraklês' friendly grievance against Admetos is stated clearly enough: he thinks that his friend has allowed him to make a public fool of himself. This complaint may seem thin enough, in all conscience; but we should reflect (*a*) that Heraklês is not a particularly sensitive Hero, and (*b*) that Admetos, insisting upon abnormal hospitality, was actuated as much by personal vanity as by piety.

189   27   *and it is Alcestis that I see!*: It need hardly be pointed out that he is unconsciously right.

191   8   *the great god who is your father*: Zeus, by Alkmêna, wife of Amphitryon, a nobleman of Thebes. Nevertheless, the Heraklês of this play is not to be thought of as a divine personage.

192   12   *the Gorgon*: The beautiful face of the Gorgon Medûsa was marred by its power to turn the beholder to stone.

194   19   *Destiny has many forms*: The concluding verses are perfunctory. They may even be quasi-ritualistic: Euripides uses them at the end of several of his plays.

THE BIRDS
OF ARISTOPHANES
TRANSLATED BY
DUDLEY FITTS

INTRODUCTORY NOTE

The Birds was produced at the feast of the Great Dionysia of 414 B.C., and although it is certainly the most fanciful and one of the most lyrical of Aristophanes' plays, it won only the second prize. Composed during those tense months after the sailing of the Sicilian Expedition, when the disheartening war must have seemed endless in prospect and even victory a sick delusion, it is nevertheless not a war play. It is outspoken enough, particularly in its attacks upon the kind of civil neurosis that finds traitors and enemy agents in every office and that encourages, applauds and rewards the professional informer; but the attack this time is of less importance than the creation of a comic dream, the dream of Cloudcuckooland the Beautiful, that ideal commonwealth in the skies. Elaborate political reconstructions of the dream have been made—classical scholarship is ingenious and tireless—but they seem, in all their complexity, pastimes better suited to the academies of Cloudcuckooland itself than to the enrichment of our understanding. *The Birds* is not a play of escape: it is too honestly aware of its time for that; but it is primarily an entertainment, and as such, I think, it should be read and weighed.

For the *rationale* of my translation I must refer those interested to my remarks prefatory to *Lysistrata* and *The Frogs*. In general, however, I hope that I have reduced the number of liberties that were conscious on my part, and that my ignorance, not my arrogance, is to blame for the errors. At the same time, I demand a certain licence in rendering the choral passages and in handling mythological or topical references. Many difficulties can be taken care of in the Notes; but there are times when only a loose paraphrase, or maybe the incorporation of explanatory ideas into the text itself, can save the poem. And it is my faith that the poem is what matters most.

The text followed is the Budé, established by Coulon. In the distribution of a few speeches I have preferred the reading of other editors, and have sometimes relied upon otherwise unreliable MSS. sources because they made better theatre sense. Once or twice I have followed myself alone, so amorous is *hybris,* and assigned a speech or two as it has never been assigned before.

For many corrections and the best of suggestions I am indebted to my colleague Alston Hurd Chase, and to the poet and Hellenist Robert Fitzgerald.

DF

CONTENTS

PERSONS REPRESENTED:
  EUELPIDES
  PISTHETAIROS
  A BIRD SERVANT
  EPOPS
  CHORUS OF BIRDS
  A PRIEST
  A POET
  A TRAVELLING PROPHET
  METON
  AN INSPECTOR
  A DECREE-VENDOR
  THREE MESSENGERS
  IRIS
  A HERALD
  A PARRICIDE
  KINESIAS
  AN INFORMER
  PROMETHEUS
  POSEIDON
  A TRIBALLIAN GOD
  HERAKLES

The supernumeraries include various servants and liturgical attendants, PROKNE *the Nightingale wife of* EPOPS, MANES *a slave, and* BASILEIA *the bride of* PISTHETAIROS.

🎜 PROLOGUE

[*A waste region. Rocks, low bushes, a few thin trees. In the background, a steep rock face surmounted by a single tree. Enter two old men,* PISTHETAIROS *and* EUELPIDES, *followed by slaves carrying baggage.* PISTHETAIROS *has a raven perched upon his wrist;* EUELPIDES *has a jackdaw. Weariness and frustration.*

EUELPIDES [*to the jackdaw*]:
  Straight ahead? Over by that tree?
PISTHETAIROS [*to the raven*]:
                                        Oh, damn your feathers!
  —Euelpidês, this fool fowl keeps cawing
  a retreat.
EUELPIDES:
                    I know. What's the use?
  All this humping up and down hills,
  we'll be wrecks before we find the right road.
PISTHETAIROS:
  Miles and miles, walking around in circles,
  all because of a brainless bird.
EUELPIDES:
                                        Yes,
  tramping my toenails off for a damned jackdaw.
PISTHETAIROS:
  I wonder where we are.
EUELPIDES:
                    Do you think we could find our way back?
PISTHETAIROS:
  Exekestidês himself couldn't find his way back.
EUELPIDES:
  Hell!
PISTHETAIROS:
  That's a road you'll have to go on your own.
EUELPIDES:
  No, damn it, but I was thinking of that birdseller.
  Nice service that was,
  swearing that these two specimens would lead us straight
  to Tereus, the king who turned into a Hoopoe;
  selling us a jackdaw for a penny, the damned jackass,
  and three pennies for that raven. What a pair!
  All they can do is peck.
                                        [*to the jackdaw:*
                    —What's the matter now?
  Forgotten how to shut your beak? Or a brilliant thought
  like leading us bang up against that rock?
  I don't see any road.

PISTHETAIROS:
Not so much as a path.

EUELPIDES:
Do you think that raven of yours is still conscious?

PISTHETAIROS:
I don't know. He sort of grunts, every once in a while.

EUELPIDES:
I mean, do you think he knows what he's up to?

PISTHETAIROS:
He seems to know enough to chew on my finger.

EUELPIDES:
Silly, isn't it?
Here we are, two of us for the birds,
and we can't even find the road.

[Addresses the audience:
—Gentlemen:

Our trouble's just the reverse of Sakas's.
He isn't a citizen, and he's dying to become one;
but we,
native born, pure strain, citizens all our lives,
we can't get away from Athens fast enough.
Not that we don't like Athens:
it's a fine city, progressive, full of opportunities
to appear in court, citizens
happy as locusts droning in the shade—
only I must say they seem to do most of their droning
before a judge.

To come right down to it,

that's why the two of us are taking this walk,
fitted out with baskets and braziers and myrtle boughs.
We're looking for a less strenuous residence,
a City where we can pass our lives in peace;
and we thought of Tereus:
what with all the flying he's done, maybe
he'll know a nice restricted—

PISTHETAIROS:
Look! Look!

EUELPIDES:
What's the matter?

PISTHETAIROS:
                    The rock! Look at my raven!
EUELPIDES:
    Yes, and my jackdaw sees something: his beak's
    open again. I'll give you odds
    there's birds around that rock. Let's do something.
PISTHETAIROS:
    Why don't you go bang your foot against that rock?
EUELPIDES:
    You go bang your head. It'll make twice the noise.
PISTHETAIROS:
    Pick up a stone and knock.
EUELPIDES:
                    Anything you say.
    —Porter! Porter!
PISTHETAIROS:
                    Idiot, that's no way
    to call a Hoopoe. You should say "Hoop! Hoop!"
EUELPIDES:
    Hoop! Hoop!
    Have I got to knock again?
    Hoop! Hoop! Hoop!
            [*A door in the rock face opens; enter* SERVANT,
            wearing an enormous bird mask.
SERVANT:
                    Whoop are youp? What do you want?
PISTHETAIROS:
    Holy Apollo, what a beak! It's a canyon!
SERVANT:
    That's all we needed: a couple of bird-watchers!
EUELPIDES:
    Not so bad as all that.
                    —Come, let's think this thing through.
SERVANT:
    You'd better make it good.
EUELPIDES:
                    Well, first of all,

we're not really men, you see.
SERVANT:
                              Then what are you?
EUELPIDES:
I am a Yellowyammer, a Libyan bird.
SERVANT:
Never heard of you.
EUELPIDES:
                        Just look at the mess on my feet.
SERVANT:
I see.—And your friend: what kind of bird is he?
PISTHETAIROS:
A Crapulet, from Phartia.
EUELPIDES:
                              For that matter,
what animal are *you*, for all the gods' sake?
SERVANT:
A slave bird.
EUELPIDES:
                  You mean you were beaten by some cock?
SERVANT:
Not that, no. But when the Chief became a Hoopoe,
he made me turn into a bird, too, to keep him company
and do little jobs for him.
                              Say he wants a mess
of sardines from Phaleron: off I run with my jug
to buy some. Or maybe it's pea soup,
and we need a tureen and a ladle: well, off I go
and arrange everything. See?
EUELPIDES:
                              I'd call this bird a Kitchern.
Well, Kitch, you can do a little job for us.
Bring out Tereus.
SERVANT:
                  I wouldn't think of it!
He's just had a lunch of ant and myrtle salad,
and now it's time for his nap.

EUELPIDES:

Bother his nap!

SERVANT:

He won't like this a bit. But if you say so,
I'll do it. It's no skin off my beak.

PISTHETAIROS:

Get going!

[*Exit* SERVANT

To hell with him and that chasm he calls a beak!

EUELPIDES:

He scared away my jackdaw.

PISTHETAIROS:

You got scared,
you mean, and let it loose.

EUELPIDES:

How about you?
When you were falling flat on your face over there,
didn't you let your raven fly away?

PISTHETAIROS:

I certainly did not.

EUELPIDES:

Then where is it?

PISTHETAIROS:

Absent.

EUELPIDES:

You can wash your hands of it now, old lion-heart.

EPOPS [*within*]:

Open the door. I'm going out to meet them.

> [*Enter* EPOPS, *the Hoopoe. He is inadequately
> covered by thin drooping feathers, and wears a
> mask with a very long pointed beak and a tall
> radiant crest.*

EUELPIDES:

What in the name of High Heraklês is that?
Those feathers! That tiara!

EPOPS:

Gentlemen,
your names, if you please? The purpose of your visit?

EUELPIDES:

The Twelve Gods seem to have visited something, friend,
on you.

EPOPS:

You find my feathers laughable?
Remember: once I was a man.

EUELPIDES:

We are not laughing at you.

EPOPS:

At what, then?

EUELPIDES:

That damned funny beak of yours.

EPOPS:

I can't help it. It's Sophoklês' fault,
the way he misrepresented me in his plays.

EUELPIDES:

You are really Tereus? A bird, or a parody?

EPOPS:

Every inch a bird.

EUELPIDES:

What's the matter with your wings?

EPOPS:

Feathers missing.

EUELPIDES:

Some bird disease, or what?

EPOPS:

Every bird moults in the wintertime.
We get new feathers in the spring.

—But tell me:
who are you two?

EUELPIDES:

Mortal men.

EPOPS:

Nationality?

EUELPIDES:

Land of the Free. Home of the Brave.

EPOPS:

I suppose
you're jurymen?

EUELPIDES:
> No; you might call us *de*
jure men.

EPOPS:
> Isn't that a new crop down there?

EUELPIDES:
> If you work hard enough you can grow it in some fields.

EPOPS:
> Well, well.—But what brings you to this place?

EUELPIDES:
> We want to integrate ourselves with you.

EPOPS:
> Why?

EUELPIDES:
> Because you were a man once, like us;
> because you owed money, like us, and because,
> like us, you hated to pay it. Now you are a bird,
> with a bird's-eye view of things and a man's knowledge
> of all lands under the sun, of every sea.
> So we have come to you
> as to an authority, meaning no disrespect,
> to ask if you can tell us where to find
> a soft snug woolly city
> where a man can loaf and stretch and lie down in peace.

EPOPS:
> A nobler city than Kranaos' town?

EUELPIDES:
> Not nobler, no; but something more to our taste.

EPOPS:
> More aristocratic?

EUELPIDES:
> The Social Register
> pains me in a spot I needn't describe.

EPOPS:
> What sort of city?

EUELPIDES:
> What I have in mind
> is a place where the worst of your troubles would be
> friends crowding in early in the morning

with invitations: 'Look, Euelpidês,
'I'm giving a dinner today. For God's sake,
'get a bath somewhere, pick up your wife and kids,
'come early and stay late. If you forget,
'I'll never turn to you when I need a friend.'

EPOPS:

I can see that you're fond of troubles.

—How about you?

PISTHETAIROS:

I feel the same way he does.

EPOPS:

For example?

PISTHETAIROS:

I'd like to live in a town
where a friend of mine, father of a goodlooking boy,
would meet me and, 'You old bastard,' he'd say,
'what's this I hear about you from that son of mine?
'He tells me he ran into you outside the gymnasium,
'and though he was fresh from his bath
'you didn't say anything nice to him, or kiss him,
'or feel his balls or his biceps—
'Why, I thought you were a friend of the family!'

EPOPS:

It's clear that both of you want to live the hard life.
Well, this city of yours
does exist, after all. You'll find it on the Red Sea.

EUELPIDES:

And have the *Salaminia* turn up some morning
with a constable on board? Thanks, no sea for us!
Haven't you a Greek city you can recommend?

EPOPS:

How about Lepreon?

EUELPIDES:

No. I've never been there,
but the name reminds me of Melanthios.

EPOPS:

Then there's Opûs, over in Lokris.

EUELPIDES:

No.

You couldn't pay me enough to be Opûntios.
But tell me,
what is life like up here among you Birds?

EPOPS:
Not bad, take it by and large. No money, of course.

EUELPIDES:
There go most of your problems right away.

EPOPS:
As for food, we have poppy seed and myrtle,
white sesame, mint—

EUELPIDES:
It's a non-stop honeymoon!

PISTHETAIROS:
I have it! I have it!
I've just dreamed the most powerful dream in the world
for you Birds, if you only do what I tell you to.

EPOPS:
What's that?

PISTHETAIROS:
Well, first of all
I advise you to stop flying around aimlessly
with your beaks open. It isn't dignified.
Back in Athens when we see a man running around,
somebody asks 'Who's that?', and Teleas
or someone else says, 'Him? He's a hot bird, *he* is!
'Jittery, ants up his tail, all over the place, un-
'dependable type.'

EPOPS:
You're right, by Dionysos!
What else do you advise?

PISTHETAIROS:
I advise you to found a city.

EPOPS:
We birds? Found a city?

PISTHETAIROS:
O ye of little faith!
Look down there.

EPOPS:
I'm looking.

PISTHETAIROS:
                                    Now up there.

EPOPS:
                                                          I'm
  looking.

PISTHETAIROS:
        Look all around you.

EPOPS:
                                        Whatever you say.
  I hope you're not trying to make me sprain my neck.

PISTHETAIROS:
  Do you see anything?

EPOPS:
                                Clouds, and a lot of sky.

PISTHETAIROS:
  That's the birds' sphere.

EPOPS:
                          Sphere? What do you mean?

PISTHETAIROS:
  It's a space, really; but it revolves,
  and everything passes through it, so we scientists
  call it a sphere.
                          Very well. You settle this sphere,
  build walls around it, and you'll have a city.
  And what's more,
  you can lord it over the human race as though
  they were so many grasshoppers. And the gods—
  why, you can starve them out like the Mêlians.

EPOPS:
  How?

PISTHETAIROS:
        Just as we manage these things on earth.
  Suppose a man wants to consult the Oracle
  at Delphoi: well, he has to get a pass
  from the Boiotians, because Boiotia's on the way
  to the Shrine. And so it will be with the gods:
  there's all that air between earth and the top of Olympos,
  so if they won't pay tribute to the Birds
  you can make it illegal

for the smoke of offering to pass up to them.

EPOPS:

Oh by Earth, by Nets, by Traps, by Springes,
I never heard a cleverer idea in my life!
With you to help me, I will build that city—
that is, if we can get the other Birds to agree.

PISTHETAIROS:

Who will explain it to them?

EPOPS:

                               You.

I've lived with them so long that they have learned
to speak Man now instead of twittering.

PISTHETAIROS:

Can you call an Assembly?

EPOPS:

                            Nothing easier.

I'll just step back into the coppice here
and wake my darling wife, my Nightingale.
We'll summon them, she and I,
and they'll come racing when they hear our voices.

PISTHETAIROS:

Oh do, do! Dear Tereus, be quick!
Into the woods, wake the Nightingale!

   [*Exit* EPOPS; *presently his voice is heard singing within:*

EPOPS:

        Awake, Love, lazy sleeper,
           Awake, and pour
        The lilting glory of your golden throat
        For Itys, ours no more.
           Ah, the liquid trill
           Of the holy monody rising
        To God's house from the stillness of the woods!
           Phoibos himself, that high
        Singer, struck by your music, would sweep
        The lutestrings with his delicate fingers
          Antiphonal, and all the air along
             Lead the quiring
        Of the tireless gods responsive to your song.

EUELPIDES:
Heavenly God, what a voice that little bird has!
He is drowning the forest with honey.

PISTHETAIROS:
You!

EUELPIDES:
What?

PISTHETAIROS:
Be quiet, can't you?

EUELPIDES:
Why?

PISTHETAIROS:
The Hoopoe is going to sing for us again.
[*During the following monody, birdcalls are
heard from various points behind the scene, distant and uncertain at first, but increasing in
volume and in urgency until the* CHORUS OF BIRDS
enters for the Párodos.

EPOPS [*within*]:
Epopoí
        popoí epopopoí
    popoí
            iô
    iô
            iô
                To me,
            to
me here, here, here, O
    friends, O feathery
myriads!
            Leave your
fields now, furrows
            deep
    in seed, beak-
wielders,
            swift
    spiralers,
                melodists

of delight
    tíotiotíotì
        All you
divers for stingvoiced gnats
    in dusky wet ravines,
            you
curlew, curlew crying,
        you,
    spume-guests of the halcyon
on the enchanted water:
        Come to me, come,
hear this remarkable old man
    whose brain
brims for our common gain:
        Hear him,
        come
    here, here, here,
        hear him!
CHORUS [*within*]:
                    Tórotorotórotíx
                        totoĭx
                    whit tuwhit tuwhit
                    Tórotorotórotorolílilíx

PISTHETAIROS:
    Do you see any birds?
EUELPIDES:
                    Not a single bird.
    There's not so much as a feather in the sky.
PISTHETAIROS:
    It seems to have done no good
    for the Hoopoe to go gargling in the glade.

🕮 PÁRODOS

        [*The* CHORUS *is composed of twenty-six persons
        dressed in stylized representation of various
        birds, each with a large beak-mask. These enter
        separately from every direction, gathering about*

their leader, the Flamingo, *in the* orchêstra. *The entrance should be complete by the end of the* Hoopoe's *catalogue.*

A BIRD:
Torotìx torotíx.

PISTHETAIROS:
                    Look, there's one coming now!

EUELPIDES:
What do you suppose it is? A peacock, maybe?

PISTHETAIROS:
The Hoopoe can tell us.
                    —What kind of bird is that?

EPOPS:
That, Sir, is a water bird; you don't see
that sort every day.

EUELPIDES:
                    Nice colour; flame-y.

EPOPS:
Naturally. He's a Flamingo.

EUELPIDES:
                    Oh look!

PISTHETAIROS:
Now what?

EUELPIDES:
                    Another bird.

PISTHETAIROS:
                              I should say so!
He's a weird sister, all right, as the poet puts it.
See how he struts! I wonder what he is.

EPOPS:
We call him the Bird of Araby.

PISTHETAIROS:
                              Araby?
Did he come on a flying camel?

EUELPIDES:
                              There's another one!
By Poseidôn, he looks as if he had been dyed!

PISTHETAIROS:
This is astonishing. Do you mean to say

there's more than one Hoopoe in the world?

EPOPS:

He's the son of Philoklês and a lady Hoopoe,
and I am his grandfather. It's like the formula
'Kallias : Hipponikos :: Hipponikos : Kallias II'.

EUELPIDES:

So that's Kallias II. I see he's losing his feathers.

EPOPS:

A man about town, you know, always getting plucked
by parasites and party girls feathering their own nests.

PISTHETAIROS:

Here comes one with a crest. What's he called?

EPOPS:

That one? Gobbler.

EUELPIDES:

I thought Kleonymos was the Gobbler.

PISTHETAIROS:

This can't be Kleonymos: he hasn't thrown away
his crest.

EUELPIDES:

Speaking of that, why do birds
wear crests? To compete in the Armed Men's Race?

EPOPS:

It's like the Karians: crests make fighting safer.

PISTHETAIROS:

I never saw so many birds! They make me nervous.

EUELPIDES:

You said it.
When they lift their wings you can't see where you're
    going.

EPOPS:

That's the Partridge; and that's—let's see—that one's
the Francolin; the Egyptian Mallard; and the female's
a Hen Kingfisher.

PISTHETAIROS:

What's that in back of her?

EPOPS:

A Shavetail, of course.

PISTHETAIROS:
Do birds shave tails?

EPOPS:
Doesn't Sporgilos?
—And that's a female
Owl.

EUELPIDES:
That's an idea! Bringing Owls to Athens.

EPOPS:
Magpie. Turtledove. Lark. Warbler. Spryneck.
Pigeon. Snirt. Falcon. Ringdove. Cuckoo.
Redleg. Firepate. Purple Hatch. Kestrel.
Grebe. Bunting. Lämmergeier. Woodpecker.

PISTHETAIROS:
Birds and more birds!

EUELPIDES:
Even white Blackbirds!

PISTHETAIROS:
The way they chatter and screech at each other!

EUELPIDES:
Do you think they're dangerous?

PISTHETAIROS:
Their beaks are wide open,
and they're certainly looking hard at both of us.

EUELPIDES:
I think so, too.

CHORAGOS:
Who-oo-oo called this Assembly?
Where is he?

EPOPS:
Here I am, your tried
and trusted old friend.

CHORAGOS:
Spea-pea-pea-peak:
What clever new message have you to give us?

EPOPS:
A profitable one, safe, correct, ingenious.
These two gentlemen, both of them keen thinkers,

came here looking for me.

CHORAGOS:
                              Looking for you? Why?

EPOPS:
I am telling you.
                    —These elegant old men
have detached themselves temporarily from
the human race and brought us what I am sure
is a plan of promising proportions.

CHORAGOS:
                                        I think
you have made the greatest blunder in history.
What are you talking about?

EPOPS:
                              Be not afraid.

CHORAGOS:
                                        Why not?
What have you done to us?

EPOPS:
                              I have lent an ear
to two respectable bird-struck Senators.

CHORAGOS:
You have?

EPOPS:
            I have. And I am proud of it.

CHORAGOS:
What, in our house?

EPOPS:
                    As sure as I'm standing here.

CHORUS:
                    Oh misery!   [STROPHE
                    Duplicity!
                        Oh horror without end!
                    Who lays the snare
                    And leaves us there?
                            Our old familiar friend!
                Is this the Hoopoe of our heart,
                  Copartner of our fields and skies,

> Who bids our ancient laws depart
> And sells us to our enemies?

CHORAGOS:
　We can take care of him later. Just now
　it's a matter of these two old fools. Look at them!
　The usual penalty is clearly in order:
　death by dissection.

PISTHETAIROS:
　　　　　　　　Done for, by God Almighty!

EUELPIDES:
　Your fault, your fault entirely. Why did you ever
　lead me here?

PISTHETAIROS:
　　　　　　　So that you could follow me.

EUELPIDES:
　It's blood and tears for us!

PISTHETAIROS:
　　　　　　　　　Hardly tears for you,
　once the Birds have pecked out both your eyes.

CHORUS:

> The cock-trump sings.　　[ANTISTROPHE
> Advance both wings,
> 　O army of the air!
> The hour has struck
> That ends the luck
> 　Of this repulsive pair.
> No clouds that cluster in the sky,
> 　No raindark mountain peaks,
> Shall save them from the battery
> 　Of our insulted beaks.

CHORAGOS:
　Forward! Peck them apart! Flay them!
　　　　　　　　　　　　—Where's
　that Wing Commander? Tell him to get moving
　on the right!

[*Immense confusion of movement among the Birds in the* orchêstra. EUELPIDES *and* PISTHE-TAIROS *confer apart.*]

EUELPIDES:
That settles that.
How do we get out of this mess?

PISTHETAIROS:
Why not
stick around?

EUELPIDES:
Of course. And get pulled apart?

PISTHETAIROS:
I suppose you have figured out some way of escape?

EUELPIDES:
You know I haven't.

PISTHETAIROS:
Then listen to me.
Let them come on. We'll stand here and fight them
with these kitchen pots.

EUELPIDES:
Pots? What good are pots?

PISTHETAIROS:
They'll keep the Owl from attacking us.

EUELPIDES:
How about those fellows with the horrible claws?

PISTHETAIROS:
Stick that spit up in front of you like a spear.

EUELPIDES:
But our eyes?

PISTHETAIROS:
Use a couple of saucers.

EUELPIDES:
What a mind!
You remind me of Nikias. You ought to be
on the General Staff, in charge of secret weapons.

CHORAGOS:
Eleleú!
Ready, beaks at the charge! Let 'em have it!
Grab! Claw! Tear! Gouge! Break the pots first!

[*Much noise on both sides, but no other activity;
the Hoopoe intervenes.*

EPOPS:
Permit me. Just a minute, please.
                              —With the best intentions,
you are behaving like besotted beasts.
What is the good of killing two harmless men,
both of them perfect strangers and, what's more,
related to my wife?

CHORAGOS:
                              Are you promoting
a Be Kind to Wolves week?

EPOPS:
                              Oh, come. I'll admit,
men are our natural enemies; but these men
are different, they really mean us well.
More than that,
they have a practical plan for the good of us all.

CHORAGOS:
A practical plan? Nonsense. Our enemies,
our fathers' enemies—what can they teach us?

EPOPS:
Why, people before this have learned from their enemies.
An open mind's a weapon in itself.
It's not our friends teach us resourcefulness,
but our wise enemies. Cities and princes
have learned the use of warships and fortresses
from necessity, not from friends. Enmity saves
our homes, our children, everything that we love.

CHORAGOS:
You may be right.
                              At least it can do no harm
to hear what they have to say.
                              It may be
we may take some profit even from what we hate.
        [*The Birds cluster in doubtful conference about
        the* CHORAGOS.

PISTHETAIROS [*apart to* EUELPIDES]:
They're coming to their senses. Easy, now!

EPOPS [*to the Birds*]:
Think over what I've said. You'll thank me for it.
CHORAGOS:
We have always admired the Hoopoe's intellect.
PISTHETAIROS:
Now we can breathe again.
Leave your pot there on the ground. Pick up your spear—
your spit, I mean—and let's walk around
and see what the place is like.
                              Keep this side
of the pots, and keep your eye on those Birds. Above all,
don't act as though you were nervous.
EUELPIDES:
                              I'd like to know:
if they kill us, where'll we get buried?
PISTHETAIROS:
                              I should hope
in the National Cemetery. For a first-rate funeral
at the public expense, we'd say we fell gloriously
in combat with the common enemy
at Gettysbird.
                    [*The Birds decide upon a truce.*
CHORAGOS:
              At ease! Stack arms!
Now we must find out who these strangers are
and what they want.
                    Listen, Epops!
EPOPS:
                              I am listening.
CHORAGOS:
Who are these men? Do you know where they are from?
EPOPS:
Travelers from Greece, where education is general.
CHORAGOS:
What brings them to the Birds?
EPOPS:
                              Ornithophily.
They have heard of your laws and customs and they long
to live with you for ever.

CHORAGOS:
                         Is it possible?
   What else do they say?
EPOPS:
                              Incredible things, transcending
   utterance.
CHORAGOS:
                  What do they ask from us?
   Does 'living with us' mean living as honest friends,
   or serving their own interests at our cost?
EPOPS:
   This savant speaks of benefits to you
   that fairly rob me of words to describe them.
   It's all for you. He will tell you so himself.
CHORAGOS:
   Is the man crazy?
EPOPS:
                        His sanity defies
   definition.
CHORAGOS:
               Really?
EPOPS:
                        Pure fox, subtle, deep.
CHORAGOS:
   Then let him speak, let him speak!
   These hints of yours have got me all a-twitter.

 AGON

                  [*Order is now restored. As* EPOPS *takes command
                  of the situation, the* CHORUS *forms itself at oppo-
                  site sides of the* orchêstra *to listen to the ensuing
                  debate.*
EPOPS:
   You there, and you,
   carry these weapons in and hang them up
   in the kitchen again, next to the tripod.
   Fair fortune befall them!

[*Exeunt two Bird Servants with the pots, spits,
and other utensils*
                        —And you, friend,
inform the Birds why I have summoned them
to this Assembly. Expound.

PISTHETAIROS:
                        No, by Apollo!
Not unless they promise me first
what Monk the Knifeman made that wife of his
promise *him*: no biting, no tickling, no unseemly
prodding in the—

EUELPIDES:
                        The arse, you would say?

PISTHETAIROS:
                                        No:
I mean my eyes.

CHORAGOS:
                        Sir, you have our promise.

PISTHETAIROS:
Swear it.

CHORAGOS:
                        I swear it; but on condition that
this Comedy of ours wins First Prize
by unanimous vote of the judges and audience.

EPOPS:
NOW HEAR THIS:
Break ranks! Every private will pick up his arms
and go back to barracks. See your bulletin boards
for further announcements.

CHORUS:
    Men were deceivers ever; and it may be   [STROPHE
    Friend, that the quality of our guilelessness
        Tempts you to gull us. Nevertheless,
            Nothing risked may be gain rejected when

    Truth as a Stranger comes. If you have discerned
    New forces in us, talents earthed over, dis-
        used instruments of old artifice:

Speak out. Let age edify unfledged youth.

CHORAGOS:
  You are at liberty to say whatever you like.
  You have our promise:
  We shall not be the first to break the truce.
PISTHETAIROS:
  I thank you.
              —Gentlemen, you will find
  much to chew on in the following message.
  But first, with your permission—

                              [*To a* SERVANT
                  Boy, bring me
  a garland and a bowl of water to wash my hands.
EUELPIDES [*apart*]:
  Do you see dinner coming?
PISTHETAIROS [*apart*]:
                  No; I am trying to think
  of something to tell them, some enormous concept
  that will knock them silly.
                  —Gentlemen: My heart
  bleeds—bleeds, I say—when I reflect that you
  who once were kings—
CHORAGOS:
                  Kings? Kings of what?

PISTHETAIROS:
  Why, kings of everything! Kings of myself, of this
  poor friend of mine, yes, kings of Zeus the King!
  Before Time was, you were: you antedate
  Kronos, the Titans, Earth—
CHORAGOS:
                  Earth?

PISTHETAIROS:
                  Yes, by Heaven!
CHORAGOS:
  That's something that I never knew before.
PISTHETAIROS:
  Ignorance, acedia. There are authorities
  for what I say: Aisôpos, to go no farther.

He tells us—don't you remember?—that the **Lark**
was the first Bird born in those chaotic times
before even Earth was thought of; and the Lark's
father died—have you forgotten?—, and because
there was no earth on Earth to bury him in,
the Lark finally laid him away in her head.

EUELPIDES:
Exactly. That's how Hyde Lark got its name.

PISTHETAIROS:
You see my point, I hope? If birds existed
before the Creation, before the gods themselves,
then you Birds must be heirs apparent: the royal **power**
belongs to you.

EUELPIDES:
                        Of course. At the same time,
they'd better keep their beaks in fighting trim:
Zeus won't give in to the first woodpecker.

PISTHETAIROS:
In those glorious days it was not the gods who ruled
over men, but the Birds. Let me cite you a few proofs.
Consider the Cock.
Long before any Dareioses or Megabazoses
the Cock was King of the Persians, and such a **king**
that ever since he's been called the Persian Bird.

EUELPIDES:
That's why, even now,
Cocks strut like the Shah; and of all birds living
only they have a right to the tiara.

PISTHETAIROS:
What power he had! Why, to this very day
when the Cock sings at dawn
everyone jumps out of bed and goes to work:
blacksmiths, potters, tanners, shoemakers,
grocers, masseurs, lyre-&-shield-manufacturers—
Some of them are hard at it before it's light.

EUELPIDES:
Some of them certainly are! That's how I lost
a perfectly good new Phrygian all-wool coat.
I'd been asked to a party to celebrate

naming somebody's baby. Well, when I got there
I had a couple of short ones, so I felt sleepy
and lay down for a minute; and—would you believe it?—
some damned cock began to crow, and I woke up
and thought it was morning, before the other guests
had even sat down to dinner! Well, I started out
on the Halimos road, but I'd hardly poked my nose
past the drive when, baff! somebody boffed me
with something blunt, and I went down for the count.
When I came to, my coat was somewhere else.
PISTHETAIROS:
At that same time the Kite reigned over the Greeks.
CHORAGOS:
The Greeks?
PISTHETAIROS:
The Greeks. That's when they learned
to prostrate themselves when the kites come back in the
    spring.
EUELPIDES:
I remember I prostrated myself one day
when I saw a Kite, or I tried to, but somehow
I fell on my back by mistake and my market money
went down my throat. That day I ate no more.
PISTHETAIROS:
Then there's the Cuckoo.
Once upon a time
in Egypt and in Phoinikia the Cuckoo
was king. As a matter of fact, when the Cuckoo
said 'Cuckoo!',
all the Phoinikians went out and mowed their fields.
EUELPIDES:
'Cuckoo! Back to the furrows, you foreskinless!'
as the proverb has it.
PISTHETAIROS:
Another thing: You will find
that whenever a man managed to become a king,
an Agamemnon, say, or a Menelaos,
he would always carry a bird on the end of his sceptre
to share the royal gifts.

EUELPIDES:

That explains something.
I used to go to the theatre; and whenever Priam
came on in the tragedies, he'd have a bird
on his sceptre, just as you say. I used to think
the bird was there to keep an eye on our friend
Lysikratês when the bribes were passed around.

PISTHETAIROS:

But the best proof is that Zeus, the current King,
wears an Eagle on his head as a sign of power.
His Daughter has an Owl; his son Apollo,
as a medical man, has a Hawk.

EUELPIDES:

That's perfectly true.
Why do you suppose those gods have those birds?

PISTHETAIROS:

Why? So that when the sacrificial roasts
are offered to the gods, the birds may taste them first.
And here's something else:
In the old days men never swore by the gods,
but always by birds.

EUELPIDES:

Lampôn still does today.
He always says 'Holy Kites!' when he makes a mistake.

PISTHETAIROS:

You understand, then, that years and years ago
you were great, even holy, in the minds of men.

But now? Now you are rejects, fools,
worse than slaves, stoned
in the streets by arrogant men, hunted
down even in your sanctuaries
by trappers with nets, springes, limed
twigs, cages, decoy-
boxes;

caught, sold
wholesale, goosed, prodded
by fat fingers, denied
even the grace of wholesome frying,
but served up sleazily, choked

with cheese, smeared with oil,
sprayed with vinegar, doused
as though you were dead meat, too gamy,
in rivers of sweet slab sauce.

CHORUS: [ANTISTROPHE
   Tears, and no idle tears, Stranger, distress us
   Hearing your plain account of calamity.
      Clearly our primeval dignity
         Has lapsed in the long sliding of the years.

   You, by a happy chance or some divine influence sent to guide us, have indicated
      Future recovery, joy ahead.
         Ourselves, our wives, our chicks depend on you.

CHORAGOS:
  What can we do? Instruct us, since you say
  you have a plan. Life's no life for us
  till we win back the power that we have lost.
PISTHETAIROS:
  My plan is a great City for All Birds,
  a single City, with the surrounding air
  and all the space between encircled by
  massive brick walls like those at Babylon.
EUELPIDES:
  Bring on your Giants! What a mighty fortress!
PISTHETAIROS:
  Once the wall's built, you must send an embassy
  to Zeus and lay your grievances before him.
  If he denies them, if he temporizes,
  then you should declare a Holy War
  against the whole of Olympos: no more free passage
  for divinities in an obvious state of erection
  on their way through your land to flirt with their Alopês,
  their Sémelês, their Alkmenês! No; once across the border,
  each strutting member must be stamped and sealed.
  That should give them something to think about!

As for Mankind,
you must send another bird to them, a herald
to announce that from now on, since the Birds are kings,
the first sacrifices must be made to them,
and then (if convenient) to the Olympian gods.
But even in sacrifices to the gods
an appropriate Bird must be adored as well:
thus, Aphroditê and a Phalarope; Poseidôn
and a Duck; Heraklês and a Cormorant;
or, if the victim is offered up to King Zeus,
let the Wren, the Wren, the king of all birds, receive
the flesh of the Balled Gnat.

EUELPIDES:
                                   What price gnat-flesh?
Let the Good Gosh bounce thunderballs in the sky!

CHORAGOS:
What if men refuse to treat us as gods?
What if they say, 'Them? Jackdaws, that's all,
'flying around up there with their silly wings'?

PISTHETAIROS:
I can't believe you are serious. Why, good Lord!
Hermês has wings, and he flies; yes, and Nikê,
she has wings; and Erôs—all sorts of gods
fly, don't they? Why, even Iris,
the one that Homer refers to as 'Trembling Dove'—
Iris has wings, Iris flies.

EUELPIDES:
                            Speaking of wings,
what if Zeus drops one of his wingèd bolts on us?

CHORAGOS:
But what if Mankind is so unregenerate
that only the regulars of the Olympos clique
are recognized?

PISTHETAIROS:
                      We'll draft a regiment
of Sparrows and march them off to steal the seeds
in the new-planted fields. Deméter can set up
a Farm Program to fend off starvation.

EUELPIDES:
>   Deméter will also find a thousand ways
>   to get around any program that she sets up.

PISTHETAIROS:
>   If the Sparrows fail, we'll send some Elite Crows
>   to the grazing lands and have them bite out the eyes
>   of herdsmen and herds. Let Apollo cure them:
>   he's a doctor, he gets paid.

EUELPIDES:
>   Let me know in advance:
>   I'll want to sell my yoke of oxen first.

PISTHETAIROS:
>   But if they sense the indwelling divinity
>   of the Birds, as they should, knowing that you are God,
>   and Life, and Earth, and Kronos, and Poseidôn—
>   then everything will end as they would have it.

CHORAGOS:
>   Everything? What do you mean?

PISTHETAIROS:
>   For example,
>   locusts will not touch their budding vines:
>   the Hawks and Owls will see to that. Then, too,
>   a single platoon of indoctrinated Redwings
>   will be assigned to keep the gall-flies and emmets
>   from chewing up fig-shoots.

CHORAGOS:
>   But how shall we manage
>   money? Men seem to set great store by money.

PISTHETAIROS:
>   The Auspice birds will show them where rich mines
>   lie in the earth. The Augurs, too, will learn
>   the secret of quick returns. Shipwrecks will end—

CHORAGOS:
>   How so?

PISTHETAIROS:
>   They'll consult the Birds before each voyage:
>   'Is it safe to sail?' 'Not today; a storm's blowing up.'

EUELPIDES:
>   I'll invest in a boat. Yo-ho for the briny deep!

PISTHETAIROS:
> Then, of course, there are those buried pots
> of treasure. The Birds know. Haven't you heard
> 'A little bird tóld me where to look for it'?

CHORAGOS:
> I'll sell my boat. Me for the buried pots!

CHORAGOS:
> But what about health? That's the gift of the gods.

PISTHETAIROS:
> When business is good, health takes care of itself.

EUELPIDES:
> I never heard of a bankrupt whose health was good.

CHORAGOS:
> How will they ever live to reach old age?
> Surely that's an Olympian dispensation.
> Or must they die in the cradle?

PISTHETAIROS:
>   Not at all.
> The Birds will add three centuries to their lives.

CHORAGOS:
> Where will they get three centuries?

PISTHETAIROS:
>   From themselves.
> The poet says:
> 'One crow caws down five generations of man'.

EUELPIDES:
> Almost thou persuadest me to be a bird.

PISTHETAIROS:
> Why not be birds? They demand no marble temples
> intricate with golden doors; their shrines
> are the ilex, the sparkling shrubs. Their highest gods
> live in the sanctuary of olive trees.
> We need no Delphoi or Ammon for this worship,
> but at home, on our own ground,
> in peace among our own familiar flowers,
> we can raise hands full of grain to them in prayer,
> invoking their dear aid:
> and when our words fly up, they will be answered
> in blessings that fall upon the scattered grain.

CHORAGOS:
Dearest of old men, you have won me utterly
to your cause. From this hour your words are my words.

CHORUS:
My mind applauds.
Swear faith to me,
And I will swear
Death to the gods.
The fight is fair:
Sing Victory.

CHORAGOS:
We are ready to do whatever must be done.
The plans and stratagems we leave to you.

EPOPS:
Action, quick action. By God, this is no time
for taking naps or dawdling like Nikias!
But first, gentlemen,
this is my nest, a poor thing of twigs and straw,
but my own. Will you permit me to entertain you
inside? And will you tell me who you are?

PISTHETAIROS:
Of course. Pisthetairos is the name. That one's
Euelpidês; comes from Kriôa.

EPOPS:
Very happy
to meet you both.

PISTHETAIROS:
Not at all.

EPOPS:
Will you please step in?

PISTHETAIROS:
After you.

EPOPS:
Right this way.

PISTHETAIROS:
There, I almost forgot!
Tell me, how can a couple of men like us

live with birds? You can fly. We don't know how.

EPOPS:
I see.

PISTHETAIROS:
And speaking of Aisôpos again,
he has a fable about a fox and an eagle.
The fox lost.

EPOPS:
Really, it's no problem at all.
There's a useful little herb. You nibble it
and, presto!—you sprout wings.

PISTHETAIROS:
That's fair enough.
—Here, Xanthias, Manodôros: pick up the baggage.

CHORAGOS:
Hi! Epops! Before you go—

EPOPS:
What's the matter?

CHORAGOS:
You'll invite our venerable guests to dine, of course;
but the Nightingale,
the Muses' love, sweet cataract of song—
will you send her out and let us play with her?

PISTHETAIROS:
A sound idea, by God, and I second it.
Ask the delightful bird to step this way.

EUELPIDES:
Yes, just for a minute. You can't imagine how long
we've longed, my friend and I, for a nightingale.

EPOPS:
You are too kind.
—Proknê, Proknê,
come here and show yourself to our noble guests.
[*Enter the* Nightingale: *a flute-girl, nude except
for her mask and wings*

PISTHETAIROS:
God of our fathers, what a heavenly little bird!
So soft, so white—
How I should like to get between those thighs!

EUELPIDES:
  The gold, all the gold, like a bride on her wedding day!
  I can't help it; I am obliged to kiss this young woman.
PISTHETAIROS:
  Stupid, don't you see the little spikes on her beak?
  You'll get hurt.
EUELPIDES:
                 No, I shan't. It's like opening an egg.
  Tap her on the head, the shell falls away,
  and there's my kiss.
EPOPS [*indicating the door*]:
                 Gentlemen.
PISTHETAIROS:
                            Let's go in.
                                        [*Exeunt*

 PARÁBASIS I

          [*In the* orchêstra *the* CHORUS *turns to face the
          audience; the* Nightingale *accompanies the lyric
          passages on her flute.*

CHORUS [*a solo voice*]:
                 Tawnythroat, Partner   [KOMMATION
                 In song, dark
                 Muse, dearest of Birds:
                 Come, let the curving long
                 Line of your fluting
                 Fall, sparkling
                 Undersong to our words.

CHORAGOS: [PARABASIS
  Come now, let us consider the generations of Man,
  Compound of dust and clay, strengthless,
  Tentative, passing away as leaves in autumn
  Pass, shadows wingless, forlorn
  Phantoms deathbound, a dream. Let Men turn
  To the Birds, aerial philosophers of

Forever, safe from age, from change, from death.
Let them be humble and learn from us
The truth of Being, the essential germ,
The Bird, first Cause of Gods and Rivers,
Of Erebos, and of the great Void of Chaos.

Here is the absolute Theogony:
Professor Pródikos can lecture somewhere else.

CHAOS and NIGHT: that was the start of it,
And black Erebos, and the long nothing of Tártaros;
No Earth as yet, no Air, no Heaven. There,
In the untried lap of Erebos, sombre Night
Laid a wind-egg, whence, with the circling year,
Erôs was hatched, golden Erôs, wind-swift
Love, the world's longing. His was the sleight
Joined Night and wingèd Chaos in that first
Tartarean marriage and brought the race of Birds
To the shores of light. It was Erôs
Created the line of God also, mixing
The urgent elements in adorable ways
To make the Sky and Sea and Earth and all
The Blessèd Ones.
                    So it appears that we
Are móre ancient than these same Blessèd Ones,
Older in the line of Love. What I say is clear
In a thousand proofs:
                    We are wing'd, and so is Love.
Love is our art: how many a handsome boy
Has armed his heart with scorn, only to yield
His proud thighs to the persuasion of the Birds,
Won by a gift of quail, or geese, or cocks!

And birds are good to men in numberless ways.
We lead in the seasons. The clanging Crane
Flies towards Libya, and the sowing begins;
She it is who tells the mariner
When it is time to take his winter sleep,
The unshipped rudder hanging against the wall.

This same Crane
Inspires our friend Orestês of the Alleys
To knit himself a shirt against the cold,
Thus winning the gratitude of citizens waylaid
Who otherwise would shiver in nudity.
Later, the Kite brings back the brilliant Spring
And you barber your sheep; and then the summer
    Swallow
Suggests bargains of thin dress at the shops.

We are Ammon, Delphoi, Dodôna, Phoibos Apollo.
Are you not always taking the advice of birds
In matters of business, of marriage, of daily life?
You see Bird in everything: your rumours are what
A small Bird told you; your sneeze is a Bird, your chance
Hello in the street's a Bird; a stranger encountered;
An ass on the road: all Birds, all signs of Birds.
Are we not right to call ourselves your Apollos?

Therefore confess us gods, for so   [MAKRON
We are, to you; and you shall have
Feathery Muses to foretell
The winter wind, the summer breeze.
We will not perch like Zeus, at ease
In some remote cloud-citadel,
But live with you and with your sons,
Your sons' sons, and their sons as well,
Bringing you gifts of youth and peace,
Love, laughter, wealth, new dances, brave
Festivals, more than the human tongue
Can tell, more than the heart can know.
This is our pledge, this is our song.

CHORUS:

       Woodland Muse   [ODE
         tiotiotinx tiotinx
            Lucency
       Darting voice
            Valley

Wanderer, circling flight
> *tíotinx tíotiotinx*
>> on the bright hills:
>> My singing
Spills
> duskiness into the light
For Pan
> and thou hearest
>> For
The Great Mother, Mountaindweller,
> *tótotototótotototinx*
>> and thou
>> hearest
In air
> on the heights
>> fields
> where Phrynichos
Tastes the ambrosial finality
> *tíotinx*
>> of song.

CHORAGOS: [EPIRRHEMA
If any gentleman in the audience is interested
In a pleasant life, he should get in touch with us.
We practise what your laws forbid: You would like to beat
Your father? Good. According to your code
It's an off-color pastime and, moreover, illegal.
All right; but if you were one of us Birds,
You'd just walk up to the old man, tap him
On the snout, and say: 'Put 'em up, if you want to
    fight!'
Or say you're on the lam, branded and all that: here,
We'd refer to you as a Mottled Francolin, and forget you.
You're a sub-asiatic type like Spíntharos?
Here you'd be a Migrant Finch, Philêmon species.
Even a creeping calamity like Exekestidês
Can hatch ancestors up here and become respectable.
Why, if Peisias' son himself
Should take after the old man and cohabit

With subversives by the dozens, we'd only say
'What a clever bird he is, always drumming up trade!'

CHORUS:

So the wild Swans   [ANTODE
     tiotiotinx tiotinx
      calling
Above the roar
Of their great wings,
             cry
    tiotinx tiotiotinx
      'Apollo!'
    on the Hebros
Shore:
    The company
 Of spotted wood-beasts fly
      for dread,
The sea
    hearing
    tótotototótototototinx
      falls
     hearing
    and is still:
Olympos
   is hushed
        The Graces
    shriek back against
The liquid instancy
    tiotinx
      of song.

CHORAGOS: [ANTEPIRRHEMA
There is nothing more practical or more enjoyable
Than a pair of wings. Suppose you go to the theatre
And find it's some Tragedy or other: well, of course
You're bored, and hungry, so off you fly home,
Take care of your belly, and get back for the last act.
Or say you develop a sudden case of the runs.
Do you sit there and spoil your suit? No. You simply

Zoom up into the air, do your job, fart twice,
Catch your breath, and coast back to your seat again.
Or maybe you're an Adulterer, of all things, and there's
Your girl's husband in the front row gawking at the
    Chorus.
A flap of the wings, and you're off you know where; and
    when
You've laid the lady—a flap of the wings, and you're back.
Wings? There's nothing like them!
Look at Dieitrephês, if you want a good example:
Those wicker wing baskets he manufactures got him
A captaincy, then a colonelcy, and now, rags to riches,
He's a full-fledged Horsecock in a yellow uniform!

☙ SCENE

> [*Re-enter* PISTHETAIROS *and* EUELPIDES. *Both are*
> *now absurdly feathered, winged, and beaked.*

PISTHETAIROS:
So far, so good.

EUELPIDES:
                    By God, it's the funniest thing
I ever saw in my life!

PISTHETAIROS:
                    What is?

EUELPIDES:
                    You,
with those pinfeathers. Know what you look like?

PISTHETAIROS:
You look like a cut-rate reproduction
of an unsuccessful sketch of a goose.

EUELPIDES:
Do I?
You look like a blackbird tonsured in the dark.

PISTHETAIROS:
These similes are futile. Remember the poem:
'I shot an arrow into the air . . .'

CHORAGOS:

Next business?

PISTHETAIROS:
First we must find
a name for our City, a glorious name;
and then we must sacrifice to the gods.

EUELPIDES:

You said it.

CHORAGOS:
Let's get busy. What shall we call this City of ours?

PISTHETAIROS:
Shall we go in for a touch of Lakonian *je ne sais quoi*
and name it New Sparta?

EUELPIDES:

I want no part of Sparta.

Gosh, I wouldn't tie a name like that
to a flop-house bunk!

PISTHETAIROS:

Well, have you any ideas?

EUELPIDES:
Somewhere, what with all these clouds and all this air,
there must be a rare name, somewhere . . .

PISTHETAIROS:

How do you like

'Cloudcuckooland'?

CHORAGOS:

That's it! That's it!

What a name, what a jewel of a name you've thought of

EUELPIDES:
Cloudcuckooland. Isn't that the place
where Aischenês and Theogenês rent castles?

PISTHETAIROS:
Yes; and it's where the Giants met the Gods
and got themselves bluffed off the battlefield.

CHORAGOS:
Cloudcuckooland's a city with a future!
What god or goddess shall we choose for Patron?

EUELPIDES:
Why not Athenê?

PISTHETAIROS:
                    In a City with a Future,
'what boots a mailèd warrior goddess in arms',
since Kleisthenês tends to the weaving?
CHORAGOS:
                                        But the Akropolis?
Who will guard the Pelargic Wall?
PISTHETAIROS:
                              A bird.

CHORAGOS:
   One of us? What kind?
PISTHETAIROS:
                        Something Persian, I should say,
something with a reputation for ferocity.
An Arês-chicken, maybe?
EUELPIDES:
                        Hail, Arês, Master Cluck!
He's used to uncomfortable roosts, at any rate.
PISTHETAIROS: [*To* EUELPIDES
But now,
off you go into the air! See what the builders
are up to. Make sure they have enough stones.
Get plenty of tubs. Make the mortar yourself. (Better
strip first.) Carry the hods up—
EUELPIDES:
                        And fall off the ladder.
PISTHETAIROS:
   Bank the fires. Post sentries in the right places.
Make the round of the guards at night—
EUELPIDES:
                              And take a snooze.

PISTHETAIROS:
   Send out two heralds, one to the gods above,
one to mankind below.
When you have done this, report back here to me.
EUELPIDES:
   And here you'll be on your back! I wish to God
you'd do some of the work.

PISTHETAIROS:
                              Friend, that's not like you.
We all depend on you to get things done.
I shall be busy too:
                                        [*Exit* EUELPIDES

I must arrange for the dedication service
and collar a priest to recite the liturgy.
Boy!—You, boy!—Bring me the basket and the lavabo.

CHORUS:
                    Inevitably right! My mind   [STROPHE
                        Melts in your mind's embrace.
                    High rituals of any kind
                        Are proper in this place.
                    Here let our piety devote
                    To the blest gods one skinny goat.

                    So may they look down from above
                        Upon our sacred feast,
                    Accept our sparsely offered love,
                        And overlook the rest.
                    Sing one, sing all! Sing deaf, sing mute!
                    Chairis, assist us with your flute.

PISTHETAIROS [*to the* Fluteplayer]:
    You, there, stop that futile tooting!
    What a man! I swear by my God, I've seen
    strange sights in my life, but this is the first
    crow I ever saw with a leather beak-rest.
                                        [*Enter a* PRIEST

    Holiness, get busy. Sacrifice to the gods.
PRIEST:
    I would fain do so.
                        —Where is my acolyte?
    LET US PRAY:
    TO HESTIA NESTIARCH, TO THE HIGH HAWK
        OF THE HALL, TO ALL OLYMPIAN BIRDS AND
        BIRDETTES—

PISTHETAIROS:

Hail Storkissimo! Hail, Super of Sounion!

PRIEST:

—TO THE PYTHODELIAN SWAN, TO LETO CORNCRAKE, TO ARTEMIS SISKIN—

PISTHETAIROS:

That's a pretty association of ideas!

PRIEST:

—TO SABAZIOS THE PHRYGILLATOR, TO THE GREAT OSTRICH MOTHER OF GODS AND MEN—

PISTHETAIROS:

Lady Kybelê, Ostrichess, Mother of Kleokritos!

PRIEST:

THAT THEY MAY VOUCHSAFE HEALTH AND LENGTH OF DAYS TO ALL CLOUDCUCKOO-LANDERS, and also to the Chians—

PISTHETAIROS:

My heart leaps up when someone mentions the Chians!

PRIEST:

AND TO ALL HERO BIRDS AND BIRDSONS OF HEROES: MORE ESPECIALLY TO THE POR-PHYRION, THE WRY PECKER, THE PELICAN, THE PYROPHLEX, THE RUDDY GUINEA, THE PEACOCK, THE MAJOR OUSEL, THE TEAL, THE BANDED BITTERN, THE HERON, THE DISTEL-FINK, THE BALMY PETREL, THE PIPIT, THE GOATGREEN TITMOUSE, THE—

PISTHETAIROS:

Birds, birds, birds! Enough! Why, what a man
you are, to summon all those vultures and sea-eagles
to our Eucharist! Can't you see that a single hawk
could take our entire victim at one gulp?
Go away, and take your portable altar with you.

[*Exit* PRIEST

I'll finish the service myself.

CHORUS: If that is so, it seems that I   [ANTISTROPHE

Must tune my voice again
In sacramental hymnody
    Of even deeper strain:
O Gods, and thou our Patron's God,
Exact no more from us than laud.

Behold our sacrificial beast,
    Sick bones and stringy hair:
If you partake of the thin feast,
    How shall we laymen fare?
Reject our poor oblation, then,
And feed your worshipers. Amen.

PISTHETAIROS:
Let us propitiate the Feathery Gods.

[*Enter a* POET, *singing*

POET:
Cloudcuckooland, my happy home,
    Sung by the Muses Nine—
PISTHETAIROS:
How did this one get in?
                        —Who are you?

POET:
Who am I? A honeythroated bard,
    a 'willing slave of the Muse', as Homer puts it.
PISTHETAIROS:
A slave? With that haircut?
POET:
                        You misunderstand.
I am a poet. All we poets are
'willing slaves of the Muse', as Homer puts it.
PISTHETAIROS:
That cloak of yours has seen service, willing or not.
Speak, O Bard: What catastrophe brings you here?
POET:
In honour of Cloudcuckooland, that great City,
I have composed the following lyric items:
    a] a batch of cyclic verses
    b] a few simple virginations

c] some odes in the manner of Simonidês.

PISTHETAIROS:

God forbid. When did you start writing them?

POET:

Long have I meditated on this City, long.

PISTHETAIROS:

Impossible. Why, only a minute ago
I was dedicating the place, giving it a name!

POET:

Ah, swift is the speech of the Muses,
Yea, swifter than swivelling steeds!
Mark me, man:

Thou Author of Aitna, Father,
At whose dire doom do foregather
All the high hierarchs—
Och! wad
Thy nod
Some giftie gi'e me:

I don't care what, just a token of your regard.

PISTHETAIROS:

He'll be around all day if we don't pay him off.
Here, you in the new overcoat:
take it off and give it to this lyric has-been.

—Put it on. You look as though you were catching cold.

POET:

Thy, Sir, high gratuity
Compels gratitudinity.

Brace yourself. I will now address you
in the vein of Pindar.

PISTHETAIROS:

It's a vein I can do without.

POET:

Ill fares the man amid the Skythian spears,
Beset by Nomads, who no 'pparel wears.
Nil is his number, nameless is his name,
Who hath no garment to refúge his shame.

Do you get me?

PISTHETAIROS:
  I get the idea that you want some underwear.
  —Take that off too, man, and let him have it.
  He's a poet, after all.
                    —There you are. Get out!
POET:
  Out, out, poor poet!
    Sing, O Muse in gold enthroned,
      This chilly City!
    Naked in many a snowbank have I moaned,
      Which seems a pity.
        But still I'll chant, where'er I roam,
          Cloudcuckooland my happy home.
  Alalai!

                              [*Exit* POET

PISTHETAIROS:
  God, what a nuisance! I hope I never meet
  another one like that. How did he hear so soon
  about our City? Well . . .
                    —You, there:
  Go around again with the holy water.
                    [*Enter a* TRAVELLING PROPHET
  DEARLY BELOVED: WE GATHER TOGETHER
    IN—
PROPHET:
              Silence!
  Begin not the sacrifice of the goat!
PISTHETAIROS:
  Who says so?
PROPHET:
              I; an Expounder of Oracles.
PISTHETAIROS:
  Expounders be damned!
PROPHET:
                    Tut. We mustn't blaspheme.
  I come to reveal an oracle of Bakis
  that bears directly on Cloudcuckooland.
PISTHETAIROS:
  In God's name, why did you wait to reveal it

until I'd gone and founded Cloudcuckooland?

PROPHET:
God moves in a mysterious way.

PISTHETAIROS:
                              He does.
Well, since you're here, let's have your revelation.

PROPHET:
    WHAT TIME WOLVES AND WHITE CROWS
    CONFECT BUNGALOWS
    'TWIXT SIKYON AND KORINTH—

PISTHETAIROS:
It's a lie! I never had any dealings with Korinth.

PROPHET:
That is Bakis' way of referring to the Air.
Now listen:
    TO PANDORA THIS DAY
    A WHITE RAM THOU MUST SLAY,
    AND TO WHOSO DIVINES ME THOU SHALT
        NOT REFUSE
    A WARM WINTER SUIT AND A PAIR OF NEW
        SHOES.

PISTHETAIROS:
Does it say shoes?

PROPHET:
                              Look in the book.
    PLUS A GENEROUS CUP,
    PLUS A SLICE OFF THE TOP—

PISTHETAIROS:
A slice off the top, hey?

PROPHET:
                              Look in the book.
    AND IF, GODLY INFANT, THOU DOST AS I SAY,
    A HEAV'N-KISSING EAGLE SHALT THOU BE
        TODAY,
    NOT SO MUCH AS A TITTYMOUSE IF THOU
        SAY'ST NAY.

PISTHETAIROS:
Is that there too?

PROPHET:
Look in the book.

PISTHETAIROS:
Strange. It's so unlike the oracle
I took down from Apollo's dictation.

PROPHET:
What was that one?

PISTHETAIROS:
BUT IF BY ILL HAP A CHEAP ORACLE-MONGER
DISTURBETH THE SERVICE WITH LIES BORN
OF HUNGER,
THOU SHALT BASH IN HIS RIBS—

PROPHET:
I don't believe it says that.

PISTHETAIROS:
Look in the book.
AS FOR HEAV'N-KISSING EAGLES AND ARSE-
KISSING SEERS,
TO HELL WITH THEM ALL. END OF MESSAGE.
[LOUD CHEERS]

PROPHET:
Is that there too?

PISTHETAIROS:
Look in the book.
[*Suddenly losing patience*
Damn you, get out of here!
[*Strikes him with his staff*

PROPHET:
Ouch! I'll go! Ouch!
[*Exit* PROPHET

PISTHETAIROS [*calling after him*]:
Peddle your damned oracles somewhere else!
[*Enter* METON, *wearing a saffron gown embroi-
dered with geometrical figures*

METON:
My aim in coming here—

PISTHETAIROS:
Another headache!

What's your project? And, above all,
why that absurd costume?

METON:

I have come
to subdivide the air into square acres.

PISTHETAIROS:
May I ask who you are?

METON:

You may. My name is Metôn.
The word's a commonplace in Greece and Kolonos.

PISTHETAIROS:
What's that you've got with you?

METON:

An aerial straight-edge.
Observe:
The conformation of the air, considered as
a total entity, is that of a conical damper.
Very well. At the apex of this cone we apply
the ruler, bracketing in the dividers to allow
for the congruent curve. Q.E.D.

PISTHETAIROS:

Q.E.D.?

METON:
We calculate the declination by cathexis
according to the sine. Thus we square the circle.
In the centre we postulate a forum, the focus
of convergent streets that, stelliform,
subtend the radii extended from this point.
Q.E.D.

PISTHETAIROS:
Q.E.D.! The man's a Thalês!
Metôn.

METON:
Yes?

PISTHETAIROS:
I admire you. I really do.
Take my advice and subdivide somewhere else.

METON:
Why? Is it dangerous here?

PISTHETAIROS:
                              Yes, here and in Sparta.
You know how they're treating aliens these days:
nasty demonstrations in the streets.

METON:
You apprehend
seditious manifestations in Cloudcuckooland?

PISTHETAIROS:
God forbid.

METON:
                    Then what?

PISTHETAIROS:
                              Well, we've passed a law
that charlatans shall be whipped in the public square.

METON:
Oh. Then I'd better be going.

PISTHETAIROS:
                              You're almost too late.
Here's a sample, God help you!
                              [*Knocks him down*

METON:
                              My head! My head!

PISTHETAIROS:
I warned you. On your way, and be quick about it!
            [*Exit* METON; *enter an* INSPECTOR, *elegant in full
            uniform, carrying two urns for balloting*

INSPECTOR:
Summon the Consuls.

PISTHETAIROS:
                        Who's this Sardanápalos?

INSPECTOR:
My good man, I am a legally designated
Inspector, empowered to investigate
the civic status of Cloudcuckooland.

PISTHETAIROS:
Your warrant?

INSPECTOR:
                    This illegible document
endorsed by Teleas.

PISTHETAIROS:
                    My dear Inspector,
  it seems a pity to waste your valuable time.
  Suppose you collect your pay and go right home?
INSPECTOR:
  A first-rate idea! As a matter of fact,
  I ought not to have left Athens at all.
  There are certain sensitive foreign affairs—you know?—
  that Pharnakês leaves to me.
PISTHETAIROS:
                              Is that so?
  Here's your pay.
                              [*Slaps his face*
INSPECTOR:
                    Sir, I demand the meaning of this.
PISTHETAIROS:
  It's a sensitive foreign affair.
INSPECTOR:
                    I make formal protest
  that you have assaulted and battered an Inspector.
PISTHETAIROS:
  Take your voting-jugs and get out of my sight!
  It's an outrage:
  Inspectors before there's a City to inspect!
            [*The* INSPECTOR *withdraws, but hides behind one
            of the Acolytes; enter a* DECREE-VENDOR, *who be-
            gins to read from a scroll:*
DECREE-VENDOR:
  'AND IF ANY CLOUDCUCKOOLANDER WHATSO-
  EVER SHALL CAUSE INJURY OR DISTRESS TO
  ANY ATHENIAN CITIZEN WHATSOEVER—'
PISTHETAIROS:
  Another one! A walking law-book this time.
DECREE-VENDOR:
  Your Honor, I am a dealer in the latest decrees.
  Satisfaction guaranteed.
PISTHETAIROS:
                    As for example?

DECREE-VENDOR:

'VOTED: THAT FROM THE DATE HEREINUNDER SUBSCRIBED ALL WEIGHTS MEASURES AND STATUTES WHATSOEVER OF CLOUDCUCKOO-LAND SHALL BE IDENTICAL WITH THE SAME OBTAINING IN OLOPHYXOS.'

PISTHETAIROS:

That ought to fix us.

                 —Look here, you!

DECREE-VENDOR:

What's the matter with you? Something you ate?

PISTHETAIROS:

Go back where you came from with your silly laws,
or you'll get some rough and ready legislation.

         [Strikes him; exit DECREE-VENDOR *hurriedly; the* INSPECTOR *reappears.*

INSPECTOR:

I charge Pisthetairos with felonious assault,
returnable April Session.

PISTHETAIROS:

           How did *you* get back?

           [The DECREE-VENDOR *re-enters.*

DECREE-VENDOR:

'AND IF ANY MAN SHALL SCUTTLE A MAGIS-TRATE AFTER THE NAME OF SAME HAS BEEN POSTED ON THE PILLAR IN ACCORDANCE WITH THE LAW—'

PISTHETAIROS:

Holy God! You too?

           [Drives him away with blows

INSPECTOR:

I'll have your license! This will cost you a cool thousand!

PISTHETAIROS:

I'll smash those jugs of yours in a thousand pieces!

INSPECTOR:

Do you remember the evening you polluted the pillar?

PISTHETAIROS:

Go pollute yourself!

> —Grab him! That's it!
>> [INSPECTOR *escapes.*

Let's hope that's the end of him.
>> —Gentlemen:
If we're going to sacrifice our goat at all,
I'm afraid we'll have to do the job inside.
>> [*Exeunt; manet* CHORUS

🎴 PARABASIS II

>[*The* CHORUS *again address itself to the audience:*

CHORUS:
>We are Lords of Earth and of all upon it, [ODE
>Marking all, all-knowing, in tireless session
>Guiding, weighing, judging the varied drama.
>>Come and adore us!

>Guardians of young fruit in the open orchards,
>Our swift beaks transfix the insect marauder,
>And he falls, struck down by the feath'ry ictus
>>Whirring from heaven.

CHORAGOS: [EPIRRHEMA
You see CRIMINAL WANTED notices everywhere:
'Whoever kills Diágoras the Mêlian,'
So much reward; 'Whoever kills
'A dead tyrant or so,' still more
Reward. Well, then, I proclaim:
'Whoever kills Philokratês the Birdseller,
'One talent, cash; whoever brings him in
'Alive, four talents'—twice as much
As for poor old Diágoras. This Philokratês
Hangs bullfinches on hooks in his shop
And sells them at cut rates; he inflates thrushes
With air pumps and exposes their abused puffy
Bodies for sale; he mutilates blackbirds; he
Stuffs live pigeons into nets and makes them

Act as decoys. That's Philokratês for you!

                                                —And

If any members of this audience
Maintain a bird in a gilded cage at home,
We beg you let it go. Refuse, and you'll see
How quickly the Birds will make decoys of you!

CHORUS:

Joy of birds! In summer the long thick sunlight   [ANTODE
When the locust drones in the trance of noontime:
Mad with sun we shout, and the forest dances
    Heavy with music.

Wintertime is sun on the tropic headlands
Where the Nymphs play counterpoint to our singing;
Spring is myrtle, pang of the pink sweet prickling
    Buds of the Graces.

CHORAGOS:

Now for a word or two, Judges, about   [ANTEPIRRHEMA
This Competition. If you give us the Prize,
We'll pay you better for it than Prince Paris
Was paid by the Goddess. First of all,
The Owls of Laureion will never desert you:
They'll be everywhere in your houses, nesting
In your purses, maniacally producing
Miniature Owls. Judges are fond of Owls.
More than that, we'll add new wings
To your houses: you'll dream that you dwell
In marble halls, and you'll be right.

                                        If your jobs
Are slow pay, if your fingers begin to itch,
We'll send you a little confidential Hawk
To perch on your wrist. For state dinners you can have
The loan of a bird-crop to solve capacity problems.
But if we lose the Prize,
Take portable canopies with you on your strolls,
Or your new white robes will suffer
Avine criticism dropping from the skies.

🎜 SCENE

[Re-enter PISTHETAIROS *with his attendants*

PISTHETAIROS:
The omens are favourable, I'm glad to say.
Strange that we've had no news
about the wall.
—But here comes a messenger now,
puffing like an Olympic sprinter.

[Enter FIRST MESSENGER, *wildly*

MESSENGER:
Where is he? Where is he? Where is he?

PISTHETAIROS:
Where is who?

MESSENGER:
The Chief. Pisthetairos.

PISTHETAIROS:
Here.

MESSENGER:
Great news! Great news!
Your Wall is finished!

PISTHETAIROS:
That *is* great news.

MESSENGER:
Oh how
shall I describe the splendor of that Wall,
the apocalyptic hugeness? Take two chariots,
hitch four fat Wooden Horses to each one,
let Theogenês and old Proxenidês
of Belchertown meet head-on—, they'd pass each other
without a scratch. It's that big.

PISTHETAIROS:
Holy Heraklês!

MESSENGER:
And tall? Look, I measured it myself:
it stands six hundred feet!

PISTHETAIROS:
Merciful Poseidon!

What workmen could build a wall as high as that?

MESSENGER:

Birds, only birds. Not a single Egyptian
hodcarrier or stonemason or carpenter
in the gang; birds did it all, and my eyes
are popping yet.
                                    Imagine thirty thousand Cranes
from Libya, each one with a belly full of stones
for the Rails to shape up with their beaks; ten
thousand Storks, at least,
all of them making bricks with clay and water
flown up by Curlews from the earth below.

PISTHETAIROS:

Mortar?

MESSENGER:

            Herons with hods.

PISTHETAIROS:

                                    How did they manage it?

MESSENGER:

That was a triumph of technology!
The Geese shovelled it up with their big feet.

PISTHETAIROS:

Ah feet, to what use can ye not be put!

MESSENGER:

Why, good Lord! There were Ducks to set the bricks,
and flights of little apprentice Swallows
with trowel tails for the mortar in their bills.

PISTHETAIROS:

Who wants hired labor after this?
—But the joists and beams?

MESSENGER:

                                    All handled by birds.
When the Woodpeckers went to work on those portals
it sounded like a shipyard!
                                    —So there's your Wall,
complete with gates and locks, watchfires burning,
patrols circling, the guard changed every hour.

But I must wash off this long trek of mine.

You'll know what to do next.

[Exit FIRST MESSENGER

CHORAGOS:

Surprises you, hey? That quick job on your Wall?

PISTHETAIROS:

Surprises me? Why, it's a lie come true!
But here's another non-stop messenger,
and this one looks like trouble.

[Enter SECOND MESSENGER: *tragic manner*

MESSENGER:

Alas! Alas! Alas!

PISTHETAIROS:

What's the matter with *you?*

MESSENGER:

Confusion now hath made his masterpiece!
One of the gods, I do not know his name,
has invaded our air and slipped through the gate
right under the beaks of the Jackdaws on day duty.

PISTHETAIROS:

Murther and treason!

—What god did you say?

MESSENGER:

Identity not established. But he has wings,
we know that.

PISTHETAIROS:

Alert the Air Cadets!

MESSENGER:

Cadets! We've alerted everything we have.
Ten thousand mounted Arrowhawks,
to say nothing of claw-to-claw raiders
of every calibre: Kestrels, Buzzards,
Kites, Vultures, Nighthawks, Eagles—
every mortal inch of air
they've ploughed up with their wings, looking for that
    god.
He won't get away,
he's somewhere around here; I feel it in my feathers.

PISTHETAIROS:

Slings and arrows, slings and arrows! All of you,

here: get shooting, quick! Give me my bow!

CHORUS:

> War to the end,   [STROPHE
> Inexpressible war,
> God against Bird!
> Arm to defend
> Our fathers' Air!
> Olympos' host
> Must not get past
> Our border guard!

CHORAGOS:

Each one of you keep watch on every side.
I hear, or seem to hear, an ominous clack
of wings, as though some Deity were descending.
  [*The goddess* IRIS *appears from above, suspended
  in the* machina; *she has broad static wings and
  wears a large rainbow around her head and
  shoulders.*

PISTHETAIROS:

Heave to! Let go halyards! Lower the flaps! Easy all!
          [*The* machina *stops with a violent jerk.*
Who are you? Where are you bound? What's your home
    port?

IRIS [*tragic tone*]:

I come to you from the Olympian gods.

PISTHETAIROS:

Your name? Are you sea-going, or a flying
hat-rack?

IRIS:

          Fleet Iris am I.

PISTHETAIROS:

                    Deep sea or
inland waters?

IRIS:

          What *are* you talking about?

PISTHETAIROS:

Some of you birds had better get on the balls

and board this crate.

IRIS:
                    Board me? I never
heard such a thing!

PISTHETAIROS:
                    Well, you heard it now.
We'll give you something to squawk about.

IRIS:
                                        Well, really!

PISTHETAIROS:
    All right, all right. What gate did you come through?

IRIS:
    How should I know? Gates mean nothing to me.

PISTHETAIROS:
    Oh. So that's the way it is.
                    —Well, then,
    did you report to the Chief Jackdaw? Say something!
    Did you get your passport countersigned by the Storks?
    You did not?

IRIS:
                    Are you in your right mind?

PISTHETAIROS:
                                        Not a single
    bird there punched your card for you?

IRIS:
                                        No, or punched
    anything else for me, you poor idiot.

PISTHETAIROS:
                            So
    you're flying over foreign territory
    without any papers.

IRIS:
                    How else should gods fly?

PISTHETAIROS:
    Good God, how should I know?
                            But they can't do it here!
    I don't care if you're a whole fleet of Irises;
    you've committed a violation, and the penalty
    for that is death.

IRIS:

Mortal, I am immortal.

PISTHETAIROS:

Death just the same!

Things have come to a pretty pass
if we set up a system of border controls, only to have
you gods flying back and forth whenever you feel like it.
But tell me:
What was the destination you had in mind?

IRIS:

Destination? I am about my Father's business.
He has commanded me to remind mankind
that they must sacrifice to the eternal gods,
smiting the hornèd beasts upon their altars
and filling their streets with the smoke of immolation.

PISTHETAIROS:

What do you mean? Sacrifice to what gods?

IRIS:

Why, to us gods in Heaven.

PISTHETAIROS:

So you are gods too?

IRIS:

Can you think of others?

PISTHETAIROS:

I am thinking of the Birds.
So far as mankind is concerned, Birds are now gods.
It's they must have sacrifices—not God, by God!

IRIS:

Alas, deluded worm, think not to stir
the guts of wrath eterne: else heavenly Justice,
with Zeus's pitchfork arm'd, drops from on high
to man's undoing and leaves not a rack
behind. Fried and consumèd shalt thou be,
as i' th' Euripidean Tragedy!

PISTHETAIROS:

Madam, wipe the foam from your mouth,
and do stop quivering so. Am I a slave,
some Lydian or Phrygian slave, that you imagine
you scare me with talk of this kind?

As for Zeus:

you can inform your Zeus
that if he gets in my way I'll burn him out,
yea, I will blast him in Amphíon's hall
with eagles lightningbeak'd that heed my call.
Notify him furthermore
that I command a squadron of six hundred
sky-scaling porphyrion birds in panther skin.
That will hold him, I think: a single Porphyrion once
kept him busy enough.

          —And if *you* get in my way,
Iris or no Iris, messenger or whatever you are,
I'll just hoist up your legs and get in between:
then, by God, you can tell your wondering friends
how you met an old battleship with a triple prow!

IRIS:

No gentleman would address a lady so.

PISTHETAIROS:

On your way! Scat!

IRIS:

          I shall certainly tell my Father.

PISTHETAIROS:

Next time, consume someone your own age!

          [Exit IRIS *in the* machina

CHORUS:

      My word is sure: [ANTISTROPHE
      Children of Zeus,
      No entrance here!
      And it shall stand.
      Let no man dare
      Cajole the skies
      With ritual brand
      Or sacrifice.

PISTHETAIROS:

Speaking of mankind, I am worried about our herald.
It's strange that his commission should keep him so long.

          [Enter a HERALD, *in haste*

HERALD:
  O Pisthetairos! O Blessedest! O Sagaciousest!
  O Superlativest! O Sagaciousest! O Perspicaciousest!
  O Thrice Blessedest! O And-so-forth!

PISTHETAIROS:
                                  Did you speak?

HERALD:
  I crown you with this golden crown, the gift
  of your admiring public.

PISTHETAIROS:
                        I thank you.
  Tell me: Why does mankind admire me?

HERALD:
  O Pisthetairos, mighty father of
  Cloudcuckooland the Beautiful, how slight
  your skill in understanding human thought
  if you must ask that question!
                          What is man?
  Or, rather, what was man before your triumph?
  An abject Spartomaniac—long hair,
  infrequent baths, bad honest food, knobbly
  accessories, the Sokratês pose.
                          What is man now?
  Mad about birds! Birds, birds, from the moment
  they get out of nest in the morning: eggs and birdseed
  for breakfast, and then bird business,
  reeding and piping till clucking-off time.
  They even affect bird names:
  'Partridge' is any man gone in one leg;
  Menippos is 'Swallow'; Opûntios,
  'Monocle de Mon Oncle'; Philoklês
  is 'Lark'; Theogenês, 'Gypsy Goose'; Lykûrgos,
  'Ibis'; Chairephôn, 'Bats'; Syrakosios, 'Jaybird';
  and Meidias, of course, is called 'Goon Quail'—
  one look at that bashed-in face of his
  will tell you why.
                  As for song-writing,
  you can't so much as buy a hearing unless
  you stuff your lyrics with assorted wild ducks

and swallows, or doves, or geese, or maybe
a few last feathers from a cast-off wing.

That's what it's like down there. And mark my words:
you'll soon be getting visitors by the thousands,
all sorts of men begging to be fitted out
with wings and beaks and claws. Take my advice
and lay in a pile of pinions.

PISTHETAIROS:

                        Heavens, yes!
I can see we'll be busy.
            —Quick, you:
                          [*To a* SERVANT
fill every last basket you can find with wings
and tell Manês to bring them out to me here.
I want to be prepared for these gentlemen.

CHORUS:

      My city is Cloudcuckooland,   [STROPHE
         And men of every nation
      Confer on us, I understand,
         Ecstatic approbation.

PISTHETAIROS:

      And surplus population.

CHORUS:

      What wonder though it should be so?
         Here Love and Wisdom dwell,
      And through the streets the Graces go,
         And Peace contrives her spell.

PISTHETAIROS:

      The servant problem's hell!

CHORUS: [ANTISTROPHE
      Manês, awake! New wings, new beaks!
         Surely there never was
      A slower slave. Your master speaks!

The precious moments pass!
                    [*Enter* MANES *emptyhanded*

PISTHETAIROS:
        This Manês is an ass.

                            [*Exit* MANES

CHORUS:
        Wings make the man; let each man wear
            The crest that suits his bent:
        Musician, merchant, privateer,
            Cleric, or laic gent,
                    [*Re-enter* MANES *as before*

PISTHETAIROS:
        Or slave of snail descent.

    Manês, I swear by All Hawks, I'll haul you
    hairless if you don't get busy! Come on; service!
            [*General confusion.* MANES *and other servants
            appear and reappear carrying wings of all shapes
            and sizes. These are arranged on a bench.*
PARRICIDE [*within, singing*]:
    'Ah that the eagle's eager wings were mine,
    To gyre above the waste of bloomless brine!'
PISTHETAIROS:
    That messenger seems to have been right.
    Here comes somebody singing about eagles.
                            [*Enter a young* PARRICIDE
PARRICIDE:
    Here we are!
    I vow, there's nothing like flying.
                                —Sir,
    I'm mad about birds, I'm
    always up in the air. More than that,
    I apply for citizenship under your laws.
PISTHETAIROS:
    What laws? We Birds have many laws.

PARRICIDE:
    All of them; especially that glorious statute
    that gives Birds the right to strangle their own fathers.

PISTHETAIROS:
    We *do* consider it a sign of manliness
    when a chick stands up to his father and faces him down.

PARRICIDE:
    Exactly my own motive in emigrating:
    I propose to throttle the old man for his property.

PISTHETAIROS:
    At the same time we have an ancient decree
    (you'll find it in the Book of Storks) that says:
    STORKLINGS CARED FOR BY THE STORK THEIR
        SIRE
    AND BY HIM TAUGHT TO FLY SHALL IN THEIR
        TURN
    CARE FOR THE STORK THEIR SIRE IN HIS OLD
        AGE.

PARRICIDE:
    What was the use of my coming all this distance
    if I've got to support my father after all?

PISTHETAIROS:
    Come, it's not so bad.
    You obviously mean well, and we'll make
    a decent orphan bird of you yet, young man.
    But first
    permit me to recite a useful thought
        'that was given me
        at my mother's knee':
    Sons, don't beat your fathers. It's unkind.

           [*During the following speech* PISTHETAIROS *arms*
           the PARRICIDE *with a top sword, shield, and*
                          helmet.

    Stick out your hand: receive this bright cock-spur.
    Your other hand: receive this shining wing.
    Stick out your neck: receive this crested helm.
    Now you're in the Army, cock.
    Keep awake on guard duty, live on your pay. and let
    your father alone. If you feel like fighting,

take a trip to Thrace: there's always a war on there.
PARRICIDE:
You're right. I'll do it, by God!

[*Exit*

PISTHETAIROS:

By God, you'd better!
[*Enter the dithyrambic poet* KINESIAS

KINESIAS [*singing*]:
'Lifted aloft on wings of song,
Towards high Olympos winging—'
PISTHETAIROS:
This man needs wings if ever a poet did!
KINESIAS [*singing*]:
'Pure in mind, in body strong,
Ever of thee, love, singing—'
PISTHETAIROS:
Kinêsias, as I live. Old limpety-lop,
why did your limping feet bring you up here?
KINESIAS [*singing*]:
'I aim, nor shall my purpose fail,
To be a Neo-Nightingale.'
PISTHETAIROS:
Damn your aim. I suppose you can talk sense?
KINESIAS:
Oh, ay. Enwingèd, man, by thee I'd be,
that from the gravid clouds I may charm down
a meed of music for my sacred soul,
'Batter'd by ev'ry wind that blows,
And snow'd upon by snowing snows.'
PISTHETAIROS:
This meed of music: you find it in the clouds?
KINESIAS:
Yea, i' the clouds my Muse doth perch and preen.
Wottest thou not that th' dithyrambic gene
burns in the air, most dark, and bright with gloom?
Plastic with pinions, too.
I'll give you an example.
PISTHETAIROS:
Never mind.

KINESIAS:
> No trouble at all. For instance,
here's a description of the upper air:
> *Pteroid shapes*
> *Thro' th' aether traipse,*
> *Longneck'd wrynecks—*

PISTHETAIROS:
Hard alee!

KINESIAS:
> *Zigging upon the zagging blast,*
> *Free in the vast anemoplast—*

PISTHETAIROS:
By God, I'll free your blast!

KINESIAS:
> *Free to fly at the wind's behest,*
> *Now north, now south, now east, now west:*
> *Furrowing with my feather'd feet*
> *Those fields where eagles eagles meet,*
> *Praying a blessing on thy name,*
> *Old Architect, for this high game.*

PISTHETAIROS:
Stop and put on your wings, damn it, your wings!

> *[A brief scuffle about the stage*

KINESIAS:
And is it thus thoudst serve a modern poet?
A poet to whom so many tribes lay claim?

PISTHETAIROS:
Let Leotrophidês claim you to train his squabs!

KINESIAS:
Thou mockest me, proud Patriarch. Farewell.
These wings I'll flap, high water come or hell.

> *[Exit* KINESIAS. *Enter an* INFORMER, *singing, un-*
> *noticed at first in the confusion of the poet's*
> *departure*

INFORMER:
> 'What birds are these whose patchwork dress
> Reveals that they are penniless?
> O Swallow, Swallow, tell me.'

PISTHETAIROS [*aside*]:
  That Kinêsias was a rough customer.
                                —And, by God,
  here comes another one!
INFORMER:
      'O Swallow, Swallow, tell me.'
  I repeat.
PISTHETAIROS:
        He seems to be singing about his coat.
  Can't blame him: it would take more than one swallow
  to make that bearable.
INFORMER:
                A little service, please!
  Who's distributing wings here?
PISTHETAIROS:
                  Just step this way.
  Now then: what do you want?
INFORMER:
                  Wings, man, wings.
  You deaf?
PISTHETAIROS:
        I suppose you're in a hurry
  to get to a clothier's.
INFORMER:
                Wrong. Plumb wrong.
  I am a process-server for the Islands.
  Also an Informer.
PISTHETAIROS:
              Thanks for the information.
INFORMER:
  Also a professional accuser. So I need some wings.
  Great thing for this Island Circuit. Big business.
PISTHETAIROS:
  A pair of wings will make your business bigger?
INFORMER:
  Couldn't. But the pirates, you know: always hanging
      around.
  With wings I could fly right over them like a crane,

belly full of lawsuits for ballast.

PISTHETAIROS:

Of course you could.
Tell me: are you good at spying on aliens?

INFORMER:
Well, a man's got to live. I never learned how to work.

PISTHETAIROS:
Aren't there enough honest jobs in the world,
that a healthy man like you
must pick up money selling false information?

INFORMER:
Wings I came for, not sermons.

PISTHETAIROS:

I just gave you wings.

INFORMER:
The devil you did. All you've done is talk.

PISTHETAIROS:
Haven't you ever heard of 'wingèd words'?

INFORMER:
Wingèd words?

PISTHETAIROS:

Yes, or wingèd actions?
Say you go into a barber's. Well, they're all
sitting around there, swapping lies
about their sons and grandsons. 'I swear to God,'
one of them says,
'I don't know what to make of that boy of mine.
'The horses have got him. Can't keep his feet on the
    ground.'
Another one says, 'That's nothing.
'Mine wants to take a flier at writing plays.
'The tragic bug's bitten him.'

INFORMER:

So you think
words can make wings?

PISTHETAIROS:

That's it exactly.
Words heighten concepts; words raise a man
out of himself. You came to me for wings:

all right, you can have them; and, what's more,
I'll throw in a word or two of good advice
about getting a job that you won't have to blush for.
INFORMER:
No good. No good at all.
PISTHETAIROS:

                    Why not?
INFORMER:
Family pride. Can't let the old name down.
There's been Informers in our family
since I don't know when.
                                        —But come:
give me a couple of good swift wings, I don't care
what model, and I'll get back,
denounce a few aliens, get them indicted here,
and then I'm off.
PISTHETAIROS:

                You mean you'll have these men
indicted before they get a chance to appear?
INFORMER:
You said it.
PISTHETAIROS:

                And while they're on their way to court
you'll swoop down on the Islands and grab their goods?
INFORMER:
You get the idea. I'm busy as a top.
PISTHETAIROS: *[Takes a long whiplash from the bench*
Top? Here's something to make tops spin:
first-class gods from Korkyra.
INFORMER:

                            Put it away!
PISTHETAIROS:
Call it a pair of wings. By God, it'll send *you*
into a nose-dive!
                                [Lashes him
INFORMER:

            Stop it! Police! Stop it!
                            [Exit INFORMER

PISTHETAIROS:
  All of a flap, hey? Can't wait around? Too bad!
  You sneaking patriot,
  this time you pay the court costs!
                              [*To his attendants*
                        Come,
  let's gather up these wings and go inside.
          [*Exit, followed by attendants carrying the bench,
          wings, and the rest of the paraphernalia*

🎭 CHORIKON: CHORAL INTERLUDE

CHORUS: [STROPHE
  Numberless are the world's wonders, and we
  Have roosted on most of them. In wicked Thrace
  There grows the remarkable Kleonymos tree,
  Immense, heart-rotted, that in summer yields
  Informative fruit; but in winter time its grace
  Forsakes it, and its boughs shed unused shields.

  And we have seen a region of the dead   [ANTISTROPHE
  Where men with Heroes dine before nightfall,
  But where the reveller walks home in dread
  Lest from the shades a new Orestês come,
  Accost him at the turning of the wall,
  Strip him, beat him, and leave him bare and numb.

🎭 SCENE

          [*Enter* PROMETHEUS, *muffled from head to foot
          in a red and yellow cloak and carrying a large
          black open umbrella.*
PROMETHEUS:
  I hope to God Zeus can't see me!
                              —Pisthetairos!
  Where's Pisthetairos?
                              [*Re-enter* PISTHETAIROS

PISTHETAIROS:

What's going on here?
Who are you in the blankets?

PROMETHEUS:

Look:
is any god following me?

PISTHETAIROS:

God? No.
Who are you?

PROMETHEUS:

Can you give me the correct time?

PISTHETAIROS:

Noon. Maybe a little later. But who
are you?

PROMETHEUS:

Noon, you said?

PISTHETAIROS:

Oh, for God's sake!

PROMETHEUS:

What's the weather like?

PISTHETAIROS:

Hey?

PROMETHEUS:

I said, 'What's
the weather like?'

PISTHETAIROS:

Go to hell!

PROMETHEUS:

Splendid. I'll just
take off these cerements.

[*Throws off the cloak and stands revealed in
scarlet tights.*

PISTHETAIROS:

Well, I'll be damned! Prometheus!

PROMETHEUS:

Sh, sh, keep your voice down!

PISTHETAIROS:

What's the matter?

PROMETHEUS:
   Just don't mention my name. If Zeus finds me here
   he'll scalp me. You don't know the half of it.
   I'll tell you; only,
   please hold this umbrella over my head
   so the gods can't look down and see me from up there.
PISTHETAIROS:
   The same old Prometheus! All right; get under,
   and begin to talk.
PROMETHEUS:
   Listen.
PISTHETAIROS:
         I am.
PROMETHEUS:
               Zeus is through.
PISTHETAIROS:
                        Since when?
PROMETHEUS:
   Since you organized Cloudcuckooland.
   There's not been so much as a sniff of sacred smoke
   coming up to us from a single human altar.
   I swear, we're hungrier
   than a Thesmophoria fast-day; and, what's worse,
   the damnedest lot of starving yowling gods
   from the back country are talking about revolt
   if Zeus doesn't manage to get a decent consignment
   of sacrificial cuts to keep us going.
PISTHETAIROS:
   Do you mean to tell me the Barbarians
   have gods of their own?
PROMETHEUS:
            What about Exekestidês?
   Doesn't he have to pray to something?
PISTHETAIROS:
                              I see.
   But these godforsaken gods: what are they called?
PROMETHEUS:
   Triballians.

PISTHETAIROS:
          Tribal totems.

PROMETHEUS:
               I suppose so.
—But this is what I have come down to tell you:
Zeus and these Triballians
are sending a delegation to look into
what's going on here. Take my advice:
laugh at every offer they make to you
until they swear to restore the Birds to power
and give you Basileia for a wife.

PISTHETAIROS:
Basileia? Who is this Basileia?

PROMETHEUS:
She's the prettiest girl you ever saw:
manages Zeus, takes care of his thunderbolts
and all the rest of his weapons—sagacity,
legislation, rearmament, ideology, ultimatums,
revenue officers, jurymen—

PISTHETAIROS:
               She does all that?

PROMETHEUS:
That's only an outline. When you get Basileia,
you've got everything.
             I thought I ought to tell you:
I have a certain stake in humanity.

PISTHETAIROS:
A well-broiled one, thanks to your foresightedness.

PROMETHEUS:
And I hate the gods.

PISTHETAIROS:
           And the gods hate you.

PROMETHEUS:
Yes. I'm a regular Timôn.
           —But it's late.
I must be getting back.
          Give me my umbrella:
Zeus will think I'm a Virgin of the Escort.

PISTHETAIROS:

Take this footstool with you; it will make a better effect.

[*Exeunt*

⚜ CHORIKON: CHORAL INTERLUDE

CHORUS:

> There is a mystic river   [STROPHE
> In the land of the Shadowfeet
> Where Sokratês the Bathless calls
> The souls of men to meet.
>
> There Chickenheart Peisandros
> Made sacrifice one day
> To conjure up his own dim soul
> And hear what it would say.
>
> Odysseus-like he cut the throat
> Of a kind of camel-cat;
> But all he raised was the squeaking ghost
> Of Chairephôn the Bat.

⚜ SCENE

> [*Enter the Ambassadors from Olympos:* PO-
> SEIDON, HERAKLES, *and a* TRIBALLIAN GOD. *The
> first wears a sea-weed crown, a cloak embroidered
> with large horse-heads, and carries a trident and
> a rigid stuffed fish; the second wears a lion skin
> and carries a club; the third, blackface, wears
> a stovepipe hat and is desperately entangled in
> a multicoloured cloak.*

POSEIDON:

So this is Cloudcuckooland. Very well,
let us proceed to act like a Delegation.

[*To the* TRIBALLIAN

You, there,

what are you up to now? Don't you know better
than to drape your cloak on the left side? Look,
you celestial rustic, it ought to hang on the right,
gracefully, like this. Do you want these people
to take you for Laispodias? Hold still,
can't you? There!
Democracy, what sins are committed in thy name!
Damn it, of all the barbarous gods I've met
you're the barbarousest.

                                  —What's your plan, Heraklês?

HERAKLES:
You heard what I said. Just croak the guy
what shut the gods out with this here Stone Curtain.

POSEIDON:
Yes, my good fellow; but we're supposed to discuss peace.

HERAKLES:
All the more reason for croaking him, I say.
            [Enter PISTHETAIROS *attended by various birds*
            in kitchen costume; he elaborately disregards the
            Ambassadors.

PISTHETAIROS:
                                            Quick, now,
let's have the cheesegrater. Where's the horseradish?
Grate that cheese, somebody. Keep the fire hot.

POSEIDON:
In the name of the Divine Authority,
three gods greet thee, O Man.

PISTHETAIROS:
                        The horseradish.

HERAKLES:
Say, Mac, what kind of a roast is that?

PISTHETAIROS:
Bird roast. Subjects condemned for subversion
of the Authority of the Birds.

HERAKLES:
                        And you use
horseradish?

PISTHETAIROS:
            Why, it's Heraklês! Good

afternoon, Heraklês.

POSEIDON:

                    The Divine Authority
empowers three gods to consider conciliation.

A COOK:

Oil's out. What do I do now?

HERAKLES:

                              No oil?
Damn bad. You can't barbecue without oil.

POSEIDON:

Regarded disinterestedly, this war
subserves no aim of the Divine Authority.
Similarly, your Delegates should reflect
how much you have to gain from a friendly Olympos:
I instance only
fresh rain water for your swamps, and halcyon days.
Shall we initiate talks?

PISTHETAIROS:

                         I don't see why.
In the first place, we were not the ones
who started hostilities. But let that pass.
As for peace, we are perfectly willing to agree
if the gods will meet our terms. We demand
restoration of our ancient sovereignty
and the return of the sceptre to the Birds.
Let Zeus accept that much, and I'll invite
all three of you to dinner.

HERAKLES:

                          I vote Yes.

POSEIDON:

You gastric monomaniac, would you vote away
your own Father's crown?

PISTHETAIROS:

                        That's a silly question.
Do you gods imagine that you will be losing power
by delegating the imperium of the skies?
Surely you know that all over the earth
men are hiding under clouds and breaking your laws
with impunity. Suppose you had the Birds

on your side: then if a man swore
by Zeus and the Crow, say, and broke his oath,
we'd simply have a Crow swoop down upon him
and peck out his right eye.

POSEIDON:

Good, by Myself!

HERAKLES:
I think so too.

PISTHETAIROS [*to* TRIBALLIAN]:
What do *you* say?

TRIBALLIAN:

Wockle.

HERAKLES:
The poor fish says Yes.

PISTHETAIROS:

And here's something else.
Suppose a man promises an offering
to some god or other, and maybe greed
gets the better of him, and he thinks: *Well,
the gods are used to waiting:*

we birds
will know how to handle him.

POSEIDON:

How? Instruct me.

PISTHETAIROS:
Well, say that man's
sitting in his office some day, counting his money,
or say he's in the tub enjoying a nice hot bath:
down comes one of the Kites when he isn't looking
and zooms off to Olympos with a couple of his sheep.

HERAKLES:
I say it again: give the Birds what they ask for.

POSEIDON:
What do *you* think?

PISTHETAIROS:

Speak, you divine Mistake.

TRIBALLIAN:
Treeballs beetee gnaw ouch, Glapp.

HERAKLES:

> He says Yes.

POSEIDON:

> If you say so. I suppose I must say so too.
> Very well. Divine Authority cedes the Sceptre.

PISTHETAIROS:

> Hold on! I nearly forgot.
> The Birds are prepared to confirm Zeus' right to Hêra, but in return
> they insist upon my having Basileia.

POSEIDON:

> I can see that you are not interested in peace.
> Good-bye.

PISTHETAIROS:

> It makes no difference to me.
> —Now this gravy, cook: see that it's thick enough.

HERAKLES:

> Hey, damn it, Admiral, hold on, what the hell?
> Who wants to fight a war for a damn woman?

POSEIDON:

> What else can we do?

HERAKLES:

> Damn it, make peace!

POSEIDON:

> Idiot, can't you see he's trying to ruin you?
> And you walk right into the trap.
> Think a moment: if Zeus
> gives the Birds what they ask for, and then dies—
> Where are you then? Where's your inheritance?

PISTHETAIROS:

> Heraklês, don't listen to the man.
> Every word he speaks is a delusion.
>
> *[Beckons him aside*
>
> Step over here a minute.
> —My poor fellow,
> that Ancient Mariner is just leading you on.
> *You* inherit from Zeus? You couldn't, not a penny.
> You, being a bastard—

HERAKLES:
Me, a bastard?

Say, listen, you—

PISTHETAIROS:
Well, your mother

was an alien, wasn't she? Besides, Athenê
is heir apparent, and how could she be that
if she had legitimate brothers?

HERAKLES:
What if the Boss

says I'm his heir, bastard or no bastard?

PISTHETAIROS:

Illegal. And suppose he does:
Poseidôn will be the first to contest the will,
as the decedent's brother.
Here is the law,

straight from Solôn:

A BASTARD SHALL NOT INHERIT IF THERE BE
    LEGITIMATE ISSUE. IF THERE BE NO LEGITI-
    MATE ISSUE, THE PROPERTY SHALL PASS TO
    THE NEXT OF KIN.

HERAKLES:

So I can't get nothing out of the Old Man's estate?

PISTHETAIROS:

Nothing at all.
—For that matter,

has your Father enrolled you yet?

HERAKLES:
No. I guess I know why.

Come, what's the use of snapping at empty wind?
Join the Birds:
you'll live like a king and feed on pie in the sky.
[They return to the others

HERAKLES:

About that dame we were beating our gums about:
I said, and I say it again: Give him what he wants.

PISTHETAIROS:

You, Poseidon?

POSEIDON:
                    No.
PISTHETAIROS:
                    Then the Triballian
must break the tie. Vote, heavenly Hayseed!
TRIBALLIAN:
  Quiffing gamsel cockitty, gotta tweet tweet.
HERAKLES:
  He says Yes.
POSEIDON:
                    I doubt very much if he says Yes
or anything else that matters. But let it pass.
HERAKLES:
  He's ready to pass her over, anyhow.
POSEIDON:
  Have it your way, you two. Make your peace,
and I'll hold mine.
HERAKLES:
                    These here top-level talks
are all over, and we say he gets the green light.
Come on, man, you got a date up in the sky
with Basileia and any other damn thing you want.
PISTHETAIROS:
  It's a lucky thing that I had these roasts ready.
They'll do for the wedding.
HERAKLES:
                    You birds run along:
I'll stick around here and keep an eye on the cook.
POSEIDON:
  Can't you rise superior to food? You come with us.
PISTHETAIROS:
  And somebody bring along my wedding clothes.
                    [*Exeunt omnes; manet* CHORUS

❧ CHORIKON: CHORAL INTERLUDE

CHORUS:
  Phonéya is that far country   [ANTISTROPHE

Where the Englottogasters dwell:
They plough the fields there with their tongues
And sow and reap as well.

Oh blest Englottogasters!
And yet we need not roam
In search of tongues as versatile—
They twitch for us at home:

The tongue that tells for ready cash,
The slimy tongue that smiles,
The paid, applauded, patriot tongue
That guards us, and defiles.

 ÉXODOS

[*Enter* THIRD MESSENGER

MESSENGER:
Thrice happy generation of Birds, O winged
with joy beyond words' contriving: receive
your great Prince in his palace of delight!
His glory burns: no star
flames brighter in the wheeling vault, no sun
has ever blazed so pure. He comes,
and beauty walks beside him crowned
with lightning from God's hand, his divine
Bride, veiled i' th' smoke of incense rising.
Your King, your Queen!
Sing them a song of the Nine Sisters' devising.

[*Re-enter* PISTHETAIROS, *splendidly gowned, with
newly gilded wings; he is accompanied by*
BASILEIA, *in cloth of gold, crowned, her face
hidden by a veil.*

CHORUS:
Back!
Make way there!
Circle them!
Dance!

Beat on the bright ground with quick feet
For the Prince of Luck, for his Bride—
 Oh sweet! Oh fair!—
Dance, dance the marriage in the air.

CHORAGOS:
Dance in the sky,
 joy in the sky!
Dance in the reign of the Birds,
 dance in
The augury of his polity:
Dance Hymen
 the wedding chorus
 dance

CHORUS:
 When heavenly Hêra was the bride   [STROPHE
 Of Zeus in his high hall,
 The Fatal Ladies danced and sang
 This for their festival:
 Round the royal pair we go:
 Hymen O! The wedding O!

 Erôs flicked his golden wings   [ANTISTROPHE
 To be their charioteer,
 And through the swaying skies their car
 Darted in sweet career.
 Round the royal pair we go:
 Hymen O! The wedding O!

PISTHETAIROS:
For your songs, for your good wishes, thanks:
I am gratified, and I am sure
that I speak for my wife as well. I should be
even more gratified to hear you perform
two or three odes in honor of my triumph
over the dangerous thunderbolts of Zeus,
the difficult lightning.

CHORUS:

      O fire lancing the black night,   [EPODE
        O rage of voices under ground,
      Thunder, hurly of rain, bright
        Tempest of sound:
      Sing, sing his audacity
        Who draws down from God's throne
      God's Basileia, Sovereignty,
        And crowns her his own.
              Round the royal pair we go:
              Hymen O! The wedding O!

PISTHETAIROS:

   Follow the bridal, follow, fortunate friends,
   to the high lands of God, to the happy bed.
   And oh my darling, take
   my wings in your shining hands, and I
   will lift you, lift you above the sky
   in the Birds' dance, the whirring dance.

CHORUS:

      Iô! Iô!
          Iê Paián! Alalaí!
        See the conquering hero go!
        Hymen O! The wedding O!

NOTES

Σ = Scholiast

Page	Line

207   1   *Persons Represented*: The Protagonist's name is in doubt. 'Peisthetairos', attested by most of the MSS., is unsatisfactory; of various other forms, 'Pisthetairos'—'trusty friend'—seems to be the best.

207   26   The scene is deliberately vague. Although Pisthetairos and Euelpidês have come on foot from Athens, the site of the future Cloudcuckooland seems neither terrestrial nor aerial: a dream region, suitable for a dream city. If the transformed King Tereus has chosen to remain in the country that he ruled as a man, the location is Thrace—northward, at any rate, in the direction of witchcraft and delusion.

208   16   Tereus was a king of Thrace who violated Philomelê, the sister of his wife Proknê, and tore out her tongue so that she should not tell. The sisters avenged themselves by cooking Itys, Tereus' infant son, and serving him up to his father at dinner. The gods' criticism of this Faulknerian episode took the form of changing all three agonists into birds: Tereus became a Hoopoe, Proknê a Swallow, and Philomelê a Nightingale. It is worth noting that A. follows the variant that transforms Proknê, not Philomelê, into the Nightingale. Moreover, she seems to have forgiven Tereus for his affair with her sister, and Tereus has forgotten the dreadful business about Itys. The Nightingale and the Hoopoe are on exemplary domestic terms with each other.

209   9   A losing war is hard on the national nerves, but A.'s grievance against Athens is that of any intelligent citizen whose government has yielded to fanaticism and public hysteria. Certainly there were traitors and dangerous malcontents in Athens, working for Sparta or for their own interests, but it is also true that the

292

inevitable Informer was providing harmless citizens and defenceless aliens with all too many 'opportunities/to appear in court' on 'loyalty' charges. After the scandals that attended the sailing of the Sicilian Expedition (415 B.C.) professional patriotism had become a golden racket.

213   1   *The Twelve Gods*: Zeus, Hêra, Poseidôn, Deméter, Hephaistos, Arês, Athenê, Artemis, Aphroditê, Hestía, Apollo, Hermês.

213   5   *It's Sophoklês' fault*: The reference is to the *Tereus* of Sophoklês, a play no longer extant.

215   19   *the Red Sea*: 'He means Arabia Felix,' says Σ. Actually he means Cockaigne or Arcady, Bali or Boston, or whatever your personal Eldorado may be.

216   7   *It's a non-stop honeymoon!*: Bridal wreaths were made of mint leaves and myrtle-berries. Poppy seeds dipped in honey were esteemed as an aphrodisiac and eaten at weddings. The sesame plant was associated with Aphroditê.

220   26   *gargling in the glade*: The word (ἐπῷξε) is unexpectedly harsh. Pisthetairos is disappointed by the Hoopoe's apparent failure to attract an audience.

221   1   The *Párodos* is the formal entrance of the Chorus into the *orchêstra,* and in *Aves* it is almost entirely spectacle. There is relatively little singing for the Chorus, and the chief interest lies in the costumes of the individual Birds and in the commenting dialogue. Here, as throughout the play, the Choragos is spokesman for the Chorus as a whole.

221   10   *Bird of Araby*: This is the Cock, the Persian Bird, here called *Mêdos*, 'the Median'. (The phallic pun is the same in Greek as in English.) My 'Araby' is a licence, intended to make the 'camel' more assimilable.

222   4   *'Kallias : Hipponikos : : Hipponikos : Kallias II'*: The names are *ad hoc*, for illustrative purposes. In ordinary circumstances the grandson takes his grandfather's name. The Hoopoe is explaining the presence on stage of a younger Hoopoe, whom we may call Hoopoe II. Philoklês was a tragic poet of unsavory

reputation (Σ) who plagiarized the *Tereus* of Sophoklês: that is to say, the monstrous cohabitation of Philoklês with Sophoklês' 'Lady' Hoopoe produced Hoopoe
II. Kallias, grandson of Kallias I, was a real enough
person: dissolute and wasteful ('always getting
plucked'), he is best remembered for Plato's making his
house the scene of the *Protágoras*.

223   4   *Magpie,* &c. Some of A.'s birds, in this list and later,
are no longer identifiable—'a bird of some sort,' says
Σ—; and the translation reflects this uncertainty.

226   8   *They'll keep the Owl from attacking us*: Athenê invented pottery; hence the Owl, sacred to her, will not
attack pots.

227   5   *related to my wife*: Proknê was the daughter of King
Pandiôn of Athens, hence of the same 'tribe' as
Pisthetairos and Euelpidês.

228   10   *National Cemetery*: Here were buried those Athenians
who died in battle for their country. The reservation
was called Kerameikos, which is 'Pottersville' rather
than 'Potter's Field'.

228   13   *Gettysbird*: The bloodless one-day siege of Orneai
(416 B.C.); hence, no one died in that battle. The
Greek name makes the pun inevitable.

230   5   *Monk the Knifeman*: From the disorderly gossip of Σ
we gather that this was one Panaitios, a grumpy ugly
cutler who had an actively amorous wife. The general
purport seems to be: 'You lay off me, and I'll lay
off you'. Panaitios' nickname was Pithêkos, 'Monkey'.

231   9   *Do you see dinner coming?*: Pisthetairos, in accordance
with correct procedure at the beginning of an address,
has asked for the ceremonial wreath and the lustral
water. Euelpidês affects to mistake this for preparation
for a formal dinner.

232   7   *Hyde Lark*: The Greek says that when the Lark's
father died he was encephalated, or hidden in the
Lark's head—an absurd allusion to the gestation of
Athenê. Euelpidês sees a chance for a joke about the
place-name Kephalai, which means 'heads'.

233   13   *to prostrate themselves*: Probably a genuflection (Σ). At any rate it is to be taken literally: the Kite was so greeted as the harbinger of spring. Euelpidês, carrying his market money in his mouth, seems to have genuflected too vigorously.

233   24   *'Cuckoo! Back to the furrows . . .'*: The meaning of the proverb is obscure; *sed latet,* as the Commentators happily remark, *spurci aliquid.*

234   17   *'Holy Kites!'*: Lampôn, possibly because he didn't want to be bound by his oracles, used to confirm them with this diluted oath; or maybe he was one of those mistaken persons who think that 'My Cow!', or something of the sort, avoids the profanity of 'My God!'

236   7   The attendant or surrogate birds are appropriate. Aphroditê's phalarope is suggested by *phallos*; as a sea god, Poseidôn should have a water bird; cormorants, like Heraklês, are greedy; and it has always been the wren, not the eagle, who is King of the Birds.

236   13   *the Good Gosh*: Not a softening, like Lampôn's oath noted above, but a whimsical variation: *Zan* for *Zeus.*

238   13   *'One crow caws down . . .'*: A parody of a line of Hesiod (Frag. 50): 'Nine generations lives the cawing crow'. [Σ]

239   14   *A poor thing of twigs and straw*: The Hoopoe's nest is proverbially filthy, Proknê being a career musician rather than housewife.

241   14   PARÁBASIS: At this point the action of the play is suspended while the author, speaking through the Choragos, addresses the audience. The Parábasis proper begins as a parody of the Theogonies, the philosophical accounts of the origin of the gods and the creation of the world; but this tone, which is precariously balanced between the solemn and the bantering, passes into mild topical satire.

242   12   *Laid a wind-egg*: This is an unfertilized egg, appropriate for the genesis of Love. Σ obscurely alludes to the Ledaian egg from which the Heavenly Twins, Kastor and Polydeukês, were hatched.

Page   Line
243   2   *Orestês of the Alleys*: This hoodlum with the glorious
              nickname, who is mentioned again on p. 278, seems
              to have impressed A. rather deeply. He must also
              have had a sense of humor, for there is something
              comic, to the non-participant, in his habit of stripping
              his victims of all their clothes after robbing them.

243   12   *You see Bird in everything*: Birds as omens, a fashion-
              able fad.

246   11   *a full-fledged Horsecock*: An unhappy Aischylean com-
              pound, which A. ridicules again in *Ranae*. Aischylos
              intended it as a kind of heraldic beast, half fowl, half
              horse, a figurehead for a ship.

246   20   '*I shot an arrow . . .*': Pisthetairos quotes a verse
              from the lost *Myrmidones* of Aischylos, where a
              wounded eagle recognizes his own feathers on the
              shaft of the arrow that struck him.

248   2   '*what boots a mailèd warrior goddess*': The whole
              speech parodies a passage from the lost *Meleagros* of
              Euripidês.

248   4   *the Pelargic Wall*: This was a part of the fortifications
              of the Akropolis. The more common name was 'Pelas-
              gic'; 'Pelargic', however, has the advantage of meaning
              'Stork [Wall]'.

248   13   *And fall off the ladder*: There is no authority for
              assigning this interpolation and the next one to
              Euelpidês, but surely the conjecture is allowable.
              Incorporated in Pisthetairos' speech they have no
              comic force at all.

249   22   *a leather beak-rest*: The Crow, as *auletês*, or flute ac-
              companist for the singing, would be wearing a leather
              lip-guard.

250   3   *Artemis Siskin*: One of the mystical names of Artemis
              was Kolainis (Σ). The *Akalanthis* is a bird, the siskin.
              This is straining for a pun; but a pun of sorts emerges.

252   9   *Author of Aitna*: The Poet's lyrics are a farrago of
              imperfectly remembered fragments from the standard
              poets. Here he is mutilating a Pindaric ode on Hiero,
              Tyrant of Syracuse and founder of the town of Aitna.

Page	Line	
261	18	*Owls of Laureion*: Coins begetting smaller coins; see Index of Names *s.v.* LAUREION.
263	2	*Egyptian hodcarrier*: A. is thinking of the accounts—Herodotos, for example—of the building of the Pyramids by the slave workmen of Cheops.
263	5	*Cranes from Libya*: Because of their improbable shape, cranes were supposed to need a ballast of stones in order to fly.
263	14	*Ah feet . . .* : A proverb; but Pisthetairos substitutes 'feet' for the 'hands' of the original.
267	22	*Euripidean Tragedy*: 'In the [lost] *Likymnios* of Euripidês, somebody or something gets struck by lightning'. [Σ]
267	25	*some Lydian or Phrygian slave*: A parody of Euripidês: *Alcestis* 675, Pherês to Admêtos.
269	12	*An abject Spartomaniac*: It is curious that in a long war it should become fashionable among certain people to ape the manners of the enemy.
269	14	*the Sokratês pose*: Here, as in the *chorikon* on p. 282, A. reveals his inability to admire the Great Martyr. The full-dress attack takes place in *Nubes*, but even in these minor skirmishes the animus is apparent, and only by shutting our minds to the plain sense of words can we conclude that this is a friendly raillery.
271	10	*'Ah that the eagle's . . .'*: Σ notes that these verses are quoted [in parody?] from the lost *Oinomaos* of Sophoklês.
272	16	*a decent orphan bird*: A male war-orphan would be educated by the State. There are vestiges of a dim ornithological pun.
273	3	*'Lifted aloft . . .'*: Kinêsias enters singing a love-poem by Anakreôn.
273	13	*Oh, ay. Enwingèd . . .* : The absurd diction parodies the manner of the dithyrambic poets, but there is a serious criticism implied: the poetry of Kinêsias is 'wingèd' not because of its exaltation, but because of its vain triviality (πρὸς τὸ κοῦφον, says Σ).

Page   Line

274   18   *so many tribes:* Although there may be a comic allusion here to the many cities that claimed Homer as
a native son, the central irony is more topical. The
office of Choragos, or Trainer of the Chorus for the
dramatic festivals, was important and much sought
after. A. suggests that Kinêsias, a vapid poet, would
be much in demand among the various tribes com-
peting at the festivals, but that no one could have
a better claim to his services as Choragos than Leotrophidês, himself a silly unsubstantial dramatist.

274   22   *'What birds are these . . .':* Parody of a song by
Alkaios of Mytilenê.

275   11   *the Islands:* The Greek Islanders, not being Athenians,
would be easy prey for the Informer.

276   1   *belly full of lawsuits:* For the cranes' ballast, see note
on p. 263:5.

276   3   *I never learned how to work:* See Luke 16:3: *Ait
autem vilicus intra se: Quid faciam quia dominus
meus aufert a me vilicationem? fodere non valeo,
mendicare erubesco.*

278   5   CHORIKON: In this short ode the Birds begin to describe
the strange places that they have seen in their migra-
tions. The Thracian tree stands for the recreant bully
Kleonymos, the shed 'unused shields' representing his
own shield, disgracefully thrown away in battle.
Kleonymos made part of his living as a paid informer:
the money would come in during the summer sessions,
slack off during the winter. The Antistrophe, which
at first sight seems to change the subject, actually
pursues it. Kleonymos is being equated with the
notorious bandit Orestês (see Notes for p. 243), while,
at the level of myth, he becomes a kind of burlesque
Aigisthos accosted by Agamemnon's avenging son: the
double allusion enforces a shift in the point of view.
Σ explains 'numb' by recalling that a chance encounter
with a Hero (the bandit had an heroic nickname) was
supposed to paralyze one's side.

281   8   *Basileia:* Her name means Sovereignty, Imperium.
She has no place in the official Pantheon, but is an
ad hoc creation to provide Pisthetairos with a mate

equivalent to Zeus' Hêra. The final mockery of this drama, of course, is the apotheosis of the bungling Hero.

281 18 *A well-broiled one*: Prometheus first taught men the use of fire.

282 1 *Take this footstool*: At the Panathenaia Festival the daughters of Athenian aristocrats were attended by wealthy girls of foreign ancestry who carried ceremonial footstools and parasols. Prometheus hopes that Zeus, looking down from Olympos, will mistake him for one of these attendants.

282 2 CHORIKON: The Birds' travel lecture proceeds. The Shadowfeet were a remarkable tribe, said to live in Libya, who enjoyed feet so large that they could be used as parasols during siesta time. This is a fit setting for the deplorable Sokratês, who is represented as 'leading the souls of men'—leading them, that is to say, as Odysseus did the souls in Hadês, but also misleading them by perverse teaching, a charge that A. constantly makes against this philosopher. The Strophe is a comic *Nekuia*, parodying the eleventh book of the *Odyssey*. The fainthearted Peisandros, having lost his own soul, goes to the land of the Shadowfeet to conjure it back.

282 13 *the Ambassadors from Olympos*: This theophany seems outrageous to us, but our ideas of what constitutes blasphemy are different from the Greeks', who would find A. brilliantly but conventionally comic.

283 7 *Democracy, what sins . . .* : Zeus, to be fair, has decided that even the Barbarians should be represented in this embassage.

283 17 *The horseradish*: Literally, *silphion*.

285 4 *by Myself!*: Poseidôn swears 'By Poseidon!'

285 5 *Wockle*: The Triballian speaks a murky language rather like that of Muta and Juva in *Finnegans Wake*. Much needless ingenuity has been expended by Professors attempting to reduce it to sense.

286 12 *Who wants to fight a war for a damn woman?*: As the Trojan War was fought for Helen.

Page Line

287 17 *has your Father enrolled you yet?*: In the register of citizens; as the illegitimate son of a foreign woman, Heraklês would be ineligible.

287 20 *pie in the sky*: The Greek phrase was 'birds' milk', but this seems too esoteric.

288 17 CHORIKON: The travelogue resumed. The Englottogasters, 'men who live by their tongues', are nearer home than the Shadowfeet: they are to be found wherever men make money by informing on their fellows, and are particularly flagrant in times of political uncertainty.

289 12 ÉXODOS: The conclusion of the play is dictated not only by dramatic appropriateness—the marriage and deification of the Hero—, but by ritual inheritance. Comedy culminates in marriage, and the final scene (*cf.* the *Pax* and, though slightly different in vein, the *Lysistrata*) has overtones of an ancestral fertility rite. The Chorus sings of the wedding of Zeus and Hêra, thus equating Pisthetairos and Basileia with the King and Queen of Heaven. The ordinary man has found Cloudcuckooland, his Utopia, and now becomes God. Like God, he insists upon the recital of his own meritorious exploits.

291 17 *Iê Paián!*: The play ends with a volley of ritual phrases, among which rings the Athenian battle-cry, *Alalaí!*, which had been *Eleleú!* among the Birds.

❧ INDEX OF NAMES

There is no fixed rule for the transliteration of Greek names. One method, the most familiar, is to derive the spelling through the Latin, as in the MacNeice translation of *Agamemnon*; another keeps more closely to the Greek forms; and there are all kinds of variations and gradations between. In the following Index variant forms are noted unless the discrepancy is negligibly slight.

ABBREVIATIONS

AG. *Agamemnon*
ALC. *Alcestis*
AV. *The Birds*
OT. *Oedipus Rex*
Σ Scholiast

ADMETOS: Son of Pherês; husband of Alcestis.

AEGEAN: The sea between Greece and Asia Minor.

AEGIPLANCTUS: A mountain in the district of Megaris, southwest of Cithaeron.

AEGISTHUS, AIGISTHOS: First cousin of Agamemnon; lover of Clytemnestra.

AGAMEMNON: King of Argos; commander-in-chief of the Greek forces at Troy.

AGENOR: A Phoenician king, son of Poseidon and Libya; father of KADMOS, *q.v.*, & hence an ancestor of Oedipus.

AISCHINES: AV.] An impoverished braggart politician; his 'castles' [p. 247] are what we should call 'castles in Spain'.

AISOPOS, ÆSOP: A semi-legendary writer of fables.

AITNA, ÆTNA: A town on the slope of the Sicilian mountain, founded by Hiero of Syracuse.

AKASTOS: Son of Pelias, King of Thessaly; brother to Alcestis.

AKROPOLIS: The Citadel of Athens, sacred to Athenê; AV.] the inner fortress of Cloudcuckooland.

ALCESTIS: Daughter of Pelias, King of Thessaly; wife of Admêtos.

ALKMENA: Wife of Amphitryon; seduced by Zeus impersonating her husband, she bore him Heraklês.

ALOPE: A mistress of Poseidon.

AMMON: A name for Zeus at his great shrine in Libya.

AMPHION: Husband of Niobê; the quotation [p. 268] is an absurdly jumbled parody of a passage in the [lost] Niobê of Aeschylus.

ANTIGONE: A daughter of Oedipus and Iokastê.

APHRODITÊ: Goddess of Love.

APOLLO: God of the Sun, of Life, of Healing, of Prophecy; AG.] as frustrated lover of Cassandra, curses her with a gift of prophecy never to be believed; ALC.] obliged to serve Admêtos, a mortal, as herdsman.

ARACHNAEAN STEEP: 'Spider Crag', a hill in Argolis, near Mycenae.

ARÊS: God of War.

ARGOS: Agamemnon's city; capital of Argolis, a country of the Peloponnese.

ARTEMIS: Sister of Apollo; goddess of the Hunt, of Virginity, of Childbirth.

ASKLEPIOS, ASCLEPIUS: A son of Apollo; the first physician among men, killed by Zeus because of his presumptuous skill.

ASOPUS: A river in southern Boeotia, flowing into the Strait of Euripus.

ATHENÊ, ATHENA: Daughter of Zeus; patron goddess of Athens.

ATHOS: A Macedonian mountain, about forty miles west of Lemnos.

ATREUS: Son of Pelops; father of Agamemnon and Menelaus; brother of Thyestês, whom he caused to eat the flesh of his own sons.

AULIS: A port in Boeotia; rendez-vous of the Greek fleet on the expedition to Troy.

BABYLON: The Assyrian capital, on the Euphratês River; Herodotos (I:178 sqq.) describes its enormous and complex walls.

BACCHOS: A name for DIONYSOS, q.v.

BAKIS: A celebrated and indefatigable Boeotian soothsayer.

BASILEIA: 'Sovereignty', or 'Empery', personified as a housekeeper of Zeus and, later, the bride of Pisthetairos.

BOIOTIA, BOEOTIA: A country north of Attika.

CALCHAS: High priest and prophet of the Greeks on the Trojan Expedition.

CASSANDRA, KASSANDRA: A daughter of Priam; awarded as concubine to Agamemnon upon the fall of Troy.

CHAIREPHON: An Athenian friend of Sokratês, nicknamed 'Bat'
[p. 282] because of his squeaky voice and sallow complexion.
CHAIRIS: A musician, 'somewhat frigid' according to Σ, who seems
to have offended Aristophanes' sense of propriety; here [p. 249]
a crow accompanying the Chorus.
CHALCIS: Chief city of Euboea, across the Strait of Euripus from
Aulis.
CHALYBÉAN: Pertaining to the Chalybês, a people living on the
southeast shore of the Black Sea, noted for their iron mines.
CHAOS: A pre-Olympian deity; primal matter.
CHARON: The ferryman of Hadês who transported the dead across
the River Styx.
CHIAN: The Island of Chios supported Athens early in the Peloponnesian War, and a clause for the Chians was accordingly
added to prayers for the public good. After the Sicilian Expedition, Chios defected to Sparta.
CITHAERON, KITHAIRON: A mountain range near Thebes, in Boeotia; OT.] scene of the exposure of the infant Oedipus.
CLYTEMNESTRA: Daughter of Tyndareus (or Zeus) and Leda, qq.v.;
wife of Agamemnon; mother of Iphigeneia, Electra, and Orestes;
mistress of Aegisthus, her husband's first cousin.

DAREIOS: King of Persia (549-485 B.C.).
DAULIA: A city of Phokis.
DELPHI, DELPHOI: A city of Phokis; seat of a celebrated Oracle of
Apollo.
DEMETER: A sister of Zeus; goddess of Agriculture.
DIAGORAS: A native of Mêlos, professor of Philosophy in Athens,
accused and condemned in absentia for atheism.
DIEITREPHES: A self-made man, manufacturer of wicker baskets,
who bought his way into the upper echelons of the Government.
DIOMED: A Thracian King, son of Arês, owner of a team of man-
eating horses.
DIONYSOS: God of wine.
DODONA: A notable oracle of Zeus.
DORIAN: Native of Doris, a country of Greece.

ELEKTRYON: A king of Mycenae; son of Perseus and Andromeda,
father of Alkmêna, q.v., and grandfather of Heraklês.
ELIS: A city in the Peloponnese, noted for its horses and for a
shrine of Zeus.
ENGLOTTOGASTER: 'Belly-tongued'; used [p. 289] of political informers and the officials who employ them.
EPOPS: The Hoopoe, Upupa epops; see Notes on p. 208.

EREBOS: A pre-Olympian deity; usually, son of Night and Chaos; the infernal depths.

EROS: Son of Aphroditê; god of love.

ETEOKLES: A son of Oedipus and Iokastê.

EUMELOS: Son of Admêtos and Alcestis.

EURIPUS: A strait between Boeotia and Euboea.

EURYSTHEUS: A king of Argos and Mycenae; permitted by Zeus to compel Heraklês to perform the Twelve Labors.

EXEKESTIDES: A parvenu alien living in Athens.

FURIES ('Ερινύες): The infernal spirits of Divine Vengeance.

GORGON: Medûsa, one of three monstrous sisters, whose eyes had the power to turn the beholder to stone.

GORGOPIS: A bay in the Gulf of Corinth.

GRACES (Χάριτες): Aglaia, Thaleia, and Euphrosynê, daughters of Zeus and Aphroditê, goddesses of delight.

HADES: The world of the dead; also, the god of the dead, brother of Zeus and Poseidon.

HALIMOS: A town in Attika, south of Athens.

HEBROS: A river in Thrace.

HELEN: Daughter of Tyndareus (or Zeus) and Leda, qq.v.; sister of Clytemnestra; wife of Menelaus, whom she deserted for Paris Alexander.

HELIOS: A name for Apollo as god of the Sun.

HEPHAESTUS, HEPHAISTOS: God of Fire; son of Zeus and Hera.

HERA: Sister and wife of Zeus.

HERAKLES: Son of Zeus and Alkmêna; the legendary hero and Strong Man of the Greeks, typically represented (e.g., AV.) as a glutton; AG.] sold as slave to Omphalê, a queen of Lydia, at whose table he endured to eat the bread of servitude.

HERMES: Messenger of the gods; ALC.] guide of souls passing to Hadês; AG.] 'Hermes' cliff': a mountain on the island of Lemnos.

HESTIA: AV.] Goddess of the Hearth; as 'Nestiarch' [p. 249], absurdly assimilated to the Birds.

HIPPONIKOS: An illustrative name; see Notes on p. 222.

HOMER: The epic poet.

HYMEN: God of marriage.

IDA: A mountain near Troy.

ILION, ILIUM: Troy.

IOKASTE: Mother, and later wife, of Oedipus.

IOLKOS: A Thessalian city, ruled by Pelias; birthplace of Alcestis and Akastos.

IPHIGENEIA: Daughter of Agamemnon and Clytemnestra; sacrificed to Artemis at Aulis by her father in order to make possible the sailing of the Greek fleet.

IRIS: The rainbow goddess; confidential messenger of Hêra.

ISMENE: A daughter of Oedipus and Iokastê.

ITYS: Son of Tereus and Proknê, *qq.v.*; hence a name expressing the lament of the nightingale.

KADMOS: The legendary founder of Thebes; father of SEMELE, *q.v.*

KALLIAS: A wealthy and dissolute Athenian amateur of philosophy. On p. 222 the name is illustrative; see Note *ad loc.*

KARIAN: A native of Karia, a country of Asia Minor. The Karians were said to prefer fighting on mountain tops as offering better opportunities for flight; hence [p. 222] the pun on 'crests'.

KINESIAS: A dithyrambic poet of Thebes in Boeotia; he is amusingly attacked by Aristophanes in *Lysistrata*.

KLEISTHENES: An Athenian bravo noted for his effeminacy.

KLEOKRITOS: An effeminate fat man with large feet who looked like an ostrich (Σ).

KLEONYMOS: A cowardly officer who became famous for having thrown away his shield in battle; see Notes, p. 278.

KOLONOS, COLONUS: A small town, suburb of Athens.

KORKYRA: The modern Corfù; the 'first-class goods' [p. 277] are whips, which were manufactured there.

KRANAOS: One of the mythical founder-kings of Athens.

KREON: Brother of Iokastê; becomes Regent of Thebes after the fall of Oedipus.

KRIOA: A deme of Attika.

KRONOS: Father of Zeus.

KYBELE, CYBELE: An Asiatic goddess worshipped as Magna Mater, the Mother of gods; on p. 250 she is the Great Ostrich.

KYLLENE: An Arcadian mountain, birthplace of HERMES, *q.v.*

KYPRIS: A name for Aphroditê.

LABDAKOS: An early king of Thebes; ancestor of Oedipus.

LAIOS: A king of Thebes; father of Oedipus, killed by him in fulfillment of an oracle.

LAISPODIAS: AV.] An Athenian general with a limp (Σ), or possibly the reference is to his sexual incapacity [Σ]. The Triballian has draped his cloak as though to conceal his left leg—most inelegant behaviour.

LAKONIA: A country of the Peloponnese; chief city, Sparta.

LAMPON: A noted soothsayer.

LARISSA: A city in Thessaly.

LAUREION, LAUREUM: A town in Attika famous for its gold mines; AV.] the Owl of Athenê was stamped on coins: hence, on p. 261 we should say 'coals to Newcastle'.

LEDA: Wife of King Tyndareus of Sparta; seduced by Zeus in the shape of a Swan, she bore him (and Tyndareus) Clytemnestra, Helen, Castor, and Pollux.

LEMNOS: An Aegean island.

LEOTROPHIDES: A dithyrambic poet, thin and corpselike in appearance (Σ).

LEPREON: A town in Elis; the name suggests leprosy.

LIBYA: A region of Africa.

LIBYAN: Pertaining to Libya, in Africa.

LOKRIS: A district of Greece, extending from Thessaly to Boeotia.

LYCEAN: An epithet of Apollo, of doubtful meaning: as 'born in Lycia' [Λυκία]; as 'god of light' [*λύκη]; as 'wolfslayer' [λύκος].

LYDIAN: Pertaining to Lydia, a region in Asia Minor that supplied the Greeks with slaves.

LYKAON: 'Wolf-man'; a son of Arês, vanquished by Heraklês.

LYKIA: ALC.] A District of Asia Minor where, at Patara, there was a celebrated shrine of Apollo.

LYKOURGOS: 'Called Ibis either because of his Egyptian extraction or because of his skinny legs. There is a redundancy of the ibis in Egypt (Σ).'

LYSIKRATES: A venal Athenian official.

MACISTUS: A mountain in Euboea.

MANES: Name for a servant.

MANODOROS: Name for a servant.

MEGABAZOS: A Persian nobleman, general in the service of King Dareios, q.v.

MEIDAS: A corrupt and perverse politician; 'Quail' seems to have been a cant word in boxing, as we might say 'Punchy', and apparently refers to Meidias' dazed and glazed expression.

MELANTHIOS: A tragic poet, effete and afflicted with leprosy (Σ) or some disease resembling it.

MELIANS: AV.] Inhabitants of Mêlos, which, in the year preceding this play, had been blockaded by Nikias and starved into submission.

MENELAUS: King of Sparta; brother of Agamemnon; husband of Helen, cuckolded by Paris.

MENOIKEUS: Father of KREON and IOKASTE, *qq.v.*

MEROPE: Wife of King Polybos of Corinth; foster-mother of Oedipus.

MESSAPION: A mountain on the coast of Boeotia.

METON: A famous astronomer and architect. He opposed the Sicilian Expedition and feigned insanity in order to avoid serving on it.

MUSES: Nine goddesses presiding over the arts and sciences; daughters of Zeus and Mnemosynê ('Memory').

NAUSIKAA: A princess of Phaiakia; daughter of Alkinoös, who befriended Odysseus.

NIKIAS: A prominent and disastrous Athenian commander in the Peloponnesian War.

ODYSSEUS: Wiliest of the Greek chieftains at Troy, and hero of Homer's *Odyssey*; in AV. [p. 282] the allusion is to his performing the sacrificial rites necessary for summoning up the dead in Hadês (*Od.* XI).

OEDIPUS: Son of Laios and Iokastê of Thebes; unknowingly kills his father and marries his mother; father (and brother) of Antigonê, Ismenê, Eteoklês, Polyneikês.

OLOPHYXOS: A town near Mt. Athos, in Macedonia. In AV. [p. 259] the name was chosen for the sake of a heavy pun.

OLYMPIANS: The gods, as living upon Mt. Olympos, *q.v.*

OLYMPOS, OLYMPUS: A mountain in Thessaly, traditionally the seat of the gods.

OPOUNTIOS: A one-eyed grafter; the word is also the proper adjective from Opous, *q.v.*

OPOUS: A town in Lokris, *q.v.*

ORESTES: Son of Agamemnon and Clytemnestra; given shelter by Strophius, King of Phocis, during Agamemnon's absence at Troy; AV.] a street brigand who assumed the heroic name [see Notes, p. 243].

ORPHEUS: A philosopher, poet, musician and magician, famous in the early legends; ALC.] descended into Hadês in search of his dead wife, and by his music won permission to bring her back to the world above.

ORPHIC: Adjective pertaining to Orpheus, *q.v.*

OTHRYS: A mountain, home of the Centaurs, in Thessaly.

PAIAN: Physician of the gods; a name transferred to Apollo in his healing aspect.

PALLAS: An epithet of ATHENA, *q.v.*

PAN: A sylvan deity.

PANDORA: AV.] 'The Earth, since it gives us everything necessary to life' (Σ); not to be confused, at any rate, with the Greek equivalent of Eve.

PARIS: A prince of Troy; son of Priam; steals Helen from Menelaus, thus precipitating the Trojan War; known also as Alexander.

PARNASSOS: A mountain sacred to Apollo; at its foot are Delphi and the Castalian Spring.

PEISANDROS: A notoriously craven politician.

PEISIAS' SON: AV.] Apparently a traitorous citizen; but the evidence is very vague, in spite of lurid hints by Σ.

PELARGIC WALL: The Stork Wall, Pelargikon, of the Akropolis at Athens.

PELIAS: A king of Iôlkos in Thessaly, father of Alcestis.

PELOPS: A son of Tantalus; father of Atreus and Thyestes.

PERSEPHONÊ: A daughter of Zeus and Deméter; Queen of Hadês.

PERSEUS: A son of Zeus and Danaê; great-grandfather of Heraklês.

PHALERON: A port of Athens, notable for its sea food.

PHARNAKES: A Persian nobleman operating as an 'enemy agent' in Athens; the Inspector [p. 258] is in his pay.

PHERAI: A city in Thessaly, seat of Pherês and Admêtos.

PHERÊS: A king of Pherai in Thessaly; father of Admêtos.

PHILEMON: 'Lampooned as a foreigner, and a Phrygian one into the bargain' (Σ).

PHILOKLES: A tragic poet, nicknamed 'Lark'; he wrote a play called *Tereus,* or, *The Hoopoe,* much of it, apparently, plagiarized from Sophocles.

PHILOKRATES: The proprietor of the shop where Euelpidês and Pisthetairos bought their bird guides.

PHOCIAN: Adjective pertaining to Phokis, a district on the Gulf of Corinth adjoining Boeotia.

PHOIBOS: A name for Apollo.

PHOINIKIA: Phoenicia, a country in Asia Minor.

PHOKIS: See PHOCIAN.

PHONÉYA: An invented name. The Greek is Phanês, the root of which suggests the pseudo-patriot Informers who are supposed to live in that country.

PHRYGIA (PHRYGIAN): A land in Asia Minor, one of whose cities was Troy; mentioned in ALC. as a source of slaves.

PHRYNICHOS: A tragic poet, fl. 500 B.C.

PINDAR: Lyric poet (552-442 B.C.)

PLEIADS: The constellation Pleiades; AG.] the 'setting of the Pleiads' = late autumn, the beginning of the winter storms.

POLYBOS: King of Corinth; foster-father of Oedipus.

POLYDOROS: A son of KADMOS, *q.v.*; great-grandfather of Oedipus.

POLYNEIKES: A son of Oedipus and Iokastê.

PORPHYRION: One of the Titans in the conflict with Zeus; [p. 268] the Purple Waterhen, *Porphyrio veterum.*

PRIAM: King of Troy.

PRODIKOS: A prominent sophist, reputedly a teacher of Euripides and Sokratês.

PROKNE: The Nightingale, wife of Tereus, *q.v.*

PROMETHEUS: A son of the Titan Iapetos, and hence a semi-divine being; reputed to have created man and to have stolen fire from Heaven for the comfort of his creation: for both of which acts he was persecuted by Zeus.

PROXENIDES: An irresponsible boaster; he comes from the wholly imaginary town of Kompasai, a word derived from the verb κομπάζω, 'shoot off the mouth.'

PYTHIAN: An epithet of Apollo as god of the Delphic Oracle (Πυθώ); οτ] 'P. hearth': the Oracle itself.

PYTHODELIAN: The Swan, sacred to Apollo, takes Apollo's epithets; Pythian, as god of the Delphic Oracle, and Dêlian, as native of Dêlos.

SABAZIOS: A Phrygian god, assimilated to Dionysos.

SAKAS: Popular name for a foreigner aspiring to Athenian citizenship.

'SALAMINIA': A state galley in the Athenian service; on p. 215 a kind of glorified police boat.

SARDANAPALOS: A lavish and splendidly dissolute king of Assyria.

SARONIC GULF: A body of water between Attika and the Peloponnese.

SCAMANDER: A river of Troy.

SEMELE: A mistress of Zeus; mother of Dionysos.

SIMONIDES: An Ionian poet (556-467 B.C.).

SOKRATES, SOCRATES: Philosopher and teacher (460-399 B.C.); see Notes on p. 282.

SOLON: The lawgiver (639-559 B.C.).

SOUNION, SUNIUM: An Attic promontory and town, site of a temple of Poseidon.

SPARTA: The chief city of Lakonia, in the Peloponnese.

SPHINX: A riddling she-monster who killed herself when Oedipus solved her riddle.

SPINTHAROS: Lampooned for the same reason as Philêmon, *q.v.*; otherwise unknown.

SPORGILOS: An Athenian barber.

STHENELOS: Father of Eurystheus, *q.v.*

STROPHIUS: King of Phokis; a brother-in-law of Agamemnon and guardian of Orestes, *q.v.*

STRYMON: A river in Thrace.

SYRAKOSIOS: A politician; author of a law forbidding the comic poets to introduce real persons into their plays.

TARTAROS: The infernal and punitive depths.

TEIRESIAS: A blind prophet of Thebes; counsellor of Oedipus and Kreon.

TELEAS: An unstable Athenian, adequately described in his own words quoted on p. 216.

TEREUS: A king of Thrace, transformed, for his outrageous behaviour, into a Hoopoe; see Notes on p. 208.

THALES: Mathematician and philosopher (fl. 590 B.C.).

THANATOS: Death.

THEBES: A city in Boeotia.

THEOGENES: A boastful, showy man of largely imaginary wealth.

THESSALY (THESSALIAN): A region of northern Greece.

THESMOPHORIA: A festival of Deméter, celebrated in November.

THRACE (THRACIAN): The region north of the Black Sea.

THYESTES: Brother of Atreus, *q.v.*; father of Aegisthus.

TIMON: A celebrated Athenian misanthrope.

TIRYNS: A city of Argolis; usual home of Heraklês.

TITANS: Pre-Olympian divinities who revolted against Zeus and were defeated by him in a battle on the Phlegraian Plain; AV.] the great combat is reduced to a riot of boasters.

TRIBALLIANS: A savage Thracian tribe.

TROY: King Priam's city.

TYNDAREUS: A king of Sparta; husband of Leda, *q.v.*; earthly, or surrogate, father of Clytemnestra and Helen.

XANTHIAS: Name for a servant.

ZEUS: Father of gods and men.